TIMBERLINE LODGE

TIMBERLINE LODGE

*The History, Art, and Craft
of an American Icon*

SARAH BAKER MUNRO
with photographs by Aaron Johanson

*Foreword by Richard Moe, President,
National Trust for Historic Preservation*

TIMBER PRESS
Portland * London

Frontispiece: *Timberline Lodge in winter, looking south toward Mount Jefferson.*

The Friends of Timberline provided a generous grant to aid in the preparation of this work and underwrote oral history transcription, archive organization, and inventory projects that made historical material available for use.

Published in 2009 by Timber Press, Inc.

The Haseltine Building
133 S.W. Second Avenue, Suite 450
Portland, Oregon 97204-3527
www.timberpress.com

2 The Quadrant
135 Salusbury Road
London NW6 6RJ
www.timberpress.co.uk

ISBN-13: 978-0-88192-856-3

Printed in China

Library of Congress Cataloging-in-Publication Data

Munro, Sarah.
   Timberline Lodge : the history, art, and craft of an American icon / Sarah Baker
Munro ; with photographs by Aaron Johanson ; foreword by Richard Moe.
      p. cm.
   Includes bibliographical references and index.
   ISBN 978-0-88192-856-3
   1. Timberline Lodge (Mount Hood, Or.)—History. 2. Timberline Lodge
(Mount Hood, Or.)—Pictorial works. 3. Mountain resorts—Oregon—Hood,
Mount—History—20th century. 4. Hotels—Oregon—Hood, Mount—Design
and construction—History—20th century. 5. Stone buildings—Oregon—Hood,
Mount—Design and construction—History—20th century. 6. Log buildings—
Oregon—Hood, Mount—Design and construction—History—20th century.
7. Architecture—Oregon—Hood, Mount—History—20th century. 8. United
States. Works Progress Administration. I. Johanson, Aaron. II. Title.
   F882.H85M86 2009
   979.5´61—dc22   2008045109

A catalog record for this book is also available from the British Library.

To my family

CONTENTS

FOREWORD

IT'S HARD not to be blown away by the magnificence of Timberline Lodge's setting on the southern flank of Oregon's iconic Mount Hood. I certainly was when I was there several years ago. It's also hard to overstate this marvelous building's significance as a unique historic and cultural treasure.

Like other historic hotels across the United States, Timberline gains much of its appeal from its skillful blending of distinctive character with modern-day amenities and comforts. However, Timberline offers something extra, something that truly sets it apart. Most of us know something about the legacy of the various and innovative public-works projects initiated by FDR's New Deal in the 1930s—but at Timberline Lodge, we can experience that legacy first-hand, touch it and walk through it, even sleep in it. The architecture that deftly balances rusticity with grandeur, the furniture, the ironwork and light fixtures, the paintings and textiles, the woodcarvings that add an engaging note of whimsy to the decorative scheme—these transform Timberline into a one-of-a-kind evocation of an era in which widespread economic hardship and visionary government leadership were the twin sparks that generated an amazing outpouring of skilled craftsmanship and artistic energy.

Whether you think of it as an art gallery masquerading as a hotel or the other way around, it's a very special place, eminently worthy of the most thoughtful, careful stewardship. Fortunately, after a somewhat rocky start, Timberline's management has taken good care of it over the years, while those who love the lodge—especially Friends of Timberline, a vigilant group made up of card-carrying preservationists and those who wouldn't dream of using that term to describe themselves—have been energetic partners in its preservation. One product of that partnership is this fascinating book, in which Sarah Baker Munro expertly recounts the building's history and provides a welcome inventory of the artwork that enriches it.

From its construction in the 1930s to its expansive restoration in recent years, Timberline's story is an object lesson in how a landmark is created and preserved. It's a story worth knowing—and learning from. "Inspiring" is an adjective that doesn't often apply to hotels, but in this case, it fits.

Richard Moe is president of the National Trust for Historic Preservation.

PREFACE

Is there a place in the world where the beauties of nature have so blended with the talents of man in the creation of the beautiful as . . . in that world famous lodge?

— ORION B. DAWSON, "The Old Blacksmiths" (1964?)

BLACKSMITH Orion B. Dawson captured the sentiment that many of the builders felt as they raced to finish Timberline Lodge before September 28, 1937, when President Franklin Delano Roosevelt would arrive to dedicate this monument to workers of the Works Progress Administration. The WPA builders, artists, and craftspeople looked back with affection at their involvement in this project. Many felt that the work they did for the lodge, although rushed, was the best of their careers.

Builders appreciated the increasingly rare opportunity to work on what may have been the last hand-built building of its size and kind in the country. Constructed of stone and wood, high on Mount Hood in the northwest quarter of Oregon, the lodge combines the architectural styles of National Park Rustic, Art Deco, Cascadian, and Environmental, with a distinct nod to the still-influential principles of the Arts and Crafts movement of the early twentieth century.

The original sturdy wood lodge furniture was built and carved in the WPA woodworking shop by out-of-work carpenters and construction workers using local woods. The traditional hand-wrought iron furnishings were made in the WPA metal shop by blacksmiths who had not been able to practice their craft for years before the lodge was built. Most of the paintings, wood carvings, marquetry, glass mosaics, and linoleum carved murals are original and were made especially for the lodge by some of Oregon's finest artists. To explore this exceptional range of art and craft, there is no better place than Timberline.

Although original textiles have worn out, restoration projects since 1975 have re-created hand-woven upholstery, hand-appliquéd draperies, and hand-hooked rugs. Ongoing restoration efforts include replacing broken or missing wood furniture and hand-wrought iron lamps, fireplace tools, metal hardware, and stair railings with handmade re-creations or adaptations.

The lodge draws over two million visitors each year and is a destination for many who enjoy the craft, the art, and the ambience of the place.

For over seventy years, skiers on Mount Hood have used the lodge as a haven to escape the cold wind and snow. Since the first Magic Mile chairlift at Timberline was constructed, the skiing and snowboarding facilities have continued to be expanded and upgraded, keeping Timberline a popular destination for winter sports enthusiasts.

As a child I learned to ski at Timberline, but my interest in the lodge began in 1975, after the nonprofit Friends of Timberline was formed to support restoration and preservation efforts. As a member of a committee of volunteers from the Junior League of Portland, I learned about and met with original builders, artists, and craftspeople, most of whom are now deceased. The result of that research was a catalog published in 1978 that I coauthored with retired Portland Art Museum curator Rachael Griffin. It included an inventory of the art and furnishings of the lodge, which I updated from the interior designer's 1938 inventory, with assistance from the Forest Service.

I have continued my interest in the lodge both as a member of the board of Friends of Timberline and as its president. When years ago Tom Booth of Oregon State University Press suggested that the real history of Timberline had not yet been written, I took that suggestion as an assignment and set about researching the history of the lodge in earnest—poring through National Archive documents and Forest Service records, interviewing surviving builders and artists, and studying 1930s art and culture. I organized the initial contributions to the Friends of Timberline Archive and directed projects in interview transcription, archive management, and botanical conservation assessment. Having laid this groundwork, I began to write this book.

Both a narrative and a guide, this book is divided into two parts—a chronology and an inventory. The five-chapter chronology starts with a brief background on the formation of national forests, the construction of the Mount Hood Loop Road, and the growth of interest in recreation in the forest. Chapters 2 and 3 cover the story of building and furnishing the lodge, ending with the dedication and opening celebration. Chapter 4 lays out the operation of the lodge from its opening in early 1938 through its closure during World War II, the phase of problematic management after the war, and the years of recovery under Richard L. Kohnstamm's leadership. The restoration efforts and expansion of facilities in the last thirty-five years described in Chapter 5 bring the lodge history into the twenty-first century.

The second part of the book is an inventory of the wonderful art and original furnishings in the lodge. The art inventory includes brief biographical sketches of the artists who created these works and lists the specific works they did for Timberline.

The selected bibliography identifies many books, theses, and articles that aided me in my work and are readily available to the interested reader. Quoted material from many letters, papers, and interviews is not documented here but is available: primary source material is in the collections of the Friends of Timberline Archive, the U.S. Forest Service's Zigzag Ranger District, and the National Archive and Records Administration (NARA), at both the Pacific Alaska Region (Seattle) and College Park (Maryland) facilities. Recorded interviews by historians in the U.S. Forest Service, volunteers of Friends of Timberline, Oregon Public Broadcasting, and me provide the first-hand perspective of architects, engineers, builders, chefs, artists and craftsmen, and operators of the lodge.

In 2004, Leslie Taylor completed an update of the 1978 inventory through an internship from Scripps College, the sponsorship of Friends of Timberline and the Oregon Cultural Heritage Commission, and the assistance of Timberline Lodge curator Linny Adamson. I revised the inventory for this book. Material for the biographical entries of Oregon artists was drawn from a variety of sources. In particular, Ginny Allen's and Jody Klevit's *Oregon Painters: the First Hundred Years (1859–1959)*, Roger Hull's monograph *Charles Heaney: Memory, Imagination and Place*, and Kitty Harmon's *Pacific Northwest Landscape: A Painted History* were invaluable sources of information on the Oregon artists whose work is at Timberline. Ginny Allen provided extensive additional information on Oregon artists and their work. I collected further information on other American artists through interviews with artists, research at the Archives of American Art, and searches on the Internet.

In 2006 and for the first time since Timberline was built, all botanical watercolors at the lodge were removed from their frames, identified, and assessed for conservation needs by conservator Elizabeth Chambers and by me, with assistance from Friends of Timberline board member Lenore Martin, curator Linny Adamson, and other employees of R.L.K. and Company. Attribution of many of the botanicals would have been impossible without this project, which was generously funded by a grant from the Kinsman Foundation.

Many of the photographic images in this book are historical; for those, I have provided as much data as I could find. All recent photographs without historical data or dates were taken by Aaron Johanson between 2005 and 2008.

Interior designer Margery Hoffman Smith believed a spirit inhabits objects made by loving hands. Timberline Lodge exudes the heart and spirit of its makers, and enriches all of us who come to know it.

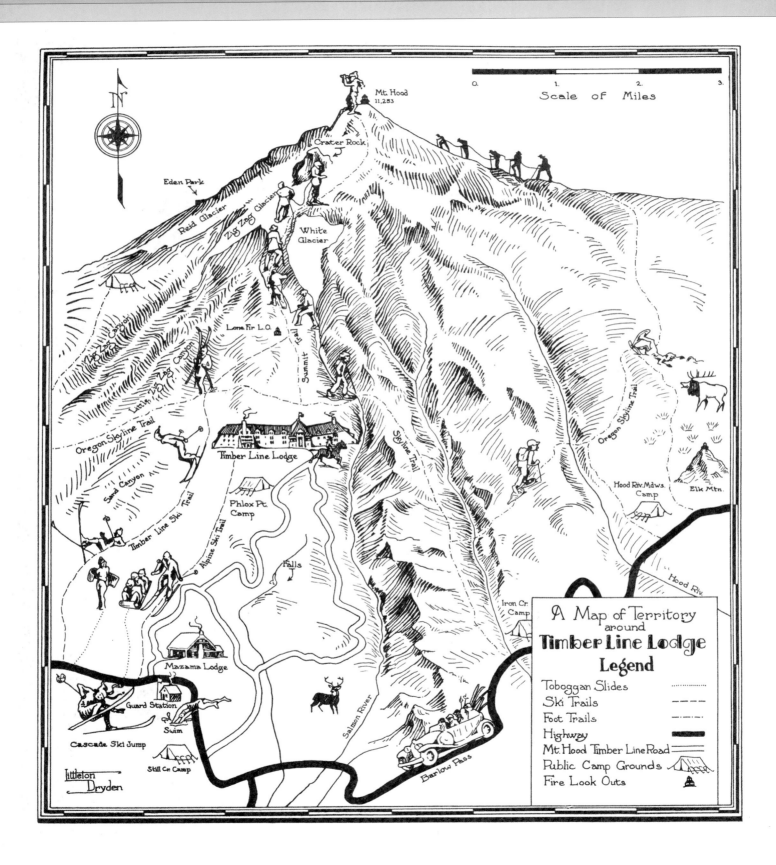

ACKNOWLEDGMENTS

MANY INDIVIDUALS provided generous assistance during the research for and preparation of the manuscript. Although I am unable to thank all by name, I want to express my appreciation to the following: Linny Adamson, Ginny and Bill Allen, Ike Bay, Lucy Berkley, Randi Black, Larry Bollinger, Tom Booth, Richard Brown, Margaret Bullock, MaryAnn Campbell, Corinna Campbell-Sack, Jim Carmin, Elizabeth Chambers, Christy Covington, Tara Crookshank, Marilyn Deering, Thomas P. Deering Jr., Professor Jacqueline Dirks, Annette Dixon, Mike Dryden, Shauna Gandy, Patricia Haim, Carol Hardwick, Henry Harth, Paul L. Havel, George M. Henderson, Joan Hoffman, Professor Roger Hull, Jeff Jaqua, Robert Joki, Marjorie Kerr, Jeff Kohnstamm, Molly Kohnstamm, Frank Kuo, Susanna Kuo, Moshe Lenske, Lois Leonard, Hank Lewis, Eric Lien, Donald Livingstone, Douglas Lynch, Lenore Martin, Kate McCarthy, Rick McClure, the McLean family, Patty McNamee, David Milholland, John A. Mills, Katharine L. Mills, Darryl Nelson, Henk Pander, Robert Peirce, Brian Reed, Roger Saydack, Jeremy Sells, Professor Robert Shotola, Donna Sinclair, Scott Skellinger, Mick Stapleton, Leslie Taylor, Jeff Thomas, Mikki Tint, Jon Tullis, Mark Vincent, Betty Walker, and Harry Widman.

The assistance of a grant from the Kinsman Foundation to Friends of Timberline enabled me to identify artists and copyists of many botanicals. I am also most appreciative of the assistance of several organizations, including Cable Huston Benedict Haagensen & Lloyd LLP, John Wilson Special Collections of the Multnomah County Library, National Archives of the Pacific Alaska Region (Seattle) and at College Park, Maryland, Oregon Historical Society, Photocraft, Portland Art Museum, and R.L.K. and Company. Many builders, craftsmen, and artists who have died also provided great assistance for which I am very grateful, including Albert Altorfer, A. P. DiBenedetto, Ward Gano, Rachael Griffin, Richard L. Kohnstamm, Ray Neufer, Francis Newton, Leverett Richards, and William Wechner. I am also greatly appreciative of those many builders, craftsmen, and artists whom I was unable to meet but who loved Timberline Lodge.

I am very grateful for the invaluable assistance of photographer Aaron Johanson. This work required the gifted editorial and publication assistance of Timber Press, including Eve Goodman, and editors Laura O. Foster and Ellen Wheat.

"A Map of Territory around Timber Line Lodge" by Littleton Dryden, published in Builders of Timberline Lodge, *Works Progress Administration, Portland, Oregon, 1937.*

Mount Hood from the south side just above Timberline Lodge, Oregon.

CHAPTER ONE

A RESORT FOR MOUNT HOOD

Not the highest of the Cascadian snowcaps, Mount Hood is called the most imposing. Its pyramid of rock and ice, sweeping to a sheer apex of noble proportions, is the predominant feature of the country. By many travelers Hood has been classed with the most beautiful mountains on the globe.

—FRED M. MCNEIL, *Wy'East, "The Mountain"* (1937)

Timberline Lodge at midwinter. The lights in the headhouse glow in the dusk.

TIMBERLINE LODGE, high on Oregon's Mount Hood, is a magnificent structure of wood and stone that blends into the surrounding trees and rocks. Just above the timberline at 6000 feet, the lodge sits on the volcano's stormy south flank. Crafted by hand during the Depression, it is not only a thriving mountain resort built from the region's natural resources but is also a museum of human artistry. Hand-wrought furnishings and fixtures in wood, iron, and textiles delight visitors. For over seventy years, families and friends have come to Timberline to ski, to play cards next to the great fireplaces, to hike, or to splash in the heated outdoor pool. Many return year after year, creating traditions and memories at one of Oregon's most beloved landmarks.

MOUNT HOOD: AN OREGON ICON

Timberline sits below the Palmer Glacier, one of twelve glaciers and named snowfields on Mount Hood. Palmer Glacier was named for General Joel Palmer, who may have been the first white man to attempt to climb Mount Hood. Between 6200 and 9300 feet and with an average annual snow depth of 102 inches, Palmer Glacier provides a year-round playground for skiers and snowboarders, and is the starting point of the most popular route for climbers who trek 3.6 miles up Mount Hood's south side from Timberline. The lodge also connects to the approximately forty-mile Timberline Trail that circles Mount Hood and to the 2650-mile Pacific Crest Trail that extends from Canada to Mexico.

At 11,239 feet, Mount Hood is the tallest point in Oregon and dominates Portland's eastern views. Only sixty miles east of the city, it is the most visited mountain in the state. It is part of the Cascade Range that also includes Mount Rainier, Mount Adams, Mount St. Helens, and Mount Jefferson. Like other mountains in this chain, Mount Hood was shaped by volcanic eruptions over the past hundreds of thousands of years, the most recent about 200 years ago. It still emits gases from at least three locations on its slopes.

Timberline Lodge on the south slope of Mount Hood looks out over the Cascade Range to Mount Jefferson. The Wy'East Day Lodge is below the lodge on the left. Bare patches on distant slopes are clearcuts. Trillium Lake and Summit Meadows are visible in the distance.

An Indian name for Mount Hood is Wy'East. The nearest Cascade peaks are Mount Adams, called Pahto or Klickitat, and Mount St. Helens, called Loowit or La-wa-la-clough by some tribes. Indian legends hint at these mountains' volcanic nature. According to one traditional story, Wy'East and Pahto fought over the beautiful Loowit, hurling rocks and sending forth streams of liquid fire. The fighting so angered the Great Spirit, Sahale, that he turned the three into mountain peaks. Mount St. Helens became a beautiful cone, Mount Adams bends longingly toward Mount St. Helens, and Mount Hood stands tall and proud.

From the summit of Mount Hood, one can see east to wheat fields in eastern Oregon, south beyond Mount Jefferson to the volcanic peaks of the Three Sisters, west past Portland to the Coast Range, and north over the Columbia River to Mount Adams, Mount St. Helens, and Mount Rainier. Mount Hood stood out to early explorers and settlers. Sailing down the Columbia River in 1792, William Broughton, under Captain George Vancouver, saw and named Mount Hood after Lord Samuel Hood, who fought the British in the Revolutionary War. As they camped along the Columbia River, Meriwether Lewis and William Clark noted Mount Hood in their journals. Pioneers on the Oregon Trail knew that they were reaching the end of their journey when they could see Mount Hood. Those who came around Mount Hood's south side along the Barlow Road (named for Samuel Barlow, who opened the toll road in 1846) had to lower their wagons down Laurel Hill by ropes before they could reach the fertile Willamette Valley.

Since the 1800s, Mount Hood has provided natural resources of timber, water, and stone to a growing population and has lured Oregonians to its slopes for recreation. Today, for many, recreation on Mount Hood means Timberline Lodge.

U.S. NATIONAL FORESTS: A RESOURCE FOR THE PUBLIC GOOD

Timberline Lodge was conceived in the 1930s as a public work relief project in the Mount Hood National Forest. But its history began about forty years earlier, when the 1891 Forest Reserve Act authorized the president to set aside the nation's timber areas. Management of the reserves meant maximizing the economic use of the forests by harvesting timber. That year President Benjamin Harrison set aside the Bull Run Timberland Reserve on Mount Hood's west side. In 1893, President Grover Cleveland created the enormous Cascade Forest Reserve, which extended south from the Columbia River through Oregon almost

Auto Road to Mt. Hood, Oregon
On line of O-W.R & N   © 1904 by Geo. M. Weister

to the California border. Twelve years later in 1905, the U.S. Forest Service was established to sustain healthy, diverse, and productive forests and grasslands. The Forest Service renamed the reserves "national forests" and carved the former Cascade Forest Reserve into four national forests. One of these, the Oregon National Forest, was renamed the Mount Hood National Forest in 1924, the name used today.

The Forest Service adopted the utilitarian credo: "Where conflicting interests must be reconciled, the question shall always be answered from the standpoint of the greatest good of the greatest number in the long run." This statement was made in a February 1, 1905, letter that, although signed by the secretary of agriculture, was probably written by the first forester, Gifford Pinchot. In the decades after 1905, increasing use of national forest land by the public for recreation caused a gradual shift in the concept of "the greatest good" from natural resource extraction to recreational uses such as hiking, climbing, and horseback riding. Some people thought that recreational uses should also include more "urban" activities, such as skiing, swimming, tennis, and ice-skating.

Auto road to Mount Hood, Oregon, on line of the O-W.R. & N., 1904. Photograph by George M. Weister. Courtesy of Marian Herron. "On line of the O-W.R. & N." may mean along a planned rail line. The Oregon Railway and Navigation Company established a rail line that traveled east from Portland. The company became the Oregon-Washington Railway and Navigation Company in 1910. It was absorbed by the Union Pacific Railroad in 1936.

Mount Hood Loop Road from Laurel Hill, 1933. Photograph by Al Monner, #1305.
Tom Robinson's Historic Photo Archive.

Opinions of hikers and skiers and among Forest Service employees differed as to whether optimal recreational uses meant solitary hiking or winter sports carnivals with 10,000 participants.

In 1919 the increasing popularity of automobiles created a demand for good roads in the Mount Hood National Forest. Through efforts of the regional forest supervisor, Thomas Sherrard, funding became available, and construction began on a loop highway around Mount Hood. A national expert in landscape architecture, Frank Albert Waugh, recommended camps at the timberline for climbers and a hut at the summit of Mount Hood: "This would make it possible to view the sunrise, and to enjoy many delightful experiences not now available." Waugh's report, written in 1920 and titled "Recreation Uses in the Mt. Hood Area," pointed out that once a roadway around the mountain was complete, tourists would come. Waugh stated, "There should be one or more resort hotels in which the average tourist could comfortably spend a week or a month, thus allowing opportunity to make the ascent of Mt. Hood, to explore the glaciers, to visit the park zone, to try the fishing or to spend a vacation in any other occupation better suited to his personal taste."

In 1925, after six years of work and delays caused in part by World War I, the loop highway was complete. Its popularity was immediately obvious because the number of visitors to the forest increased dramatically. In 1937, *Oregon Journal* writer Fred McNeil wrote that it was the "first and to date only standard constructed road to encircle one of the major snowcaps of the region." The Loop Road was a 173-mile "necklace" that started in Portland and wound around Mount Hood. Current roads follow the original route, including Highway 26 from Portland to the junction with Highway 35, north along Highway 35 to the town of Hood River, and west on the Columbia River Highway.

In 1926, a year after the road was completed, the federal government set aside 83,751 acres of the Mount Hood National Forest as a public recreation area, where economic activities would not be allowed to interfere with recreational purposes. A road to the mountain was now in place and policies encouraged tourism, but adequate recreational facilities were still lacking.

DEVELOPING A RESORT ON THE MOUNTAIN

Developers in the 1920s focused first on expanding a small, existing private resort on the remote north side of Mount Hood. In 1889, prominent Portlanders William M. Ladd and Charles Erskine Scott Wood had built Cloud Cap Inn at 5837 feet, just below the Eliot Glacier and a ridge called Cooper Spur. The lodge, which still stands, is a rustic,

Cloud Cap Inn, in 1893, from Henry C. C. Stevens's album. Oregon Historical Society Research Library negatives #56651 and #55099.

partly unpeeled log structure with stone fireplaces. Its shape, a half-hexagon facing the mountain, anticipated angles used in Timberline Lodge, although the two lodges are situated differently on the mountain. Cloud Cap was designed by William M. Whidden, a prominent Portland architect.

Sarah Langille operated the inn from about 1891 to 1907. Langille's sons Douglas and Will were local mountain guides and helped at Cloud Cap before Douglas joined the U.S. Geological Survey and Will pursued the Alaska gold rush. The Reverend Arthur J. Brown of the First Presbyterian Church in Portland remembered the pleasure of staying at Cloud Cap Inn: "It was a thoroughly homelike and hospitable place, a veritable olden time inn," he wrote, as Elisabeth Walton quoted him in *Space, Style and Structure*. Members of prominent Portland families relaxed a week or more in one of the inn's eight guest rooms or adjacent cabins. Langille's nephew, Horace Mecklem, managed Cloud Cap for several years after 1907. He was later an officer in the first company that operated Timberline Lodge.

Although the first inns on the south side of Mount Hood were built about the same time as Cloud Cap Inn, none enjoyed Cloud Cap's unique reputation as a destination resort. Inns on the south side clustered in Government Camp, a village near the summit of Barlow Pass along Highway 26. Built along the roadside, the lodges on the south side served more as overnight stops than as the destination retreats that Waugh later envisioned. Among these lodges were the Government Camp Hotel and the Battle Axe Inn, rustic structures decorated with Indian and pioneer motifs similar to the decor later selected for Timberline Lodge.

Several structures on the south side were closer to the timberline than the inns at Government Camp. All were small and none remain standing. Mountaineer Elijah "Lige" Coalman built the Timberline Cabin in 1916 at Camp Blossom (named after local pioneer James M. Blossom) about one-half mile west of Timberline Lodge in an area near current ski runs, as a halfway point for a telephone line to the summit. The cabin became a favorite way station for climbers. Coalman also built and manned a fire lookout on the summit of Mount Hood. The Timberline Hotel, also near Camp Blossom, was a tent extension of the Government Camp Hotel that John Valentine Rafferty operated between 1924 and 1930.

The area around the Timberline Lodge site was popular with climbers and skiers long before the lodge was built. Climbing groups, including the Wy'East Climbers Club and Nile River Yacht Club, had cabins in the area. As hikers from Government Camp climbed to the 6000-foot elevation, they reached the tree line where trees are smaller, twisted, and stunted due to more severe winds and snow, and eventually where no trees grow at all. At this timberline location, views become spectacular, making the spot attractive for a large resort facility.

Despite poor road access on Mount Hood's north side, private entrepreneurs applied for permits to operate and expand Cloud Cap Inn throughout the 1920s. The Cloud Cap Inn Resort Company submitted a design by architect Pietro Belluschi, then in A. E. Doyle's office in Portland, to the Forest Service as part of a permit application. The proposal resembled the rustic 1925 Multnomah Falls Lodge in the Columbia Gorge, which Doyle had recently designed. The proposal for the Cloud Cap expansion was abandoned due to a lack of investors. Twenty-one-year-old Portland architect John Yeon also proposed a design for a grand hotel in the Cloud Cap area. In a 1983 interview with Marian Kolisch for the Smithsonian Institution, Yeon stated that he later "came to hate" his design as a "youthful indiscretion."

The most controversial design was proposed by the Cascade Development Company. It included a large hotel designed by Portland architect Carl L. Linde and a tram and cableway to the summit of Mount Hood. The proposal alarmed the Forest Service and eventually induced the secretary of agriculture to retain three nationally known experts in public lands to evaluate public uses of the forest, one of whom, landscape architect Frank Albert Waugh, had written the 1920 report on recreational uses on the mountain. The other two committee members were Frederick Law Olmsted Jr., a member of the National Capital Parks and Planning Commission and son of the designer of New York's Central Park, and John Campbell Merriam, the president of the Carnegie Institute, a paleontologist and conservationist who was active in developing educational features of the National Parks. The secretary justified delaying a decision on the proposed Cloud Cap expansion by noting of Mount Hood, "We are dealing with one of the great landmarks of the continent."

The committee's report, *Public Values of the Mount Hood Area*, finally completed in 1930, did not approve Linde's hotel design. The promoters submitted several revisions, but the proposed hotel design essentially remained a large blocky structure that the committee considered better suited to the city than the forest. In a paper "Design of a Hotel at Cloud Cap," Olmsted advised that a mountain hotel should instead be integrated into the environment: "As an element in the timber-line landscape of Mount Hood, it should be as little self-assertive and conspicuous and as little incongruous as the utmost skill and ingenuity in design can make it." The tram and cableway failed for lack of financing. Through

CLOUD CAP INN

Cloud Cap Inn, a private retreat built in 1889 on the north side of Mount Hood, was sold to the Forest Service in 1942 for $2000 and was operated as a hotel for a brief time during 1946. In 1954, it was leased to the Hood River Crag Rats, the oldest mountain rescue group in the United States, who restored it for private use as a base for snow surveying, training, and mountain rescue. Over the years, the inn's appearance has been altered by renovations such as an added foundation and deck, replacements of beams and logs, and repairs to its fireplaces. Cloud Cap Inn is the oldest building remaining on Mount Hood and was listed in the National Register of Historic Places in 1974. It is accessible by a fourteen-mile gravel road and, still under lease to the Crag Rats, is only occasionally open to the public.

Cloud Cap Inn interior, circa 1900. Hostess Sarah Langille rests in a chair. Oregon Historical Society Research Library negative #2569.

PROPOSED CLOUD CAP INN - A·E·DOYLE ARCH'T
NORTH ELEV. - APRIL 28 '27

Pietro Belluschi design for proposed expansion of Cloud Cap Inn, north elevation, 1927. Oregon Historical Society Research Library OrHi 39039.

the process of considering the proposals for expansion at Cloud Cap, the Forest Service developed principles to guide future development elsewhere in the forest, including the Timberline Lodge area.

By the late 1920s, Government Camp on Mount Hood's south side had become the site of winter sports events. In 1927, the Mount Hood Ski Club was formed, one of several local outdoor recreation groups. The next year, several members of the Mount Hood Ski Club organized the Cascade Ski Club, and some of its members developed Multorpor Ski Bowl near Government Camp. Local ski clubs soon banded together to form the Pacific Northwest Ski Association, which organized competitions, including a winter sports carnival that drew up to 10,000 participants and spectators to the mountain. According to skier, climber, writer, and photographer George Henderson, tournament competition included ski jumping and downhill and slalom races at the nearby Ski Bowl Ski Area on Tom, Dick, and Harry Mountain. As Hank Lewis remembered, skiers also climbed the six miles to the timberline from Government Camp and skied down the old Timberline Road, west of

Carl Linde design for expansion of Cloud Cap Inn proposed by Cascade Development Company, circa 1929. U.S.D.A. Forest Service, Mount Hood District.

Legendary skier Otto Lang on Mount Hood in 1937. He operated ski schools at Mount Hood (including the first at Timberline Lodge), as well as Mount Rainier and Mount Baker in Washington and was known for bringing the Arlberg turning technique from St. Anton am Arlberg, Austria, to the Northwest. Lang was also a filmmaker, photographer, woodworker, and writer. He died in 2008. Photograph by Ray Atkeson, Friends of Timberline Archive.

The annual winter sports carnival at Battle Axe Inn, Governor Julius L. Meier (center) and Portland Winter Sports Association Queen Hadji with her court and association board members, circa 1931. Mount Hood booster Jack Meier is to the right and behind his father, the governor. Photograph by George Henderson, Friends of Timberline Archive.

the current Blossom Trail, to the top of Mazama Hill, and west to Government Camp, a popular route for years.

With increasing activity on the south side of the mountain, the need for more overnight facilities was becoming critical. As early as 1928, Fred W. Cleator and Francis E. "Scotty" Williamson Jr. of the Forest Service investigated a proposed site and a nearby water source. In 1932, Williamson expanded the proposal to include a recreation plan for a twenty-eight-acre area along the west side of the Salmon River at an elevation of 5800 feet. He suggested an architectural style for the proposed resort: "This chalet had best not be a regular tourist hotel, but built along the line of the Swiss alpine hospice, of stone or stone and logs. The building should be arranged for both winter and summer use." This plan for a modest chalet with cabins for hikers and climbers was later abandoned, but Tract D, the tract identified by Williamson in the 1920s, was the site later selected for Timberline Lodge.

In 1931, Mount Hood boosters, including young Jack Meier of Portland's Meier & Frank department store and son of Governor Julius L. Meier, formed the Portland Winter Sports Association (the Oregon Winter Sports Association after 1936) with the purpose of "Develop-

Sun Valley Lodge poster. The Sun Valley Lodge has not been added onto since it opened in December 1936. The building was designed in several segments, not unlike Timberline Lodge, but the scale is much larger. Courtesy of Sun Valley Company.

Ski competitions on Mount Hood increased in popularity during the 1930s. One tournament was the Midsummer Ski Tournament, where Hjalmar Hvam, a member of Cascade Ski Club, competed in the slalom in 1937. Photograph by George Henderson, Oregon Historical Society Research Library negative #010754.

ing, fostering and encouraging a love of winter sports and exercise; the promotion, establishment and advertisement of the use of Mount Hood as a center for winter sports; to hold expositions and carnivals of winter sports; to provide facilities for the enjoyment and participation in winter sports; to at all times operate said corporation without profit to the corporation or any of its members."

A ski lodge was critical to promoting winter sports on Mount Hood. In the mid to late 1930s, Oregon ski enthusiasts looked to the new Sun Valley Lodge in Idaho for inspiration. In 1935, Averill Harriman, chairman of the Union Pacific Railroad, had retained Austrian Count Felix Schaffgotsch to scout out the ideal location for a ski resort. After touring western mountain regions, including Mount Hood, Schaffgotsch identified a site near Ketchum, Idaho. Harriman purchased several thousand acres there and built the Sun Valley Lodge, which opened in December 1936. That same year, James Curran developed the world's first chairlift in Union Pacific's Omaha headquarters, and it was built at Sun Valley. Local Mount Hood Forest Service officials visited Sun Valley to observe its operation as a model for potential operators of what would become Timberline Lodge. The lodges were similar: both were ski lodges offering overnight facilities and food service, and both areas provided chairlifts.

Although the operation at Sun Valley was a pattern for Timberline, the two lodges would be very different. Whereas Sun Valley Lodge was built by private enterprise on private land, Timberline Lodge would eventually be financed with public funds on public land. While Sun Valley's somewhat remote location precluded visits from large numbers of nonpaying members of the public, Timberline Lodge's location close to Portland drew crowds of day visitors. Sun Valley was a resort hotel, constructed of concrete with manufactured furniture, and Timberline would be partly a museum, hand-built of wood, iron, and stone and furnished with handmade furniture, draperies, and bedspreads. The comparison to Sun Valley was obvious, however, and in January 1940, Richard Neuberger wrote an article in *Coast* in which he called Timberline "Uncle Sam's Sun Valley." In the same article, Neuberger (later a U.S. Senator from Oregon) observed that the ski slopes at Timberline were "superior to those of Sun Valley," and that the lodge was "almost as expensive to build per room as the most sumptuous hotels in the world."

In the early 1930s, however, neither the demand for resort facilities for skiers nor the Forest Service's recreation policies on Mount Hood were enough to guarantee that a lodge would be built. The nation's economy had been crippled by the Depression, and private financing for a resort in the forest was simply not available.

CHAPTER TWO

CHALLENGES TO BUILDING TIMBERLINE LODGE

The tremendous logs which form its interior frame are from the mountains of Oregon. The stones which form its lower walls were scoured and shaped by the Great Glacier. The heavy rough timbering of its upper walls is a part of the industry of the State. The hand-hewn slabs which sheath its roof are of the forests of Oregon. The hand-wrought bands and ties of iron which unite its log framing will be made on the ground. It will belong to the mountain and to the State.

—STANLEY STONAKER, architect Gilbert Stanley Underwood's representative on the Timberline Lodge project, 1936

Civilian Conservation Corps enroll-ees on the fire line in a forest fire in the West in 1933. Courtesy of the Franklin D. Roosevelt Library Digital Archives, NARA photo 27-0652a.

THE STOCK MARKET CRASH of Black Thursday, October 24, 1929, signaled the beginning of the Depression, but many other factors contributed to the economic crisis that culminated in the market plunge. Farming, mining, and logging industries that had begun sliding in the 1920s plummeted after 1929. Drought plagued the Midwest, consumer spending declined, construction stalled, and unemployment rose. Nationally, unemployment peaked at 25 percent by 1933. Oregonians suffered from the decline of the timber industry when construction slowed in the 1920s. Since much of Oregon was rural, the state's residents were also widely affected by drought and declining prices for agricultural products. In 1933, more than 40,000 were unemployed in Portland alone and in need of relief. Oregonians joined the rest of the nation in hoping that a political change would help.

When President Franklin Delano Roosevelt took office March 4, 1933, he immediately set up the New Deal, a series of social and economic programs to provide relief through public employment as well as measures to create private sector jobs. Among the first programs was the Federal Emergency Relief Act (FERA) of 1933, which provided states with $250 million in direct relief grants and supplanted an earlier relief program of state loans initiated by Roosevelt's predecessor Herbert Hoover. The Works Progress Administration (WPA), the agency that ultimately provided funding for construction of Timberline, was part of the Emergency Relief Appropriation Act that replaced FERA in 1935.

The Emergency Conservation Work Act, approved in March 1933, created the Civilian Conservation Corps (CCC), which immediately provided jobs for 250,000 unemployed men between the ages of eighteen and twenty-five in reforestation, building and road construction, prevention of soil erosion, and fire and flood control. A worker's earnings (thirty dollars per month) were sent directly to his family except for five dollars per month given to the worker. Many CCC workers were employed in state and national forests, including the Mount Hood National Forest.

DEPRESSION-ERA PUBLIC WORKS PROJECTS IN THE PACIFIC NORTHWEST

Between 1933 and 1934, approximately 27,000 Oregonians were put to work on public projects. Most public employees in the state worked on projects funded by the Public Works Administration (PWA), a program adopted in May 1933. That year, construction was begun on the Grand Coulee and Bonneville Dams on the Columbia River. The dams were the largest PWA projects undertaken in the Northwest. More than 3000 workers were employed at Bonneville Dam, where unskilled laborers earned fifty cents per hour. Bonneville Dam was built at a cost estimated between $51 million and $88.4 million.

The phase of projects called the First New Deal started through legislation enacted in the first three months of Roosevelt's administration in 1933. A new phase, the Second New Deal, started in 1935. The WPA was one of the best-known programs of the Second New Deal. Since the goal was to provide jobs to the greatest possible number of workers, efficiency became a secondary concern in many WPA projects. With shovels and picks, WPA workers constructed and repaired roads and tunnels in Portland and throughout the state. Rocky Butte Scenic Drive in northeast Portland began as a state relief project in 1934 and was finished by WPA workers. The drive's beautiful hand-hewn rock walls,

Bonneville Dam, excavation of the navigation lock for the second approach channel, December 21, 1934. Courtesy of the Franklin D. Roosevelt Library Digital Archives, NARA photo 27-0902a.

tunnel, railings, and summit observatory are one of Portland's most distinctive WPA projects.

The largest WPA project in Portland was the construction of the Portland–Columbia Airport, site of today's Portland International Airport, where an average of 1000 workers labored daily to cover the Columbia River bottomlands with four million cubic yards of sand dredged from the river, as described in Neil Barker's summary of Portland's WPA projects. Much of this work was done by hand with shovels.

In 1935, when government loans to private investors seemed unlikely, promoters of a lodge on Mount Hood turned to the newly created WPA for funding. With stimulating employment as the goal, WPA regulations required labor to account for 90 percent of a project's cost (materials made up the other 10 percent) and that jobs should primarily go to the unskilled. In addition, workers were limited to thirty hours per week to ensure that the maximum number of men could be employed.

A YEAR-ROUND RECREATIONAL CENTER AT TIMBERLINE

In September 1935, Emerson J. Griffith, Oregon's WPA director, submitted an application to Harry L. Hopkins, WPA administrator, for $246,893 to build a hotel on Mount Hood's south side. Griffith used cost estimates from architect John Yeon's design for a ski lodge. In addition to a lodge proposed for the Cloud Cap area, Yeon also designed a building to be situated at the edge of the Salmon River Canyon on Mount Hood's south side. The location provided a dramatic vista but Yeon also chose it because he anticipated that winter snow would blow off into the canyon and not build up on the lodge's roof.

Griffith urged WPA administrator Harry Hopkins to act on the application immediately: "We wish to get this project well underway before the heavy snows come, and your efforts to speed this application will be very much appreciated." Griffith did not explain that no working drawings had yet been completed, or that snow at Mount Hood's timberline could be expected to start within six weeks of the application being submitted. In December, the WPA approved funds for constructing a "a year-round recreational center at Timber Line on Mount Hood, including housing accommodations, roads, trails, landscaping, parking spaces, swimming tanks, toboggan and ski runs, ski jumps, tennis courts, water system, open amphitheater, barns, shelters, and a hotel of stone and wood."

For every project, the WPA required a sponsor that provided a percentage of the funds. The sponsor for the Mount Hood lodge project was obligated to contribute $28,620, of which the local booster organi-

Workman on one of the towers erected to transmit electricity generated at Bonneville Dam, 1937–1938. Courtesy of Oregon State Library, 2006.001.1244, #2825.

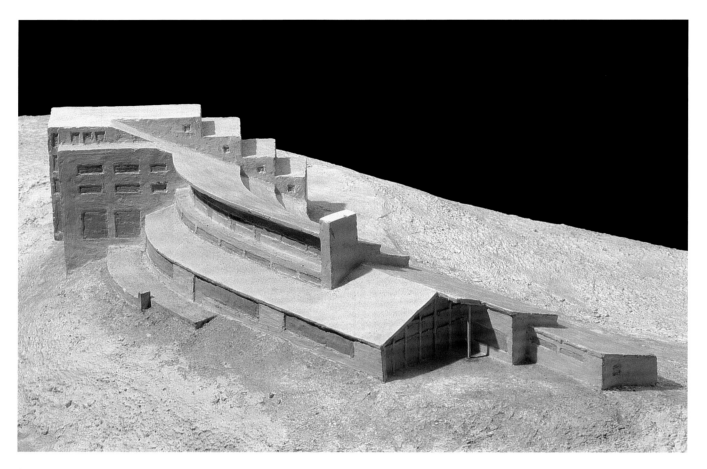

John Yeon's model of a lodge proposed for timberline on the south side of Mount Hood, 1935. Years later, in 1986, Yeon described the proposal in a letter to architect Thomas P. Deering Jr.: "The wing extended north instead of south from the highest block. The building lunged away from the mountain instead of towards it. The lounge was at the north end, reaching to the roof with a north wall of glass (floor to roof) facing the mountain. The dining room exploited the canyon view in the south block."

zation, Mount Hood Development Association, pledged $20,000 and the Forest Service $8620 for truck and machinery rentals and gravel for road improvement and construction. The initial application was followed by three additional applications for construction of the building, two for road improvements, and one for landscaping, totaling $968,636 from the WPA. Separate applications were filed for funding for art and furnishings.

The construction proposal for Timberline Lodge did not meet several WPA project standards. Material costs were higher than 10 percent (as much as 40 percent) and labor less than 90 percent. Griffith filed for exceptions to allow workers more than a thirty-hour workweek in order to frame in the lodge before winter. At the construction peak in September 1936, workers logged up to forty-eight hours per week. Griffith also filed requests for more skilled labor than was typical. The sponsor, the Forest Service, was unable to provide adequate sponsorship funding. Lack of sponsor funds in part caused the WPA to turn down an application for a ski chalet adjacent to the lodge.

EMERSON J. GRIFFITH (1884–1965)

Emerson J. Griffith was a former newspaperman and shipping manager who served as the finance director of the Democratic National Committee in 1932 and chaired the Roosevelt for President League in Oregon. An urbane gentleman and enthusiastic skier, Griffith became committed to establishing a ski resort on Mount Hood. He was interested in developing a hotel below Government Camp until Portland architect and conservationist John Yeon convinced him that the timberline site at the Salmon River Canyon was superior. In January 1935, Griffith was appointed Oregon state director of the Federal Housing Administration and in May the Oregon state director of the WPA. He was regarded as an honest and fair administrator. On October 1, 1938, a supporter wrote of Griffith: "There are Democrats, Republicans, Socialists, and Reds working on these projects. He has never demanded that a man must be a Registered Democrat to get a job. Human need is the pass word." In 1942, Griffith resigned from the WPA and ran unsuccessfully in the Oregon Democratic primary for U.S. Congress. He became rent control director for the Portland-Vancouver district, then moved to San Francisco. He lived in Tokyo from 1949 to 1952, where he opened a shipyard and participated in the reconstruction of Japan after World War II. He and his wife retired to Santa Rosa in 1953 and wrote mysteries. Griffith died in July 1965 in Burlingame, California.

Emerson J. Griffith, circa 1936. In February 1938, after Timberline's opening, Griffith wrote to Aubrey Williams, deputy WPA administrator, "Timberline Lodge stands today not only as a beautiful monument to the skill of WPA workers, but a most useful one. I believe that for many years to come it will be one of the world's most outstanding recreational centers." WPA Negatives Collection (negative #2183), Portland Art Museum, Oregon.

Colonel Francis C. Harrington, the WPA assistant administrator and successor to Hopkins, was so frustrated by the repeated applications and high cost of construction materials that on September 3, 1936, he told Oregon's deputy WPA administrator, "It is a lousy project but we are in it now and we have got to get out." Later in the same conversation he remarked, "I didn't mean it wasn't a good thing to do," but he continued to suggest that it was not suited to the WPA. Construction of Timberline Lodge as a WPA project would have been unlikely without Emerson Griffith's unflagging support.

A CASCADIAN BUILDING:
TIMBERLINE'S ARCHITECTS AND ARCHITECTURE

On December 18, 1935, regional forester C. J. "Shirley" Buck wrote to the Washington, D.C., office of Chief Forester F. A. Silcox to inform him that the plans for the lodge by architect John Yeon had been abandoned because of their high cost per rentable room. Buck asked Silcox to recommend an architect with a national reputation who might be available to design a lodge on Mount Hood. On December 26, the National Forest Service office recommended Gilbert Stanley Underwood of Los Angeles, who was then working in Washington, D.C.

Underwood's background made his selection ideal. Early in his career in southern California, he was apprenticed to masters of Arts and Crafts architecture, which featured the use of natural materials and Indian designs. He utilized these elements in his designs for several lodges for the National Park Service, including Utah's Zion Lodge and Bryce Canyon Lodge in 1924. In these lodges, Underwood used massive stones to create a sense of solidity and immense scale and wood to blend with surrounding forestland. Shortly after completing the Utah lodges, Underwood designed the Ahwahnee Hotel in California's Yosemite National Park, which opened in 1927. The following year, the Grand Canyon's North Rim Lodge opened. Underwood would have been aware of LeConte Memorial Lodge, the first visitor's center in Yosemite, which bears a striking resemblance to the main façade of Timberline. Underwood biographer Joyce Zaitlin stated that his designs for National Park lodges became the standard for architecture on public lands. These buildings, described as Rustic in style, were sympathetic with the aesthetics of the Arts and Crafts movement. Soon after the WPA application was approved, Underwood was retained as consulting architect for Timberline Lodge. His fee was paid from funds raised by the Mount Hood Development Association.

Possibly alluding to the focus on the mountain and forest, the Underwood firm referred to Timberline's architectural style as "environmental." In *Patterns of Rustic Design: Park and Recreation Structures from the 1930s*, Albert H. Good, architectural consultant to the National Park Service in 1938, stated, "The style of architecture . . . most widely used in our forested national parks, and in other wilderness parks, is generally referred to as 'rustic.' It is, or should be, something more than the worn and misused term implies. Successfully handled, it is a style which, through the use of native materials in proper scale, and through the avoidance of severely straight lines and over-sophistication, gives the feeling of having been executed by pioneer craftsmen with limited hand

Bryce Canyon Lodge, Utah, circa 1924, designed by Gilbert Stanley Underwood, is in the tradition of Rustic lodges similar to Timberline Lodge. Courtesy of National Park Service.

Architect Gilbert Stanley Underwood (left) holding a rendering of the Ahwahnee Hotel, Yosemite National Park, circa 1926. RL 1736. The Yosemite Museum, Yosemite National Park.

Gilbert Stanley Underwood drawing for Timberline Lodge, preliminary design, published in newspapers in February 1936, to help Mount Hood Development Association sell bonds for sponsor contributions. The octagonal headhouse put the wings at a right angle, south elevation. Courtesy of U.S.D.A. Forest Service.

tools. It thus achieves sympathy with natural surroundings and with the past." Timberline Lodge's use of native wood and stone, its oversize scale, and its broken architectural lines place the building both in the tradition of Rustic park structures and in the tradition of the Arts and Crafts movement.

Most of the distinctive features of the lodge's design are visible in Underwood's drawings, such as the headhouse, asymmetrical wings, short transepts near the ends of the wings that contain a dormer bisected by a chimney, dormers that extend upward from the wall beneath them, vertical board-and-batten siding combined with clapboard siding, stone facing on the ground level, and stone buttresses at the building ends. (The end buttresses are no longer visible because of additions to the lodge at each end.)

Underwood's early proposals for the lodge design featured both pioneer and American Indian motifs in conjunction with the use of local natural materials. Underwood's suggestions for a pioneer theme at Timberline were reflected in such detailing as iron bands on peeled logs

in the main lobby and exterior metal ornamentation on the chimney. Underwood also suggested using an Indian theme. In a letter written to Robert C. Dieck in early January 1936, and cited in Jean Weir's thesis, Underwood stated: "I believe that a decorative motif, based on the crude Indian forms that were common in the Pacific Northwest, would form an interesting basis of study. Certainly there will be men of ability there who can do accurate research and who can develop primitive designs in primary colors which will blend with rough oiled wood interiors." While Underwood's use of the words "crude" and "primitive" was unenlightened, his focus was on developing a design aesthetic that would be appropriate for the lodge's architectural style. In the same letter, he continued, "One note which must be kept out at all costs is sophistication," and he recommended the use of "very crude iron work in fixtures, grilles, fire irons, etc."

As the lodge developed, Underwood felt that its design was becoming too sophisticated. In October 1936, he recommended that metal hardware be simplified to suggest work created by the "average blacksmith

Gilbert Stanley Underwood drawing for Timberline Lodge, preliminary design, north elevation, February 1936. During meetings in spring 1936, designers decided to reduce the building's height from 90 to 70 feet. Courtesy of U.S.D.A. Forest Service.

Zigzag Ranger Station buildings designed in the early 1930s exhibit an arch similar to the Timberline arch that appeared not only in the lodge's architecture but also in the furniture.

who might have accompanied early pioneers." He cautioned Griffith, "There is a little tendency to 'over-design' and to use stylistic influences as against creating architecture that grows out of the conditions of the problem," again reminding the builders of the elements of ideal Rustic architecture. Carvings on the stone fireplace in the main lobby are the only motifs that follow Underwood's recommendation to use local Pacific Northwest Indian designs, although elements inspired by Native American symbols were used throughout.

The Building's Exterior

Promoters of Timberline Lodge avoided both the terms "Rustic" and "Environmental." They adopted a new term, "Cascadian," coined by Forest Service architect William I. "Tim" Turner, which suggests that the lodge's design echoes the shape of the mountain peak behind it. The goal of architecture described as Cascadian was identical to the aim of Rustic architecture. In a 1967 interview with *Oregonian* reporter Muriel Ames, Forest Service architect Linn Forrest stated: "The character and outline of the mountain peak inspired the shape of the central lounge. . . . It was our hope not to detract from the great natural beauty of the area. The entire exterior was made to blend as nearly as possible with the mountain site."

The task of supervising construction and the creation of detail drawings belonged to architect Turner, who had trained in the Portland office of David Chambers Lewis (architect of Portland's Trinity Episcopal Cathedral). Turner supervised Linn Forrest, Howard Gifford, and Dean Wright, who were brought into the Forest Service in the early 1930s to design structures funded through public works programs. Among Turner's early projects were buildings at the Zigzag Ranger Station on Mount Hood, which exhibit an arch form similar to the one used later at Timberline Lodge. Structural engineering, especially adapted to abnormal snow loads and snow creep, was done by Forest Service engineers Ward W. Gano and W. D. Smith, as Gano remembered in 1976 interviews.

Each of the Forest Service architects focused on a different aspect of the building. Forrest, who previously worked on Bonneville Dam, drew most of the floor plans and exterior elevations. In a 1976 interview, Forrest remembered that the axis of the wings was altered slightly after the site was surveyed in May 1936. As built, the wings open at an obtuse angle to the south, maximizing the view from both wings. Underwood's original design for an octagonal central headhouse that echoed the mountain behind it was altered during design to a hexagon, partly to position the wings at this angle.

The headhouse of Timberline Lodge suggests the conical shape of Mount Hood behind it.

DIRECTLY IN LINE WITH THE SOUTH ENTRANCE,
THE PEAK OF MT. HOOD SHINES ABOVE THE LODGE

Forest Service architect Linn Forrest's drawing of the final design for Timberline Lodge, south elevation, facing north toward the mountain, 1936. From Claire Warner Churchill's Timberline Lodge, Friends of Timberline Archive.

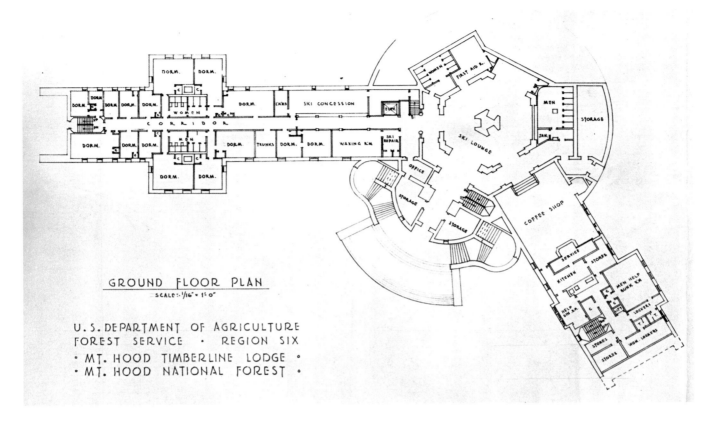

GROUND FLOOR PLAN
SCALE: 1/16" = 1'-0"

U.S. DEPARTMENT OF AGRICULTURE
FOREST SERVICE · REGION SIX
· MT. HOOD TIMBERLINE LODGE ·
· MT. HOOD NATIONAL FOREST ·

Ground floor plan of Timberline Lodge, lower lobby and wings, 1936. The full transept on the west wing was a design feature contributed by Gilbert Stanley Underwood, according to Thomas P. Deering Jr. and is echoed by the second floor windows on the east wing. Both transepts break up the asymmetrical wings and provide surface for varied exterior wall treatments—shingle, board and batten, and stone facing. Oregon Historical Society Research Library negative #37947.

Timberline's Interior Spaces

Most visitors enter Timberline Lodge at the central headhouse, which contains the public lobbies and mezzanine. Connected to the headhouse are two wings that contain guest rooms on four floors of the west wing and guest rooms on one floor and the dining room in the east wing. The lower lobby is on the ground level in the headhouse, with three large hearths set in an enormous central fireplace. From 1938 to 1981, this space was the Ski Lounge, where skiers dripped and dried in rawhide chairs, their toes warmed by the fire. (Ski concessions were moved to the Wy'East Day Lodge when it opened in 1981.)

The lower lobby also originally contained first aid facilities, a Forest Service office, and storage space (in the area that now houses the Rachael Griffin Historic Exhibition Center and model of a restored guest room). The Coyote Den, where the video *Builders of Timberline Lodge* is shown, was previously part of the men's restroom. The former Ski Grille (now the Barlow Room) is in the east wing, and the Blue Ox Bar, with its vivid murals, is tucked around a corner in the east wing. This area contains a hall leading to the Americans with Disabilities Act (ADA) elevator and entrance. The west wing once included a ski con-

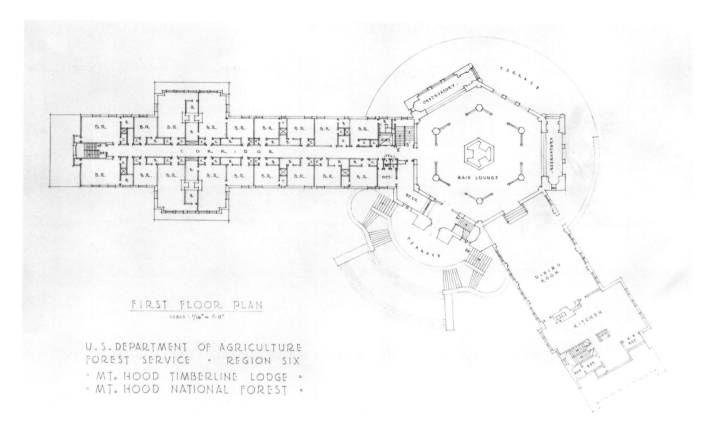

FIRST FLOOR PLAN
SCALE: 1/16" = 1'-0"

U.S. DEPARTMENT OF AGRICULTURE
FOREST SERVICE · REGION SIX
· MT. HOOD TIMBERLINE LODGE ·
· MT. HOOD NATIONAL FOREST ·

cession room, a ski waxing room, and a dormitory. Of these, only the dormitory area, where guest rooms are now called chalet rooms, is still in place. The reception desk, gift shop, and offices are also in the west wing. The lodge's heated outdoor swimming pool, built in 1958, is at the end of the west wing.

The main lobby is one floor above the lower lobby in the headhouse. It soars two stories to a conical roof. Handmade three-sided couches and hexagonal coffee tables cluster around a hexagonal stone chimney. Enormous log posts and rails encircle the room like a corral. Each of six hand-adzed, solid pine columns marks the six angles of the headhouse and rises over thirty feet to the roof. Flooring in the main lobby and the adjacent Cascade Dining Room is one-inch-thick oak planks. The C. S. Price Wing, added to the lodge in 1975, is beyond the dining room, and contains two meeting rooms and the Raven's Nest Bar, which has large view windows facing north and south.

The mezzanine looks over the main lobby. In this open seating area, guests relax at original handcrafted tables, chairs, and couches and enjoy several of the major oil paintings in the Timberline collection. The Mount Jefferson window is a favorite view window on the mezzanine.

First floor plan of Timberline Lodge, main lobby and wings, 1936. Oregon Historical Society Research Library negative #37946.

The lodge's guest rooms are located on four floors of the west wing and one floor of the east wing. The original flooring in guest rooms and corridors was fir; on the fourth floor it was hemlock. The guest room walls are knotty cedar, knotty pine, and hemlock.

SPRING 1936: THE WORK BEGINS

In the early days of the project, the lodge was called a "hotel at the timberline," "Mt. Hood Timberline Hotel," "Timber Line Hotel," or "Mt. Hood Hotel." In a letter to James Mount on February 4, 1936, regional forester C. J. (Shirley) Buck settled the name question: "The best we have been able to evolve is 'Mount Hood Timberline Lodge.' The timberline zone of Mt. Hood has received considerable attention in the past, and it seems desirable to stress this feature."

Before construction began, the Forest Service worked to clear a path to the site, not an easy job since the six-mile-long road in late winter was covered with snow four to sixteen feet deep. In March 1936, the Forest Service began to remove snow on East Leg Road, which ran along the same route as today's Timberline Road but stopped about one-half mile below the lodge site. The original road to the timberline site was West Leg Road, which stopped at Phlox Point.

In the spring of 1936, contractor Max Lorenz wrote that he anticipated clearing the road in about four weeks. Engineer Ward Gano wrote in 1989 that it ended up taking three months, with the road not fully cleared until June 11, 1936. For every foot of packed snow that was removed each day, another two feet might fall that night. In a progress report, the Forest Service engineer in charge of snow removal, Captain C. G. Jones, known as "Hurry Up" Jones, noted: "In starting this work Mar. 5, the snow depth . . . was 47″ on the level. At the end of March the Highway Dept. reported a depth of 90″."

In March 1936, a tent camp for workers opened at Summit Meadows. Formerly a CCC camp, it was almost seven miles downhill from the lodge site. At the camp, eight-man canvas tents were set on four-foot-high wood platforms. A pot-bellied stove in each tent provided heat. In winter, the tents were covered with wood roofs to prevent snow from collapsing them.

Supervisors shared the camp with workers. Engineer Ward Gano wrote that wages were ninety cents an hour for building trade laborers, seventy-five cents per hour for common laborers, and fifty-five cents per

Clearing the road to the lodge site, spring 1936. WPA Negatives Collection (negative #4368), Portland Art Museum, Oregon.

Cartoon of construction supervisors on Timberline project, by Albina, circa 1936–1937. Personalities and relationships of construction supervisors are suggested in the caricatures and comments. Courtesy of William Wechner, Friends of Timberline Archive.

Supervisory personnel on the Timberline Lodge project, November 18, 1937. Front row (left to right): William Wechner, W. I. Turner, Max Lorenz. Back row (left to right): Delmer Johnson, carpentry foreman; Roy Baxter, lead man; Leo Williams, watchman; Jim Duncan, painter; Emery Hicks, electrician; Ed Finnegan, plumber and installer of fire sprinkling system; Ed Daniel, camp transportation and watchmen supervisor; Al Burrows, labor foreman. Photograph by Paul Callicotte. Courtesy of William Wechner, Friends of Timberline Archive.

The Civilian Conservation Corps tent camp at Summit Meadows below the Timberline Lodge site, circa 1936. This camp was converted into a WPA camp for workers on Timberline Lodge. Horstmeier Collection, Friends of Timberline Archive.

Woodblock print of the Summit Meadows Camp mess hall, by Martina Gangle, from Builders of Timberline Lodge, published by the Works Progress Administration, Portland, Oregon, 1937. Friends of Timberline Archive.

WPA kitchen crew, outside the mess hall,
camp at Summit Meadows, circa 1936.
Friends of Timberline Archive.

hour for unskilled laborers. The WPA records reported that unskilled workers were paid fifty-five dollars per month, intermediate workers sixty-five dollars, skilled workers eighty-five dollars, and technical professional workers ninety-four dollars. Workers living at the camp were charged one dollar per day for room and board.

William Wechner, a construction supervisor for Lorenz Bros. contractors, remembered living in the camp through the winter of 1936–1937. In a 1977 note, he recalled: "We had six to seven feet of snow at Summit Meadows that winter. . . . Latrines in some cases 100–200 feet away, sometimes at night going through 6–7″ of new snow to the latrine." Winter camping conditions were offset by the ample hot food. Chef Albert Altorfer, professionally trained in Switzerland, was proud of the meals served at Summit Meadows Camp. For breakfast, workers ate hot cereal and had a choice of cold cereal, fried ham, fried bacon, link sausage or patties, fried potatoes, eggs, and fresh or canned fruit. Lunch was sandwiches and soup, an apple or grapes. Dinner included steak, boiled or pot-roasted beef, or fish, mashed potatoes or fried potatoes, and always two vegetables, salad, and some kind of beans or peas or corn. Dessert was bread pudding or Jell-O, cake and cookies, coffee and tea. On the table, there were always jelly and peanut butter, and pickles and radishes. With up to 470 men eating and staying at the camp during the peak of construction, perhaps the busiest workers were those in the mess hall.

Each morning, with plows clearing the roads ahead of them, open canvas-covered trucks ferried the men from the Summit Meadows Camp uphill to the construction site. The men rarely lost a day of work, but the trek sometimes took as long as an hour during the winter, with workers shivering in the unheated trucks.

WPA crews generally were switched every two weeks to provide work for the maximum number of unemployed people. In the construction of Timberline, possibly only the unskilled workers switched. The total number of workers on site varied from 100 to 470. Workers came pri-

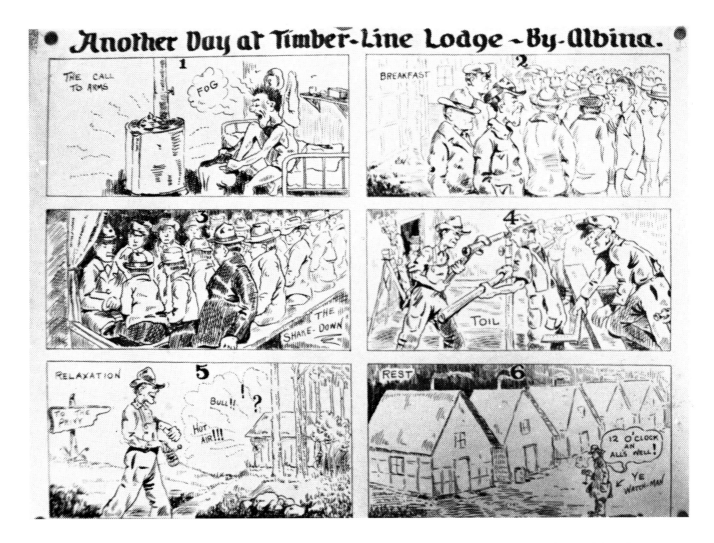

Cartoon illustrating a day in the life of a WPA worker toiling on the Timberline Lodge project and living at the camp at Summit Meadows, by Albina, circa 1936–1937. Courtesy of William Wechner, Friends of Timberline Archive.

marily from the WPA, but some jobs were performed by the younger men in the CCC, who came to the site from Camp Zigzag, west of Government Camp.

Before construction began in the spring, Griffith became concerned that the proposed lodge site was too close to the ridge above Salmon River Canyon, where a snow cornice might collapse under the weight of users around the building. After a meeting with the Forest Service, the decision was made to place the lodge to the west of the canyon edge. In May 1936, engineer Ward Gano, landscape architect Emmett Blanchfield, architect Linn Forrest, and two others spent three sunny days surveying a site about 900 feet west of the original site. In an undated paper written later, Gano recalled: "There were two major problems—an average of 14-ft. of snow that required rodding [inserting a pole through the snow for measurements] of each elevation shot and stretched the survey to a 3-day job, and beautiful cloud-free weather every day. Blanchfield and I were well-conditioned after a winter of skiing, but the other three suffered severe sun burn despite heavy application of the best lotions of the day. Fortunately, the contours developed from the survey required only minimum modification of the ground level plans to adapt the already designed building to the new site."

SUMMER TO FALL 1936: FAST AND FURIOUS

On Mount Hood, summer is short, and winter snows sometimes come as early as September. To frame and roof a building that covers 15,000 square feet in a remote location before winter storms arrived meant that every minute was of the essence. Work began before building plans were approved and before the official groundbreaking ceremony was held on June 14, 1936. George Henderson, a publicist for the Oregon Winter Sports Association, realized at the groundbreaking ceremony that the true cornerstone location would not make for an optimal photo opportunity. Henderson wrote about the groundbreaking ceremony in his 2006 memoir *Lonely on the Mountain*: "[The stone] was swinging from the boom of a power crane ready to be deposited at the site selected by the engineers when I appealed to Griffith to revise the location. The engineers were adamant and the construction crew anxious to get on with the job, but the WPA chief had a sense of history, and the clanking crane was redirected to a point a hundred yards away so that Mount Hood's majestic summit was aligned perfectly beyond the stone. Following the ceremony, the oft-moved monolith was returned to its rightful resting place to become a permanent part of the lodge's foundation."

Groundbreaking ceremony, June 14, 1936. Photograph by George Henderson. WPA Negatives Collection (negative #4381), Portland Art Museum, Oregon.

BUILDING THE LODGE

Once the ground was finally clear of snow, construction on the lodge proceeded rapidly. Only four months elapsed from the beginning of construction in mid June to completion of the exterior and roof in October 1936, a remarkable achievement. The safety record was also outstanding, especially in light of the fact that the contractor's crews were often made up of unskilled laborers.

WPA workers in line in camp, waiting to be trucked to the lodge construction site, summer or early fall, 1936. Photograph by Francis E. McIntosh. Courtesy of Oregon State Library, 2006.001.0425.2628.

The foundation and the floor of the west wing were framed during summer 1936. Gano Papers, Friends of Timberline Archive.

Construction on Timberline Lodge began with the west wing and proceeded to the east wing in the summer of 1936. Friends of Timberline Archive.

Workman on ladder at Timberline Lodge site, summer or early fall 1936. Beam in photo is for the lodge interior. Gano Papers, Friends of Timberline Archive.

Workers at the lodge construction site ate lunch supplied by the Summit Meadows Camp kitchen, summer or early fall 1936. Photograph by Francis E. McIntosh. Courtesy of Oregon State Library, 2006.001.0425.2627.

The great columns for the main lobby of Timberline Lodge were protected by temporary wood sheathing as they were raised into place, summer or early fall 1936. Photograph by Francis E. McIntosh. Courtesy of Oregon State Library, 2006.001.0425.2642.

Fortunately for the workers, significant snowstorms held off until December in 1936, although this photo, probably taken during WPA administrator Harry Hopkins's inspection of the lodge on September 14, 1936, shows some snow accumulating before the headhouse was completed. WPA Negatives Collection (negative #2379), Portland Art Museum, Oregon.

The headhouse was constructed between the wings after the wings were framed, early fall 1936. When the headhouse roof was connected to the roofs of the adjoining wings, builders were concerned about the fit, as supervisor William Wechner remembered in a 1978 interview: "These—what they call the rafters, or the hipsters, six of those, and they had to go at a certain point up there to meet this six-point tuck. They were quite worried about whether we were going to make it or not, but it happened to be that there was only about an inch or inch and a half discrepancy, which we overcame very easily." Oregon Historical Society Research Library negative #71458.

Stonework

According to Forest Service engineer Ward Gano, crushed rock for the roadbed came from a quarry about four miles below the Timberline site, and sand for concrete came from the Wapinitia Highway junction on Mount Hood's south flank. Gano recalled that most of the boulders used in facing the building were collected locally. Architect W. I. Turner told a newspaper reporter in 1938 that the flagstone for hearths and terraces was quarried near Stayton, Oregon.

Up to fifty stonemasons covered the front steps and terraces with flagstone. The stonemasons included a number of Italians who had learned their craft in Italy. Among these was Jack DiBenedetto, whose son, Americo P. DiBenedetto, became a Forest Service architect and was responsible for several lodge remodeling and upgrading projects. Jack DiBenedetto and other Italian masons had worked in the Columbia Gorge on the Vista House, the stone bridge at Eagle Creek, and the stone retaining walls along the original Columbia River Highway before they came to Timberline. Scandinavians were also well represented among the Timberline stonemasons.

Inside, eight to ten masons, using large cut stone, built the enormous fireplace that forms the center of the headhouse. They also built the smaller fireplaces in the Cascade Dining Room, fireplaces in some guest rooms, and all of the lodge's chimneys.

Above the roofline, the central stone chimney rises from the peak of the headhouse and is punctuated by arched vents. The weight of the main chimney is approximately 800,000 pounds. It was built within a wood frame during the winter of 1936–1937. A 750-pound brass and bronze weather vane rises twenty-nine feet above the chimney. Installed during a storm, the weather vane was reportedly almost blown off the roof before the concrete base set. The other chimneys are in the wings for the guest room fireplaces and the Cascade Dining Room fireplace. On October 16, 1936, A. D. Taylor, Forest Service landscape architect, wrote about Timberline's stonework to Fred Cleator of the Zigzag Ranger District: "I think it is the best stonework of this kind which I have seen in any building in any of the forests."

The chimney rises to the roof of the headhouse, where the ceiling beams join it, circa 1938. WPA Negatives Collection (negative #4522), Portland Art Museum, Oregon.

The stone chimney and brass and bronze weather vane crown the headhouse. Timberline Lodge photograph.

Framework for exterior stone facing, Timberline Lodge, fall 1936. WPA Negatives Collection (negative #4360), Portland Art Museum, Oregon.

Rock for the stone facing on the lodge was collected near the construction site. The terrain was rough and vehicle access was difficult. Photograph by Francis E. McIntosh. Courtesy of Oregon State Library, 2006.001.0425.2631.

Stonemasons outside the lower front entrance, Timberline Lodge, fall 1936. Jack DiBenedetto is second from the right. Courtesy of A. P. DiBenedetto.

Ira Davidson, the superintendent of stonemasons, in front of stonework facing being applied to the lodge, circa November 1936. Friends of Timberline Archive.

Sprinkler System

Timberline was unusual in the 1930s for having a sprinkler system installed when it was constructed, remembered Ward Gano in a paper written in the 1970s. Architect W. I. Turner wrote a memo in the Forest Service log on December 4, 1936, reporting that the first layout of the sprinkler system showed visible piping in the public areas. A meeting was held with Oregon WPA Administrator Griffith, contractor Max Lorenz, and architect Turner, and they agreed that the piping would be concealed and the only visible part of the system would be the sprinkler heads themselves. The continuing attention to detail during construction is one reason for the ultimate beauty of the lodge.

Water and Septic Systems

No plans for a sewage system or water supply were completed before construction of the lodge began. Gano, then a young Forest Service engineer, rose to the challenge of planning both systems quickly in 1936, adapting to the difficult location. The original water source was a spring in the Salmon River Canyon. A buried 50,000-gallon concrete reservoir above the lodge would conduct gravity-fed water through a six-inch cast-iron pipe to the lodge. But in the late summer, the flow of that spring dwindled to about ten gallons per minute. Gano then located several other springs, but one lacked adequate flow and two others would have required expensive high-pressure pumps to fill the reservoir.

Finally in late October, a spring with a sufficient flow of twenty-nine gallons per minute was located 300 feet upstream in the Salmon River, and it was marked with a thirty-foot mast so it could be found in winter. A reservoir and settling tank were completed by late November 1936. By February 1937, however, the water supply was low. Gano, George Henderson, George Calverley (a horse packer), and Jerry Lymph (a forest guard), and another crew member spent sixteen days camped in a cabin near the spring, digging down into the snow to locate the mast only to find dry stream beds.

In the spring, Gano used a bulldozer to continue digging in the same spot to locate the spring. After two weeks, the crew uncovered the spring only to learn that it too was dry. CCC crews under Forest Service direction excavated another spring, the current water source, between one and two miles below the lodge, which feeds the west fork of the Salmon River. The spring has been improved so that it passes domestic water standards. The pumping system includes a three-stage high-pressure pump, a buried power cable, and a pipe.

Wastewater disposal presents special problems at Timberline's altitude, in the harsh climate, and because of the unique design of the building. The original septic system plans called for a surprisingly

Ward Gano (foreground) in a snow cave during excavation of a spring to supply water to the lodge, spring 1937. Photograph courtesy of George Henderson, collection of Jeff Thomas.

small, 2000-gallon single-compartment tank. (A tank for an average three-bedroom home is 1000 gallons.) In October 1936, Gano designed a 4000-gallon, two-compartment, reinforced concrete Imhoff-type sewage tank and a 2300-square-foot drain field. Built in one month, the system lasted until 1960. The current sewage treatment plant is in an A-frame building near Timberline's parking lot. Treated sewage is piped to a drain field on the west side of the Salmon River below the main parking lot. The current wastewater treatment plant is operated under a permit from the Oregon Department of Environmental Quality.

Wood Siding, Millwork, and Shingles

The headhouse was covered with two roofs, an inner, lower roof and the more steeply pitched outer roof. The outer, split-shake cedar roof is steeply slanted, reaching almost to the ground in places, to facilitate snow sliding off of it. The roof shakes, purchased from a Milwaukie, Oregon, mill, are one and one-quarter inches thick at the bottom, tapering to one-half inch at the top, thirty-one inches long, and between four and eight inches wide. (Cedar shakes for residential use are generally one-half to three-quarters inches thick and eighteen to twenty-four inches long.) Originally, builders planned to use shakes made at the CCC Camp One and a Half at Estacada, but the project became too expensive and time-consuming to support. Construction supervisor William Wechner remembered that at the eaves, shakes were placed

Timberline Lodge's large-scale board-and-batten siding and steeply pitched wood-shingled roof make use of native materials. Shown here is the transept at the end of the west wing.

three layers thick for protection against storm winds, which have been recorded up to 100 miles per hour. Timberline's roof shakes need to be replaced every six years.

In addition to the lodge exterior's cedar shingles, the cedar and Douglas fir board-and-batten siding is another distinctive feature. In typical board-and-batten construction, battens are placed one foot apart, but for Timberline Lodge, they are two feet apart. Architect Linn Forrest stated in a 1976 interview that the scale was doubled to conform to the large scale of the building.

NATIVE AMERICAN AND WILDLIFE DESIGN ELEMENTS

Native American images and wildlife themes appear on certain exterior wood details such as the carved thunderbird and rams' heads at the front door and buffalo and bear heads under eaves.

The dramatic thunderbird carved design over the front door on the exterior of Timberline Lodge and semicircular figures on the door posts were designed by Howard Gifford. Rams' heads top the columns at either side of the front door. The chevron carving was identified as the butterfly, characterized as a symbol of everlasting life on a poster from approximately 1937 that depicted all the carved symbols used at Timberline. WPA Negatives Collection (negative #4528), Portland Art Museum, Oregon.

Bear head carving on exterior beam end at the eave near the ADA entrance of Timberline Lodge, carved by Masamichi Nitani, 1990s, replaced an older weathered carving.

The Indian head carved panel by Jim Duncan for a door in the lower lobby is an Art Deco–like design with a stylized sunburst headdress and braids, and collar beading consisting of the initials of the Forest Service employees who worked on Timberline Lodge. The initials (left to right): JF (James Frankland, regional engineer), WIT (W. I. Turner), HG (Howard Gifford), DW (Dean Wright), EDC (Ethel Daniel Chatfield, secretary), and LF (Linn Forrest).

Dining room windows form the aborted transept on the east wing. The carved wood motifs between the windows were taken from a page titled "The Year in Moons" in a 1930s Camp Fire Girls handbook.

The six headhouse columns define the main lobby, the lodge's primary public space.

Inside the headhouse, six enormous hand-hewn columns support the ceiling. Gano remembered that each column was about thirty feet long and four feet in diameter at the smallest. Thomas Howell wrote in 1982 to then Friends of Timberline President Bill White about scouting out some of these original pine timbers: "I went with Mr. Andy Anderson, one day only, to cruise for Several Timbers as I remember it. . . .These timbers were to be 60″ at Base and could not vary over 6″ in 50 [feet]. His climbing rope had a series of different colored knots to allow him to determine diameter of tree at any height he wished to measure. Andy made a remark 'Why the hell do they want such a big trees if they are going to make Totem Poles!' . . . As I recall we only marked two (2) trees that day. The price of $500.00 seems to linger per each timber. At that time was a *very good* price."

Many have said the timbers were brought from the Gifford Pinchot National Forest in Washington, but George Woodruff stated that five of the "sticks" came from his father Ralph Woodruff's timberland a few miles north of Trout Lake, Washington, just east of the Gifford Pinchot National Forest. Each log comprised a truckload in itself. Using cables and a tractor, the logs were rolled up ramps onto the truck, chained down, and "snugged up with cheese blocks," according to Woodruff. Each timber was hauled through Tygh Valley and up the Wapinitia Highway because the Mount Hood Loop Highway curves were too tight for the long truckloads.

A local cabin builder German-born Henry Steiner agreed to shape the timbers into hexagonal columns for twenty-five dollars each if the logs were turned at his request after he finished hewing each of the six sides. He struck a line where he wanted an edge and cut down to the line with a saw. In a 1976 interview, architect Forrest recalled that Steiner straddled the log and shaped down to his mark, using only hand tools, a foot adze, and broadaxe. In 1990, Gano remembered that Steiner finished all six columns in less than two weeks. These timbers were pulled into place by a hoisting engine and with the aid of a gin pole. Before the lodge was completed, Steiner's son John was asked to fill out one column where the natural wood shape was concave. John Steiner stated that he nailed in a wedge to make the edge square. That column is in the northeast side of the main lobby. Henry Steiner built many cabins in the area around Rhododendron that feature imaginatively shaped rough-hewn log beams, stairways with split log steps, and distinctive irregular log detailing.

Landscape Plan and Amphitheater

Plans for stables, tennis courts, and trails were in the original landscape designs for Timberline drawn by Forest Service landscape architect A. D. Taylor in late 1936. He stressed the importance of retaining the site's natural alpine vegetation and preserving its fragile volcanic ash soils. Taylor suggested that the north terrace take a free-form shape and that the road to the turnaround in front of the entrance steps should continue to the west of the lodge. Emerson Griffith favored putting the parking lot on the east side of the building, where it was ultimately placed. Griffith also supported installing a reflecting pond as part of the landscaping plan. The reflecting pond is on the north side of the lodge. The Forest Service directed that the area around the building be kept in a natural condition, and that planting be initiated only in the area disturbed by construction. Within the five acres surrounding the lodge, the plan included putting in such native alpine plants as paintbrush, spreading

Timberline Lodge in summer, circa 1994. Photograph by Jon Tullis, Timberline Lodge.

Amphitheater facing south toward Mount Jefferson, circa 1938. Courtesy of Oregon State Library, 2006.001.0319.

phlox, aster, penstemon, lupine, juniper, mountain ash, mountain hemlock, and whitebark pine. It is doubtful that funding existed to carry out the landscape plans.

Before the construction of the C. S. Price Wing in 1975, Timberline could accommodate large audiences or groups only in the summer in an outdoor amphitheater west of the lodge building. With a seating capacity of 500, the amphitheater was finished in late summer and dedicated on September 9, 1938. The seats were built of yellow cedar logs. WPA administrator Harry Hopkins wired Griffith at the dedication: "The amphitheatre you are dedicating today is another important element in an outdoor recreational facility surpassed in few places, if any, in the world." Hallie Flanagan, director of the Federal Theatre Project, was more extravagant in her praise, writing to Griffith in 1938: "You are too conservative when you say the Timberline amphitheatre is the most beautiful theatre in the world. There should be something in that comparison which would bring in the entire cosmos, for what theatre in the world, or even on Mars, could duplicate your backdrop with Mount Jefferson marked with pine."

The original amphitheater was damaged over decades of severe weather that destroyed the wood seats and loosened the stonework. In 2006, Friends of Timberline completed a renovation of the amphitheater; the benches were replaced, and the site was made accessible to wheelchairs. At the same time, access paths from the lodge were developed. This beautiful location has become a popular setting for summer weddings, concerts, and receptions.

Lodge builders received a boost from WPA administrator Harry Hopkins's inspection with a party of thirty-five guests on September 14, 1936. Architect Turner's memorandum for the log stated that twelve inches of snow covered the site and flurries fell during their visit. Turner noted that two of the six hexagonal columns for the main lobby remained to be installed due to the inclement weather and that rafters were being placed in the east wing. Turner wrote that Hopkins 'expressed himself as being an enthusiast relative to the development." According to the Portland *News-Telegram*, Hopkins said: "We have built lodges in national parks and other recreational areas, but nothing like this."

Despite the early snow, the building was completely framed by October 1936, and workmen began the interior finishing work that would last through the winter. In Portland, workshops and studios, craftsmen and artists were making the wrought-iron furnishings, wood furniture, and textiles - hooked rugs for the floor, and woven fabric for upholstery and draperies in guest rooms.

Timberline Lodge, 1937. When Albert Altorfer had a day off from his work as chef at Summit Meadows WPA camp, he took photos of the progress of construction on the lodge. Many appeared in the local newspaper, but one achieved greater prominence. He hammered slats into the trunk of a tree to get a higher vantage point for photographing the lodge. He sent the resulting photograph to President Franklin Roosevelt, who signed it and returned it to Altorfer. It is on display at the lodge. Friends of Timberline Archive.

CHAPTER THREE

A LIVING MUSEUM FOR OREGON

You know I am a fanatic on handicraft, and the lodge has been proof of what results from a hand-wrought object. It might seem sentimental, but I feel that there is a spirit in objects that are made by loving hands. Every workman on the job was thrilled by his work because he felt that his creative skill was becoming an integral part in a very significant whole.

—MARGERY HOFFMAN SMITH,
in Gwladys Bowen, "A Study in Harmony" (1938)

*Main lobby, Timberline Lodge, circa
1938. Oregon Historical Society Research
Library negative #bb003325.*

TIMBERLINE LODGE is a living museum of handcrafted furnishings, where small children run their hands over carved animal newel posts in lodge stairways, friends visit on hand-built loveseats in the Ram's Head Bar, skiers relax on rawhide and iron chairs, and families play ping-pong in the Barlow Room surrounded by carved linoleum panels of mountain activities. The immense time pressures under which the lodge was built could have led to shoddy workmanship, but Timberline's architects and designers, urged on by Oregon's WPA director Emerson J. Griffith, rose to the challenge and accomplished some of their best work. Many later said working on Timberline was the highlight of their life. Ann Claggett Wood, in her thesis on the architecture of Timberline, quoted Forest Service architect Dean Wright, who designed light fixtures, door hardware, and some furniture: "It is only once in a lifetime that an Architect gets to do a job like this."

THE FEDERAL ART PROJECT: ART FOR EVERYDAY LIVING

Funds for Timberline Lodge's furniture, furnishings, and artwork came mostly from the Federal Art Project (FAP). The FAP, which ran from 1935 to 1943, was part of the WPA and fostered work in the fine arts, music, theater, writing, and historical records. Historian William McDonald stated that the FAP "in material size and cultural character was unprecedented in the history of this or any nation."

The goal of the FAP's director Holger Cahill was to encourage an interest in art as an everyday part of living and working. Consequently, Cahill took a broad view of what qualified as art. In a 1937 letter to Griffith, he wrote, "It seems to me that it is one of the functions of the fine arts to bring order and design into the visual environment created by society, and that everything the Art Project can do to help along these lines, it should do." The Timberline project embodied Cahill's goals of encouraging all types of people to regard the functional furnishings they were creating as objects of art.

Lower lobby, formerly the Ski Lounge, with wrought-iron, wood, and rawhide chairs designed to let melting snow drip from skiers' clothing.

Many details were worked out during construction, initially in an effort to spend allocated funds before holds were put on spending, and later in a terrific rush to complete the lodge before President Roosevelt arrived for the 1937 dedication. Master blacksmith O. B. Dawson wrote of the free-wheeling atmosphere during construction: "[Architect] Tim Turner approved everything I drew up, but there were some objections by others about the designs for the big fireplace andirons, so Tim suggested that I draw up designs using heavy railroad ties [rails]. I did and Tim liked them and told me to get busy and make them before someone else had time to argue. We did and those andirons still stand." Engineer Ward Gano and architect Linn Forrest remembered that Turner's management technique was simple. When they suggested a solution for an engineering or architectural problem, Turner's response was typically, "Do it."

TIMBERLINE'S DECORATIVE THEMES: PIONEERS, INDIAN MOTIFS, AND LOCAL WILDLIFE

Oregon's pioneer heritage was the theme for Timberline Lodge's furnishings from the beginning. Just a few miles downhill from the lodge are the famous pioneer-era Barlow Road and treacherous Laurel Hill. Around the nation, pioneer themes were popular subject matter in New Deal murals and art. Pioneers embodied heroic self-reliance, independence, and the ability to survive through hard work, all traits that encouraged spirits that were sagging in the face of the Depression. When Griffith promoted the state's pioneer heritage as a decorative theme in Timberline's funding application, he was suggesting a theme typical for government buildings of the period and acceptable to WPA officials. Even prior to the Depression, Americans often decorated mountain lodges and recreational retreats with rustic objects from the pioneer period, such as wagon wheels, oxen yokes, and lanterns. Other objects used in Rustic decoration, including skins and antlers, suggested local wildlife and Indian culture as well as pioneer traditions.

Architect Howard Gifford sketched designs for the heavy, rustic furniture in the Blue Ox Bar and writing desks in the alcoves, and designed the carved panels of pioneers traveling west over the front stairway. Gifford and fellow architect Dean Wright discovered a discarded ox yoke in the region. As Thomas P. Deering Jr. has pointed out in his thesis on mountain architecture, Underwood proposed the ox yoke as one motif in the pioneer decorative theme, and Gifford and Wright used it to create accurate proportions in the ox yoke light fixtures by the reception desk and in the gift shop.

Carving by Melvin Keegan on front stairway of lodge, 1936–1937, showing Oregon Trail pioneers crossing the plains and descending Laurel Hill west of Mount Hood.

Battle Axe Inn at Government Camp, early 1900s. A Mount Hood resort, the inn was decorated with rustic objects, a bearskin rug, mounted animal heads, an ox yoke, and stick furniture. Courtesy of Jeff Thomas.

Ox yoke light fixture at Timberline Lodge.

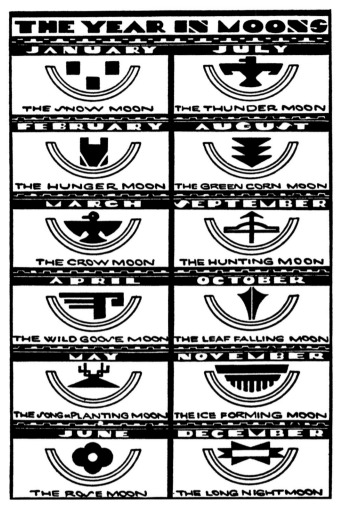

"The Year in Moons," from Wo-He-Lo: The Camp Fire History, *1980, Camp Fire Girls handbook. Courtesy of Camp Fire USA.*

Tower, *by Charles Heaney. Woodcut circa 1937. The weather vane on the headhouse chimney was designed by Forest Service architect Tim Turner, circa 1937. The weather vane form included the Camp Fire Girl symbol for the Wild Goose Moon, or April, in "The Year in Moons." The weather vane was later adopted as the logo for Timberline Lodge.*

The second major design element of the lodge was Indian motifs. The carved Indianlike designs in the lintels around the Ski Lounge (now the lower lobby) were not created by consulting with local Native Americans, but were instead taken from a page in the Camp Fire Girls handbook belonging to architect Gifford's daughter. The page "The Year in Moons" illustrates twelve symbols, one for each month. The founders of Camp Fire Girls may have adapted the symbols from northern Plains

Drum light fixture in Cascade Dining Room, with zigzag design, circa 1937.

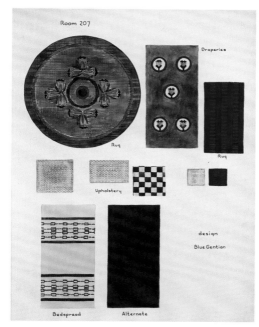

Watercolor of room design scheme for Blue Gentian guest room, circa 1937. Watercolor in John Wilson Special Collections, Multnomah County Library, Portland, Oregon.

Indian culture, as suggested by Columbia River Indian basketry historian Mary Schlick.

Some Indianlike motifs at the lodge reflect aesthetics of the Art Deco style of the 1920s and 1930s, with characteristic parallel lines, stripes, zigzags, triangles, and other geometric shapes. These motifs are included in the beautifully proportioned chevron carving over the front door, the drum light fixtures, and some of the geometric shapes of the wrought-iron coyote head gates to the dining room. Geometric Native American designs were also incorporated in appliquéd draperies and in hooked rugs.

The third decorative theme at Timberline is wildlife. Animals native to Timberline's alpine region are depicted in the carved rams' heads outside the front door. Mosaic, carved wood, and marquetry cougars, coyotes, bears, deer, and eagles, for example, populate panels in the main lobby, the Cascade Dining Room, and the top stairway newel posts. The guest room fireplace andirons depict beavers, rabbits, squirrels, and woodchucks (according to tradition, but actually marmots at this alpine altitude). Plants of the area are illustrated in botanical watercolors in the guest rooms and in the glass mosaic mural surrounding the drinking fountain.

Owl, *from a plaster cast by Florence Thomas, a carved newel post on a staircase, circa 1937.*

Cougar Resting in Forest *by Florence Thomas, circa 1937. This wood relief carving was originally over the fireplace in the Cascade Dining Room of the lodge, but is now in the main lobby. Albert Altorfer Papers, Friends of Timberline Archive.*

SIGNATURE SHAPES:
THE TIMBERLINE ARCH AND HEXAGON

An architectural feature seen throughout the lodge is the curved post-and-lintel arch. This haystack-shaped arch is so prevalent in the building that it has become known as the "Timberline arch." The arch also appears in lodge furniture. Interior decorator Margery Hoffman Smith told reporter Gwladys Bowen, "We made great use of the curved arch—bedroom mirrors, table legs, backs of dining room chairs." Another repeated design in the lodge is the hexagon—the shape of the headhouse, which is repeated in hexagonal windows at the front entrance and main lobby coffee tables and suggested in angled couches.

A Timberline arch frames the west wing staircase.

UNIFYING THE DESIGN: MARGERY HOFFMAN SMITH

As construction proceeded, someone was needed to coordinate the interior furnishings, to provide what WPA administrator Emerson Griffith called "a woman's touch." Portland architect John Yeon recommended interior designer Margery Hoffman Smith. The recommendation was an inspired one. Smith integrated and elaborated on the lodge's three design themes, creating harmony among Timberline's structure, its art, and its furnishings, which still delights visitors and has transformed the building into a beloved Oregon icon.

Margery Hoffman Smith, circa 1930s.
Friends of Timberline Archive.

Smith's background prepared her perfectly for the job. Her mother, Julia Hoffman, was a painter and photographer. In 1907, Hoffman established Portland's Arts and Crafts Society (now the Oregon College of Art and Craft). Hoffman also sponsored the first art classes at the Portland Art Museum. After a childhood immersed in art, Margery attended Bryn Mawr College, Parsons School of Design, and the Arts Students League in New York. During World War I, she married Ferdinand C. Smith, a Portland stockbroker. She became an interior designer in 1929.

Smith's work at the lodge was described in a 1941 article in *The Weaver* magazine: "One's impression on seeing Timberline is that surely some master mind did the planning and some master hand guided the chisel, torch and shuttle to produce such perfect harmony and keep everything on the same magnificent scale. A harmony such as is seldom seen exists between the lodge, its furnishings and its setting. Only an artist would have the fine feeling for proportion that characterizes Timberline Lodge. That artist is Mrs. Margery Hoffman Smith."

At a time when few women were in the work force, Smith's professionalism and imagination affected the final design of the building in important ways. She influenced several significant architectural adaptations during construction. Architects initially designed the window on the mezzanine that faces Mount Jefferson with small panes. Smith supported Griffith, who was adamant that a large sheet of glass be installed so that visitors could savor the breathtaking view. The glass pane is now protected by springs that absorb the force of winds. And when Smith noticed the absence of a bar in the drawings, she found space in a room designated for wood storage. The Blue Ox Bar, tucked back in a corner of the building, was the only bar at Timberline until 1950.

After Timberline Lodge was completed, Smith chaired the WPA exhibition at the New York 1939 World's Fair, taking charge of the Arts and Skills Section. She also furnished Secretary of Commerce Harry Hopkins's offices in Washington, D.C., and consulted on furniture for state public buildings in Alaska. Smith moved to San Francisco in 1940, and after her husband's death in 1959, she opened an interior design studio there.

Iron gate, hand-wrought by restoration blacksmiths, at entrance to the Blue Ox Bar, Timberline Lodge.

FINE ARTS AT THE LODGE

Burt Brown Barker, a lawyer and past vice president of the University of Oregon, was appointed in 1935 as the Federal Art Project director for the western region. Barker was charged with designating artists who were on relief to the Timberline project. In October 1936, the position of regional director was given to Joseph Danysh of San Francisco. Barker continued as the state director of the FAP, and Margery Hoffman Smith became the assistant art director. The selection of art and craft at Timberline is primarily the result of these three administrators working together with Griffith.

Darrel Austin

The first artwork created for the lodge was probably a series of five paintings by Darrel Austin illustrating mountain activities, completed in 1936 before construction had even begun: *Dishwashers, Musicians, Skier, Woodcutters,* and *Fish Story.* Only *Dishwashers* and *Musicians* were placed at the lodge at the end of the project. *Skier* was left at Jefferson High School in Portland, where it remained until the school loaned it for display at the lodge in the 1990s. Sometime later, *Woodcutters* was hung at the lodge, on loan from the Portland Art Museum. *Fish Story* was at Tongue Point Naval Station in Astoria, Oregon, for years before it was moved to Portland's Grant High School and subsequently considered for loan to Timberline. Austin also created watercolor designs for the iron and rawhide chairs in the lower lobby as well as for other furnishings.

Clayton Sumner (C. S.) Price

Along with Austin, C. S. Price was one of the first artists assigned projects for Timberline Lodge. His favored subject matter was humans in the natural landscape. Described as one of the West's first Modernist painters, Price captured the American West in the early twentieth century with representational scenes of horses, cowboys, Indians, boats, wolves, and cattle. One of his two epic murals at Timberline, *Huckleberry Pickers,* depicts Indian women and children in a traditional Northwest summer food-gathering activity.

Its companion piece, *Pack Train,* portrays packhorses and men crossing through the mountains. Price had begun his career sketching renditions of cattle and horses on the Wyoming range, where he worked as a young man. In *Pack Train,* his style had become strongly expressive, with blocky, structural forms. Frank H. Hurley of Reed College wrote about the impact of the WPA on Price's work: "His WPA paintings . . . are his largest and most ambitious works and among them are some of his finest."

Huckleberry Pickers and *Pack Train* were so large that, unfortunately, they did not properly fit the assigned spaces in the Cascade Dining Room on either side of the gate. Margery Hoffman Smith later remembered that Price was terribly disappointed when the murals were rejected from Timberline Lodge and returned to Portland. Initially *Pack Train* was loaned to the Civic Auditorium, where a stagehand recalled seeing the painting in a storeroom leaning against a wall where a chair had dented it. A furnace tender had planned to burn the mural, but the stagehand

Dishwashers, by Darrel Austin, 1936. Oil on canvas, 45 × 37 inches. Lodge mezzanine.

*Huckleberry Pickers, by C. S. Price, 1937. Oil on canvas, 56 × 136½ inches.
C. S. Price Wing of lodge.*

*Pack Train, by C. S. Price, 1937. Oil on canvas, 57¾ × 139½ inches.
C. S. Price Wing.*

rescued it and gave it to the Portland Art Museum. *Huckleberry Pickers* was held by Portlander Hugh Laing from July 1945 to May 1946, when the Portland Art Museum took possession of it. Eventually in 1975 both murals were installed at the lodge in the newly constructed wing named the C. S. Price Wing in the painter's honor.

Two smaller easel paintings that Price completed under the FAP were hung on the mezzanine: *The Team*, or *Plowing* and *Mountain Landscape*. These works have been part of the lodge's collection since they were loaned to the lodge in 1938.

Huckleberry Pickers *(1937) and* Pack Train *(1937) by C. S. Price briefly hung in the Cascade Dining Room flanking the entrance but were sent to Portland before the lodge opened in 1938. WPA Negatives Collection (negative #4472), Portland Art Museum, Oregon.*

The Mountain, by Charles Heaney, 1937. Oil on canvas, 34¼ × 42½ inches. Main lobby of lodge.

Charles Heaney

Painter C. S. Price referred Charles Heaney to FAP Western Regional Director Burt Brown Barker. Heaney was thrilled to be assigned by Barker as a painter under the Federal Art Project. In July 1937, interior designer Margery Hoffman Smith took Heaney to visit Timberline Lodge while it was under construction and asked him to do an oil painting for the lodge. The result was *The Mountain*, considered one of his most significant works. In an article written in 1969, journalist Carl Gohs described the painting: "The mountain is not Hood. I think. It

Symbolizing Lodge Builders: Wood
Workers, *by Howard Sewell, 1937.*
Oil on canvas, 48 × 117⅛ inches.
Mezzanine.

is fine. Who ever thought of painting a mountain with the top cut off.
Whoosh . . . like that. The top isn't there. The effect is astonishing. You
look up the wall over the painting to see if there is any more of it. How
high DOES it go? The feeling is that it goes up forever." Heaney completed another painting of this size, *Mountains*, the next year. It is in the
collection of the Portland Art Museum.

Heaney was in his late thirties when he was employed on the FAP,
and as a result of this work he began supporting himself as an artist, a
goal that FAP director Holger Cahill sought for artists employed by the
FAP. Art historian A. Joan Saab used the term "cultural democratiza-
tion" to describe changing attitudes in the 1930s that allowed artists
to be employed as artists, and quoted Cahill's view of these broadened
opportunities: "The public . . . has learned to accept the artist as a useful, producing member of the social family." After the end of the FAP in
1939, Heaney pursued a career as a painter and printmaker.

Howard Sewall

Howard Sewall, a student of C. S. Price and Clyde Leon Kellar, painted
two large murals for Timberline Lodge. He also painted other murals
in Portland and Oregon City under the FAP. His murals for Timberline
pay homage to craftsmen who built the lodge: *Symbolizing Lodge Builders: Wood Workers* and *Symbolizing Lodge Builders: Metal Workers.*

Throughout the country, and in fact the world, in the 1930s labor
and workers were favored themes especially for public art. Sewall's lodge
builders are rendered as stylized Egyptian figures, their movements simplified and angular and their focus entirely on their work. The central
figure in *Wood Workers* is finishing a beam with an adze. The central
figure in *Metal Workers* is hammering a bar on an anvil. The portrayal of
the workers as Egyptians idealizes the common man in his daily tasks.
These murals were intended for the lower lobby, but historically hung in

the Cascade Dining Room where the Price murals were first installed. The Sewall paintings were placed on the mezzanine after they were restored in the 1970s.

While the works of Austin, Price, Heaney, and Sewall were appropriate for some of the larger spaces in the lodge, the decoration of smaller rooms was assigned to individual artists. In April 1937, Regional FAP director Joseph Danysh met with Emerson Griffith, Margery Hoffman Smith, and architect W. I. Turner to discuss art for the lodge. Danysh recommended that the mezzanine was an ideal area to feature art by a variety of artists, and that smaller rooms such as the Ski Grille and Blue Ox Bar should be defined by the work of one artist. Having an entire room as a canvas provided the individual artist with an unusual creative opportunity.

Douglas Lynch

In accordance with Danysh's recommendations, the Ski Grille (now the Barlow Room) features a series of murals by Douglas Lynch, *Calendar of Mountain Sports*, comprising carved and painted linoleum panels. Lynch worked with his colleague John Blew to create the intricate linoleum panels, using a technique Lynch had previously developed for displays at Portland's Meier & Frank department store. The murals are Lynch's largest and most significant public art. In a 2004 interview, he summarized the process used to create this unique art form:

> I made inch-to-the-foot scale drawings of the family camping scene and of the artist sketching. Other than that, preliminary drawings were few. The full size drawings were made as the project went along, and transferred directly to the linoleum. We laid the linoleum panels flat on the floor, and lying prone on our elbows, we carved the incised lines that delineated the figures.
>
> The color glazes, however, were applied with the panels supported on a large wall easel. Color areas were built up with successive layers of oil glazes rubbed on by hand and cloth pads. Each layer was set and isolated with a coat of white shellac. Three or four, sometimes five or more layers, created a rich and glowing tone. It was a tricky process. Occasionally, an under layer would soften and wash through to the original surface. We'd curse and repeat the process. Having transformed a simple charcoal line into a carved groove in a floor covering, it didn't seem right to use it as the border for coloring in, nor appropriate for these glowing color smudges

Photographer *and* Winter, *two panels from the* Calendar of Mountain Sports, *by Douglas Lynch, 1938. Twelve carved and painted linoleum panels, each 56 inches high and between 48 and 142 inches wide. Created for the Ski Grille, now called the Barlow Room.*

Ski Grille, circa 1938. Oregon Historical Society Research Library negative #bb003324.

to be confined within a rigid outline. So, this line-color duet evolved. The French artist Raoul Dufy painted works like that and some eastern big city designers also experimented with the idea. There were two of us working. In calendar time, creating the panels took well over a year.

As of July 29, 1939, no funds were available to decorate the last two walls with linoleum panels. Administrators and Lynch decided he would paint scenes directly on the wall: "I stood on a ladder and painted these arch-shaped spaces in bright, flat poster colors: 'Fireside Folk' motifs; country chores, loggers, farm folk, streamside plant forms. These were improvised and meant to be light and whimsical. During the restoration, they were not well repainted." Lynch later taught at Portland's Museum Art School and became a well-known graphic artist.

Virginia Darcé

Virginia Darcé portrayed stories of Paul Bunyan in glass murals for the Blue Ox Bar. Paul Bunyan, the legendary super-sized logger who performed feats of unbelievable strength, was a popular image in WPA art of the Northwest and a logical choice for Timberline Lodge.

Darcé chose *opus sectile*, a technique used in ancient Egypt and Rome, in which the artist cuts marble or glass into large pieces and attaches them to a background material in patterns. It differs from mosaic in that individual pieces are not small tessarae but are large enough to form significant parts of the design. A paint and glass company in Portland, W. P. Fuller, provided European glass for the work. Darcé made full-size cartoons as patterns for cutting the glass, and another set of cartoons was used to transfer the design to the wall. Darcé described the process in a 1979 interview:

> I selected every piece as it went in and laid it out exactly how I wanted the grain of the glass to go, and so on, and Pete [Ferrarin] ground the edges, because when you cut that kind of glass, it doesn't break straight. It can break with a little slant, and it had to be straight up and down and the edges ground so they wouldn't cut anybody. So this little grinding stone here, which was run by hand, of course, was where Pete stood and ground the glass down. And [expert glass cutter Charles] Haller cut each piece from a pattern.
>
> When we went up there finally to put the mural up, the wall had to be prepared to receive the mastic, and it was painted

Virginia Darcé and Charles Haller working on the Blue Ox Bar opus sectile *murals, 1938. Friends of Timberline Archive. Photo also at Oregon State Library, 2006.001.0424.664.*

with a tarry material that would stop moisture from coming through and would make it adhere better. . . . Each piece of glass was numbered, and then the pattern was numbered underneath . . . and . . . that number was transferred on the wall. And then we went through the boxes, which were all very carefully packed, and found each piece corresponding to the number, and then that was put on. . . .

And it was started from the bottom. You start a thing like that from the bottom and work up, so the glass below supports the glass above. And that's the way . . . the tile is put on the wall. Then once it was up and adhered tightly to the wall . . . I came with the putty and filled it in . . . in different colors and made the expression in the face come to life, and so on, and that's how it was done.

Paul Bunyan
Carrying Babe the
Blue Ox, *by Virginia
Darcé, 1938. Opus
sectile, 65¾ × 56¾
inches. Blue Ox Bar.*

Prairie Farm Dam, *by Arthur T.
Kerrick, 1937. Watercolor, 18 × 28
inches. Room 108.*

One assistant, Pete Ferrarin, had learned the craft of mosaic setting in his native Italy. The Paul Bunyan glass murals took two years to
complete.

Just prior to the lodge's February 1938 opening, Griffith wrote Cahill
and requested the finest paintings created throughout the country under
the WPA for display at Timberline. In a January 14, 1938, letter to
Thomas Parker, the assistant FAP director, Cahill's assistant, Mildred
Holzhauer, suggested making some prints and watercolors available,
and Cahill responded, "I don't think prints is what they want. The scale
of T. L. is a good deal like that of Grand Central Station." In response
to Griffith's request, Cahill shipped twenty oils, watercolors, and prints
depicting various subjects for exhibition at the lodge. Administrators for
the Oregon project decided that some of the works were unsuitable for
the lodge, and they obtained permission to exhibit them at the Salem
Art Center, according to May 1938 correspondence between Holzhauer,
Cahill, and regional FAP administrator Joseph Danysh. The other works
have remained at Timberline as part of the permanent collection, and
they hang in guest rooms and on the mezzanine. The themes of these
works vary, but many are landscapes.

Other art at the lodge includes several wood carvings of local animals
or events: Erich Lamade's carved wood *Forest Scene* over the fireplace
in the Cascade Dining Room, Florence Thomas's carved wood *Cougar
Resting in Forest* in the main lobby, Aimee Gorham's intricate marquetry panels of *Coyotes* and *Mountain Lions*, and Melvin Keegan's *Pioneer
Scene.* In addition, Tom Laman's mosaic of local animals *Spring on the*

Mountain surrounds a drinking fountain, and more than 150 botanical watercolors and hand-colored lithographs of alpine plants native to Mount Hood decorate the guest rooms.

CRAFTS: IRONWORK, WOOD, AND TEXTILES OF TIMBERLINE

"It is doubtful if there is in America any other single structure which can throw more light on the craft production of the period," wrote Rachael Griffin, curator at the Portland Art Museum, in a 1977 *Oregonian* article about Timberline Lodge. The focus on craft in the Timberline project fulfilled an objective of the FAP to improve economic welfare of craftspeople by developing independence through training in skills, encouraging private enterprise, and fostering thrift. In *The Builders of Timberline Lodge* (1937), a writer with the Federal Writers' Project wrote, "Having seen how the homely materials work up into something surpassingly beautiful, a woman may not only become inspired to copy them for her own home, but may even search and find a commercial market for her work."

In a 1976 *Oregonian* article, Margery Hoffman Smith said, "Carpenters became cabinet makers, blacksmiths became art metal workers and sewing women wound up expert drapery makers." In explaining her focus in furnishing the lodge, Smith noted: "We did not have many artists. That's why we went in so heavily for crafts." Her expert direction inspired excellence in workers who had never picked up a shuttle, hooked a rug, or sewn a stitch.

While some of Timberline's fine artists launched careers as artists, few craft workers on the Timberline project were able to transfer their skills to a commercial arena after the Depression. Rug hooker Thelma Dull, for example, never did that work after the Timberline project concluded in 1938 until she joined the restoration project in 1975. Perhaps the onset of World War II and the need for skills in constructing ships and manufacturing war supplies prevented many from building on skills they developed at Timberline.

A second goal of the Oregon WPA administrators was to resurrect the flagging Oregon flax industry by using flax grown at Mount Angel in the Willamette Valley and wool produced by Oregon growers to showcase local handmade linen and wool draperies, bedspreads, and upholstery at Timberline Lodge. This endeavor may have brought some commercial success to the state's fiber industry because it flourished during World War II, providing rope, twine, thread, nets, fishing tackle, mops, rugs,

Women making hooked rugs for Timberline Lodge in the Elks Temple, Portland, circa 1937. WPA Negatives Collection (negative #2303), Portland Art Museum, Oregon.

toweling, and defense materials. The industry declined in the 1950s when foreign fiber became less expensive and more readily available.

A third goal of administrators was to encourage thrift by recycling materials into handcrafted objects. Rugs for guest rooms, for example, were hooked from strips cut from old Civilian Conservation Corps wool blankets and corduroy uniforms. Scraps of material left over from other WPA sewing projects were stitched into appliquéd draperies. Recycling was also an economic necessity. Old telephone poles became newel posts. Equipment and parts from World War I–era ships were recycled into the lodge's plumbing and electrical systems.

The use of native local materials, recycling, and teaching handicraft skills for making attractive everyday objects grew out of the Arts and Crafts movement of the early twentieth century, as Harvey Kaiser noted in his book *Landmarks in Landscape*. Kaiser credited Smith with organizing the furnishings project for Timberline in the Arts and Crafts style. In their book *The Arts and Crafts Movement in the Pacific Northwest*, Lawrence Kreisman and Glenn Mason described Timberline Lodge as one of two buildings that exemplify the culmination of the Arts and Crafts movement in Northwest architecture: "Timberline epitomized Arts and Crafts ideals through the employment of local artisans to carve wood, forge metal, and weave tapestries to embellish the interior spaces of the lodge."

Ironwork

Timberline's wrought-iron decoration—furniture and fixtures—is one of its signature attractions, both for its extensiveness throughout the lodge and for the artistry of the designs. The beauty of the ironwork is even more remarkable given the pressure to complete most of it in time for the September 28, 1937, dedication.

Orion B. (O. B.) Dawson, a master blacksmith from Portland, was a natural choice to lead this phase of the Timberline project. Dawson learned blacksmithing in high school, discovered medieval iron decoration in Europe where he was stationed during World War I, and later studied metal design in Los Angeles and at the University of Oregon. He also was employed hand-forging ornamental ironwork for Portland architects, and he had crafted the ironwork for industrialist Henry J. Kaiser's Lake Tahoe home. In 1935, he was commissioned to supervise the metalwork shop for Oregon WPA projects. Other WPA projects Dawson directed were ironwork production at the University of Oregon and at Oregon State College (now University).

The WPA ironwork was made largely by eleven workers (although the number varied) in Dawson's workshop on S.E. Boise Street in Portland. Timberline's architects designed most of the lodge ironwork produced in the shop, including wrought-iron straps that wrap around posts and rails in the main lobby; decorative door hardware such as latches, hinges, kick plates, and push plates; foot scrapers; and some light fixtures. Some distinctive pieces were designed by Dawson or created in collaboration with coworkers.

Timberline's light fixtures were a team effort of the WPA woodworking and metalwork shops, Margery Hoffman Smith, Forest Service architects, and Fred Baker of the English–Baker Company (later the Fred Baker Lighting Company) in Portland. In a December 23, 1936, memo, Forest Service architect Turner stated that the Forest Service and the WPA agreed to allocate $500 for Baker to design the fixtures and for WPA craftsmen to construct them. Forest Service architect Arthur Ulvestad remembered the design process: "I did my drawing in an office at Baker Lighting Co., and as each set of drawings progressed a man from Baker Lighting would bring me lamp holders, glass bowls, fittings, etc., which I would incorporate into the drawings. As soon as I finished each drawing for a fixture, I took the [drawings] out to the WPA shop. The men in the WPA shop were made up of artisans of vari-

Tracing shows the design for wood and wrought-iron fixtures for the Ski Lounge (now in lower lobby). Courtesy of Tom Lockhart, U.S. Forest Service.

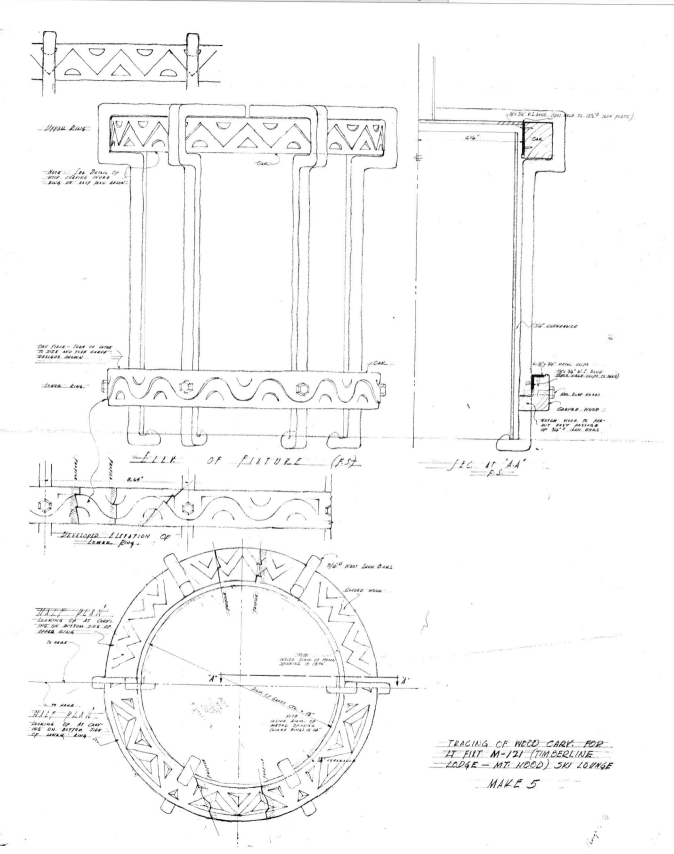

ELEV. OF FIXTURE (F.S.)

SEC. AT "A-A" F.S.

DEVELOPED ELEVATION OF LOWER RING.

HALF PLAN
LOOKING UP AT CARVING ON BOTTOM SIDE OF UPPER RING

HALF PLAN
LOOKING UP AT CARVING ON BOTTOM SIDE OF LOWER RING

TRACING OF WOOD CARV. FOR LT. FIXT. M-121 (TIMBERLINE LODGE — MT. HOOD) SKI LOUNGE

MAKE 5

Older blacksmith at work in WPA metalworking shop, circa 1937. John Wilson Special Collections, Multnomah County Library, Portland, Oregon.

ous kinds—wood carvers, metal workers, etc. These men then built the required number of each type of fixture. As work neared completion on each set of fixtures, Baker Lighting must have been drawn into the wiring of the fixtures, but I never did get to see that work or find out where it was done."

Many of the WPA ironworkers were over fifty. In his memoir "The Old Blacksmiths," O. B. Dawson recalled that some blacksmiths were addressed as "Ol' Jake" or "Ol' Bill." Ed Frisk and George Fessler, for example, were in their seventies. The hand-wrought pieces were all created using techniques similar to those that pioneer blacksmiths would have employed, with no bolts or electric welds. Many of the men in Dawson's shop had learned their trade when a blacksmith produced such widely used objects as tools and mule shoes. By the 1930s, these objects were being mass-produced. The blacksmiths were glad for an opportunity to use their skills. Dawson wrote that Ed Frisk was the only blacksmith with experience in "art metal," so he made the andirons for the fireplace guest rooms and the Dutch oven in the Cascade Dining Room. Although Frisk was not well and had to be hospitalized part of the time, he always came back to work. "Whenever he could he would be right back where he could breathe a little more coal smoke from the forge. That was all that kept him alive, so he said." Dawson described the project's impact on the men: "Timberline was such a big thing. We all wanted every piece of work to be perfect. It wasn't just a job to the men. What I mean is, they were doing something important, something that would last, and they appreciated the chance to do it."

Dawson wrote in an article in the *Oregon Historical Quarterly* in 1975 that he designed fireplace andirons, screens, and fire tools for the lodge. He also worked on the distinctive coyote head wrought-iron gates for the entry to the Cascade Dining Room. In his memoir, he noted that several motifs had been tried and rejected for the gates, including "animal motifs, wagon wheels, Indian motifs, native flowers." Smith told reporter Gwladys Bowen in 1938 that artist Gabriel Lavare also contributed to the design of some fireplace andirons, and that she rejected the original ornamental designs Dawson had proposed for the dining room gates. Smith's and the architects' inability to decide on a design left the gates unfinished in Dawson's shop. In the *Quarterly* article, Dawson recalled a phone call from contractor Max Lorenz in September 1937 before the dedication of the lodge:

> The instant I lifted the telephone receiver Max said he wanted to hang the big gates as the President of the United States was on his way out here, and he wanted those gates *now*.

Blacksmith O. B. Dawson with the ornamental wrought-iron gates for the Cascade Dining Room, before they were shipped to the lodge in time for Roosevelt's dedication visit on September 28, 1937. Forest Service, U.S.D.A.

"But Max," I said, "the gates aren't finished. . . ." There had been so much difference in opinions over the ornamentation that I had given up and had the gates leaned against the wall over in a corner and left them there. Max wanted to know if I had any ornamental motifs made. I told him that I had ornament motifs scattered all over the shop but that none of the "powers that be" could decide what they wanted. Max said to forget what anyone else says, put what ornament motifs you have in the gates and get them up here. So we did.

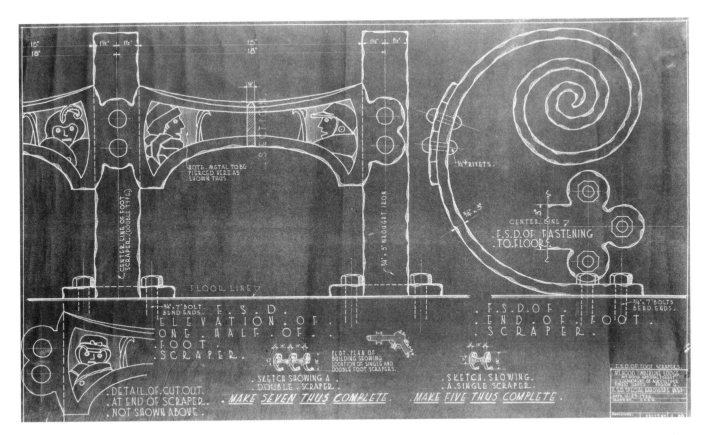

Design for etched foot scraper decorated with skiers. Drawing signed by D.R.E.W. (architect Dean Roland Edson Wright), dated December 29, 1936. Oregon Historical Society Research Library OrHi 105739.

The four vertical "Indian design" panels in the gates did not appeal to Dawson, he wrote, because he felt they did not suit ironwork but were, rather, angular. The vertical panel designs, however, may have appealed to interior designer Smith, whose taste was more contemporary and who would have appreciated elements of the gates that reflected the 1930s Art Deco style, with zigzags, sunbursts, and chevrons. The foot scrapers were similarly contemporary in design.

Unlike the flat, abstract angles of the dining room gates, the animal head on Timberline's front door knocker is representational, although ambiguous enough that it has been called a ram's head, a deer head, the "Oregon Thump," or even "Slap Bang." Dawson thought very highly of the knocker, noting, "To me it was the finest example of metal sculpture involving skilled craftsmanship that I have ever seen either in Europe or in America."

The front door, including the knocker, was designed by Forest Service architect Dean Wright. Dawson indicated that Ed Frisk crafted the door's knocker, lock, latch, escutcheons, and trim. One of the younger blacksmiths who trained in the shop, Henry Harth, remembered working on the door: "I worked with . . . Edward Frisk, who [was] an artist

Ram's head door knocker, 1937. Iron, 16¾ inches high.

with his hammer and all, and I helped him a little on making the front lock on the front door and the door . . . knocker. . . . It was supposed to be a deer head and it looks more like a goat head. . . . We just couldn't get the iron to work down far enough . . . and they were in a hurry for it so they let it go where he had it."

Dawson remembered, "When [Frisk] had [the knocker] completed, I told him to stop. . . . When I was a student of sculpture one of my teachers told me that sculptors should work in pairs, one to do the work

Front door with ram's head knocker, 1937. The wood planks in the door weigh 600 pounds; the ironwork weighs 400 pounds.

and the other to tell him when to stop." In recent years, the ram's head door knocker has been identified by restoration workers as cast iron, not wrought iron.

While many of the original iron details in the lodge remain intact, fireplace tools and screens, door kick plates and push plates, and many other pieces of iron hardware have been re-created to replace lost or damaged originals. To meet current fire code requirements, guest room door latches have been replaced with lever-style latches that can be opened with a single downward motion. The original latches have been stored. Handrails on the stairways, added for safety reasons, were also hand-wrought by restoration craftsmen working in the tradition of the WPA blacksmiths.

After he completed his contracts with the WPA, Dawson reluctantly closed his Portland shop. The Blacksmith Union sent him to work as a heavy hammer smith at Willamette Iron and Steel Company, forging with a large, steam-driven power hammer. Three years later at Swan Island Ship Yard, he worked on war ships. Shortly before his death in 1977, Dawson worked with restoration blacksmiths at the lodge. After traveling Europe and America in search of ornamental ironwork, Dawson wrote in 1964, "In Timberline is one of the most unique and outstanding exhibitions of wrought iron work to be found in any one building anywhere in America and no doubt anywhere else in the world."

Wood

In 1936, the WPA opened a woodworking shop on S.W. Corbett Avenue in Portland. Ray Neufer, who at that time was managing a cabinet shop on S.E. Hawthorne Boulevard in Portland, was asked to supervise the WPA shop. In a 1979 interview, Neufer remembered, "They hired me, putting me in charge of a shop that was supposed to do crafts work— little things for the schools." Neufer was surprised and pleased when the woodshop was asked to produce all the furniture for Timberline Lodge.

Neufer was provided with architectural drawings of the lodge and designs for some furniture, including chairs and tables for the Ski Grille, the alcove desks, and wood light fixtures such as the ox yoke light. He designed most of the remaining furniture on the spot with interior designer Margery Hoffman Smith. He and Smith designed a prototype, Smith approved it, and the shop produced the necessary number of pieces. Between 1937 and 1938, ten to twenty carpenters in the WPA woodworking shop built Timberline's furniture. WPA carpenters also constructed the looms used to weave the lodge's draperies and upholstery.

Worker in WPA woodworking shop, circa 1937. WPA Negatives Collection (negative #5330), Portland Art Museum, Oregon.

Carved wood stool for Ski Grille, circa 1937. Courtesy of Oregon State Library, 2006.001.0416.2567.

On September 30, 1939, in the script for an Oregon WPA program called "Builders of Tomorrow," Neufer described the workers who carved the newel posts as generally inexperienced carvers: "Most of the men came in from construction projects and they didn't know they COULD do some of the things they did. Most of them had been out of work a long time, then on construction jobs, and they had lost their self-confidence."

Despite some of the workers' inexperience, the project inspired excellence. After visiting the completed Timberline Lodge in May 1939, State Parks Superintendent S. H. Boardman wrote to Oregon's WPA administrator Emerson J. Griffith: "I was particularly fascinated by the interior furnishings, chairs, tables, counters, rugs, murals, spreads, tapestries—all works of art." Boardman asked Griffith if the same workers could produce furniture for Oregon's Silver Falls State Park. The WPA woodshop made furniture for Silver Falls using myrtlewood from Oregon's south coast. Some pieces are still at the park.

Northwest forests provided all the wood for the lodge. Furniture for the Cascade Dining Room and mezzanine rails in the main lobby are made of Douglas fir. Oregon white oak was used for furniture in the main lobby. Wrought-iron strapping or wrought-iron legs made in Dawson's shop added to the furniture's heavy, rustic look. Old red cedar telephone poles purchased in Portland for two dollars and ten cents each were recy-

The WPA woodworking shop made the furniture for the guest rooms, including bedside tables and corner writing desks, 1937–1938. The bedside table may be a replica made to meet current standards for hotel rooms.

cled into stairway newel posts. Artist Florence Thomas modeled animals and birds for the newel posts and cast them in plaster of Paris, and the figures were then carved in the Portland WPA woodworking shop.

Decorative elements created in the woodworking shop included carved rafter ends and animal heads for the building's exterior. The large ram's head table in the main lobby, Neufer remembered, was designed by carver Melvin Keegan, who also carved the pioneer panels over the stairway by the front door. Keegan came in to work one day,

Ram's head table made in the WPA woodworking shop, circa 1937. The table supports were carved by Melvin Keegan.

Black bear newel post, 1937.

Armchair made in the WPA woodworking shop for President Franklin Roosevelt, 1937. The chair's back incorporates the Timberline arch.

Neufer said, and without any preliminary plan carved a block of yellow cedar into a ram's head. When Smith saw it, she asked him to carve a duplicate to make the two end supports for the large table.

In a 1979 interview, Neufer recalled the pressure to complete the lodge's furniture in time for the President's dedication: "On a Friday, they told us that he was going to be there on that Monday, and we had to have a chair with arms. . . . And [they] certainly didn't make any provision for any drawings or details of architecture, or anything like that. We just went ahead and made it. . . . The President was there to dedicate the lodge, and he was suffering from polio. There is only one chair that has arms. That is the one we made for him."

Like many WPA workers, Neufer didn't attend the dedication. Some workers said that they were too tired to attend because of the rush to complete the lodge. Orion B. Dawson, after finishing a two-week rush order to install every light fixture in the building, recalled, "I was invited to attend but after getting those fixtures out not even the President of the United States could stir up any enthusiasm in me. I went home and went to bed."

Draftsman Reynold Bashaw drew each type of furniture design to actual measurements and the items were photographed. Bashaw's designs and the photographs were compiled into two volumes. Three sets of the books were made. One set is housed at the Oregon State Library, one is at Portland's Multnomah County Library (returned to Oregon by Eleanor Roosevelt), and the third is in the Friends of Timberline Archive (a donation from Margery Hoffman Smith's estate). The books met a WPA recordkeeping requirement but may also have been intended to provide blueprints for a future handcraft industry. The books were invaluable in the 1970s when restoration of the lodge began and have been used by craftsmen recreating Timberline furniture.

Textiles—The Women's Division

Timberline's interior designer Margery Hoffman Smith directed the women who created textile furnishings for the lodge. The Women's and Professional Division of the WPA housed the sewing project at 614 S.W. 11th Avenue in Portland. This building was the Elks Temple and is now part of the Governor Hotel. Up to twenty-eight craftspeople, working under the Women's and Professional Division, wove, hooked, or sewed fabrics according to Smith's designs. In 1938, *Oregonian* reporter Gwladys Bowen stated that Smith told her that fabric dyeing was done with oil paints and gasoline. Smith said that the crafts project developed a special green: "It is the color of new growth of the tips of the fir trees in spring and the new leaves of the rhododendrons. I think we should by rights call it Timberline green."

Women making appliquéd draperies for Timberline Lodge in the Elks Temple, Portland, circa 1937. WPA Negatives Collection (negative #2385), Portland Art Museum, Oregon.

Smith remembered in a later interview, "[I would] stand over the looms and tell them how to throw their shuttles, pick out the yarns and the colors. Our relief people were not very skilled but willing. They loved the work." Since only one family member could be employed by the WPA at a time, the Women's Division employed mostly unmarried, divorced, or widowed women. In 1936, of the 14,372 individuals employed on WPA projects in Oregon, 3172 were women, and of these, 2500 were employed on sewing projects, according to the December 1936 *Report of Women's and 'White Collar' Projects Operating in State.*

Smith created at least twenty-eight unique room design schemes for sixty-one numbered guest rooms. (There are currently about seventy guest rooms.) Some of the design schemes featured themes such as native wildflowers or forest and mountain symbols. Others depicted pioneer, Indian, and wildlife imagery. The designs were incorporated into the appliquéd draperies, woven bedspreads, upholstery fabrics, and hand-hooked rugs. The guest room draperies were made of colorful sailcloth, and the bedspreads and upholstery fabrics were hand-woven from local linen or wool.

The textiles in the rooms were complemented by botanical watercolors and hand-colored lithographs. While most of the original textiles have long been worn out, re-creations of the original designs were finished under restoration projects in the 1970s. Several hundred watercolors and lithographs were created between 1936 and 1939 and more than 150 were hung at the lodge, at least one in every guest room.

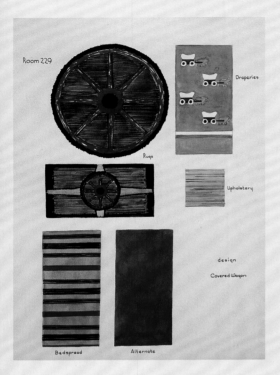

Watercolor of room design scheme for Covered Wagon guest room, circa 1937. John Wilson Special Collections, Multnomah County Library, Portland, Oregon.

ROOM DESIGN SCHEMES

The room design schemes were recorded in two copies of a hand-painted book made by WPA workers. These copies are now part of the John Wilson Special Collection at the Multnomah County Library. All the room schemes are illustrated in the book, but the names of the designs vary slightly between the two copies. The design scheme names (and alternate names, if any) include:

Anemone (White Anemone or Red Anemone)

Autumn Leaf (Maple Leaf, Mountain Leaf, or Indian Summer)

Bachelor Button (Blue Bachelor Button)

Blue Gentian (Gentian)

Blue Spruce (Spruce)

Cornflower

Covered Wagon

Fish in River (Fish and Wave or Brown Trout)

Flower Field (Dogwood or Posy)

Forest and Stream

Frond (Fern or Fern and Fronds)

Garden Gate

Indian Pattern

Indian Pipe Stem (Indian Pipe)

Indian Woman and Dog

Monks Hood

Moon over the Mountain

Mountain Flower (Shooting Star)

Mountain Range (Brown Peaks)

Mountains

Noble Fir (Blue Fir)

Paper Doll

Phlox (Blue and Gold)

Snow Flakes

Solomon Seal (Woods Flower)

Swamp Lily

Trillium

Zigzag (Skyline, Mountain Trail, or Indian Pottery)

Trilliums, probably by Karl Fuerer, circa 1936–1938. Example of botanical art hung in guest rooms. Trilliums are one of the local wildflowers, and inspired the Trillium guest room design scheme.

DEDICATION BY FRANKLIN D. ROOSEVELT, SEPTEMBER 28, 1937

In late summer 1937, President Roosevelt scheduled a visit to dedicate Bonneville Dam, one of the region's largest New Deal projects. Probably through Oregon WPA administrator Emerson J. Griffith's efforts, Timberline Lodge was added to his itinerary. Griffith pointed out that Timberline's elevator would be working by then (to accommodate the president's disability), and suggested side trips to the municipal airport in Portland, the flax plants at Mount Angel (where linen thread was made), and other Oregon WPA projects.

On September 28, 1937, the president and Eleanor Roosevelt bundled against the cold morning and left Bonneville Dam in an open touring car, accompanied by a motorcade of forty vehicles. As they entered the Mount Hood National Forest on the Mount Hood Loop Road, mounted Forest Service personnel met them in a formal military display. Later in that day, as they drove to Portland, they were greeted by Civilian Conservation Corps workers lined up to salute and wave along the roadside.

Forest Service engineer Ward Gano was assigned to security for the president's visit. In 1983, he wrote in "Some Timberline Lodge Recollections":

Motorcade carrying President Franklin D. Roosevelt, leaving Bonneville Dam and driving toward Mount Hood for the Timberline Lodge dedication ceremony, September 28, 1937. Courtesy of Robert Hadlow, Oregon Department of Transportation.

> My assignment, as a bridge engineer, was to guard the West Fork Salmon River Bridge on the east leg road (which generally followed the route of the current Timberline Road) over which the President and his party would travel. I suppose it was felt that my being under the bridge would discourage anyone having any thoughts about blowing it up. I had no weapon of any kind to back up my mere presence. As I sat out of sight under the bridge I heard the cars in the President's party rumble across its plank deck. After a decent interval, and having no instructions to the contrary, I unparked my government pickup and drove on up to the Lodge to join the assemblage there and to listen to his remarks. I saw to it that I got back to my post under the bridge before the Presidential party made its return trip.

For the dedication, most visitors were not allowed to drive up to the lodge, in part for security and also because no parking lot had been completed. Buses transported visitors from Government Camp up to the lodge site. Prior to Roosevelt's arrival, the WPA band played and a

Forest Service welcoming demonstration for President Franklin D. Roosevelt at entrance to Mount Hood National Forest, September 28, 1937. Sketch by "B. W.," dated October 5, 1937. RG 95, NARA— Pacific Alaska Region (Seattle). National Forest, Region 6. Photo D, Supervision, Mount Hood.

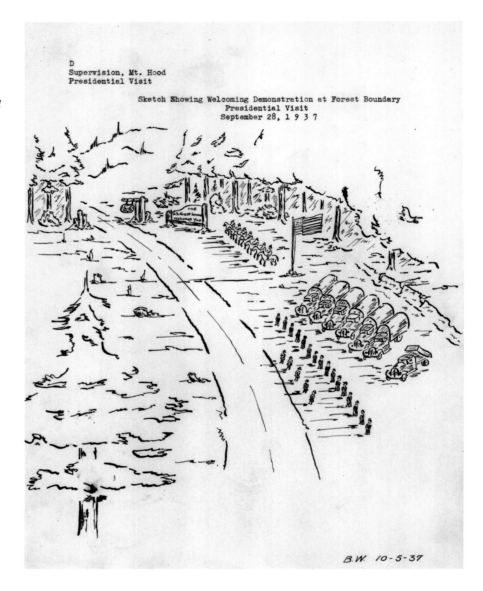

D
Supervision, Mt. Hood
Presidential Visit

Sketch Showing Welcoming Demonstration at Forest Boundary
Presidential Visit
September 28, 1 9 3 7

B.W. 10-5-37

pageant from the Federal Theatre Project was performed in the amphitheatre, with short dances, according to Karen Wickre's thesis, including: "All the Weary People," "Bonneville Dam," "Dance of the Flax-Scutching Machines," "Indian Celebration Dance," "American Negro Interlude," "Dance of the Sophisticates," and "Dance of the WPA Workers."

Prior to the Roosevelts' arrival, speeches of various administrators were broadcast over national network radio. Twelve lookouts visible from the lodge were manned by Forest Service workers who used heliographs (mirrors to reflect sunlight) to flash messages at timed intervals throughout the speeches leading up to Roosevelt's speech.

After entering the lodge, Roosevelt took the elevator to the main floor and went out on the terrace overlooking the main entrance, looking south toward Mount Jefferson. (It has since been named the Roosevelt Terrace.) Though in his speech he mentioned future recreational benefits of the lodge, Roosevelt emphasized the economic value of the forests for timber, livestock, game, and water. Last, he referred to government operation of the lodge: "This Timberline Lodge marks a venture that was made possible by WPA emergency relief work, in order that we may test the workability of recreational facilities installed by the Government itself and operated under its complete control."

After the dedication, about 150 invited guests went inside for lunch and were entertained by the WPA orchestra's string ensemble, which played on the mezzanine.

Architect Turner showed Eleanor Roosevelt around the building after lunch. She was given the use of Room 107 in the west wing, which was known as the Eleanor Roosevelt Room for many years. The room is now called the Solomon Seal guest room and is decorated with the same wildflower design as the original, although the fabrics are re-creations.

Presidential motorcade at entrance to Timberline Lodge, September 28, 1937. Roosevelt's car is first in line. A temporary ramp was built for Roosevelt's access to the lodge. Friends of Timberline Archive.

President Franklin D. Roosevelt delivering the dedication speech at Timberline Lodge, September 28, 1937. Plaque includes the dedication to the workers. Courtesy of McLean Family Collection.

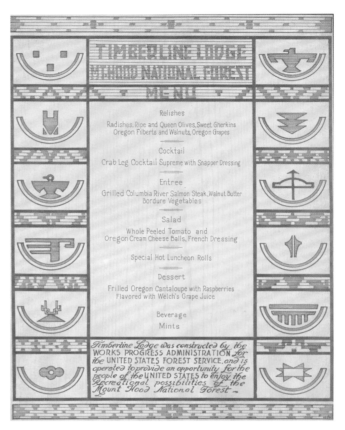

(upper right) *Menu for dedication luncheon, September 28, 1937. The meal focused on Northwest foods, and the menu design incorporates the Camp Fire Girls' "The Year in Moons" designs, an acknowledgment to the WPA, and the mission of Timberline Lodge. RG 95, NARA—Pacific Alaska Region (Seattle).*

President Franklin D. Roosevelt having lunch after the dedication of Timberline Lodge, by the fireplace in the main lobby of the lodge, September 28, 1937. Courtesy of McLean Family Collection.

"DON'T TAKE THAT PICTURE!"

At the lodge, the president was assisted from his car and up to the terrace. George Henderson, a young photojournalist for the Forest Service, waited impatiently in the press box with his camera poised. As Roosevelt disembarked from the car, Henderson pressed down the shutter, prompting a Secret Service man to point at him and mouth, "Don't take that picture." Since he was not a member of the press corps, Henderson had not known that press rules forbade pictures of President Roosevelt that showed his disability. With the shutter already depressed, however, all he could do was release his finger. The photograph he snapped that day was later sought out as one of the few images showing Roosevelt getting assistance because of his paralysis.

Like many people, architect Linn Forrest had not been aware of the extent of Roosevelt's paralysis and was surprised that construction of a ramp had been a requirement for Roosevelt's visit. He recalled in a later interview, "They put plywood all along . . . so that anybody . . . could not see the president's feet, legs." After watching Roosevelt being helped up the ramp, Forrest remembered, "We knew he was paralyzed, but you never saw it in a movie . . . . He was always with somebody, and they were actually carrying him. He had no use of his limbs at all."

President Franklin D. Roosevelt being assisted from his automobile, September 28, 1937. Courtesy of George Henderson.

Solomon Seal guest room (Room 107), with decor that is similar to the original decoration scheme in 1937.

The *Oregon Journal* quoted Eleanor Roosevelt as she was being shown the room's drapes, upholstery, and woven bedspreads: "This is the best thing I have seen. I think it is perfectly wonderful. Isn't it possible that this might lead to a permanent arts and crafts center?"

Not long after lunch, the presidential party left for Portland. Although they had been invited to spend the night, they declined, and took the train to Seattle to be with their daughter, Anna Eleanor, who for several years was an editor of the women's page for Seattle's *Post-Intelligencer*.

Griffith expressed palpable relief over the performance of the weather in a memo reporting on the event: "The sun shone warmly in a cloudless sky, the mountain peaks glistened in the clear atmosphere, and the whole setting was perfect when the President spoke from the Lodge terrace. Just five hours later a terrific blizzard gripped the mountain and left it covered with snow. I shall never again doubt the efficacy of prayer."

THE LODGE OPENS: FEBRUARY 4 AND 5, 1938

After the September dedication, the builders and craftspeople returned to work to finish building the furniture, painting and framing the botanical watercolors, and sewing draperies and bedspreads before the lodge could be open to the public.

Griffith turned the lodge over to the Forest Service in January, but an official opening was scheduled in February to publicly announce the lodge's completion. The opening festivities were to take place over two days, February 4 and 5, 1938. The event was complicated by a snowstorm that made unexpected guests out of some celebrants and members of the press. During the official opening, Griffith handed the lodge's key to Fred H. Brundage, acting U.S. regional forester, to indicate that the WPA had completed the project and that the lodge and its furnishings were now Forest Service property.

Bess Whitcomb, director of the Federal Theatre Project for Oregon, directed a cast of twenty-five singers and dancers in a tone poem celebrating the event. In addition, a musical production was performed on each of the two days by an eighteen-piece orchestra under the direction of Frederick W. Goodrich, chorus master of the Portland Symphony Orchestra and state director of the Federal Music Project.

Students at Portland's Reed College were invited to serve at the fancy opening dinner which cost the invited guests one dollar and fifty cents each. In exchange for their time, the student servers could stay overnight and ski the next day. Reed student Neil Farnham remembered that would-be waiters had to audition by successfully carrying a tray of glasses across a room with one hand. The glasses on Farnham's tray slid to one side, and he was consigned to kitchen work. That night, Farnham said, the kitchen was in chaos. At one point, the chef opened the oven to check on the dressing. When he tried to kick the oven door shut, his foot landed in the pan of dressing. It was later served to unsuspecting guests with the rest of the meal. After the dinner guests left, the student helpers poured together the champagne left in the glasses, drank it, and ate leftover ice cream.

"I GOT SO DARNED BUSY UP THERE I FORGOT TO QUIT!"

The February 4, 1938, farewell dinner for work superintendents and foremen became an emotional evening as workers said goodbye to a project that had inspired and sustained them for over two years. Griffith recalled in a paper "Timberline Lodge: An Experiment": "The banquet did not go off with the jollity that had been planned. As each man was called on to speak, he bid a faltering farewell to beams that had been shaped with loving hands—to a job that had put new hope into many hearts."

Griffith described the fervor that workers felt for their work at the lodge in a *San Francisco News* article, "Oregon's Timberline Lodge is Tribute to Relief Labor," published February 12, 1938:

> [Timberline] has proved that when men and women on relief feel that they are really doing something worthwhile, they work as hard at it as any private employee, show as much initiative, add a surprising degree of creative ability.
>
> Hour after hour of overtime have been put in by the men who built this lodge. They've suffered privations up here, cut off from civilization, to build it. And tales of heroism, of workers carrying injured comrades on their backs for miles through blizzards are too numerous to mention.
>
> When the lodge opened last week, and the last 17 WPA workers had driven the last nail, they left with tears in their eyes.
>
> And two hours later a lone relief carpenter came down from the attic into the midst of the gayety with which society was celebrating the occasion, to inquire where the truck was that was to take the WPA men back.
>
> "It left two hours ago when they finished," he was told.
>
> "Gosh!" was the reply, "I got so darned busy up there I forgot to quit!"

In 1978, Oregon's administrator of the WPA Women's and Professional Division Gladys Everett remembered: "[Timberline] was a different kind of project. . . . It wasn't just a construction project. . . . It is a monument of what unskilled, dedicated people can do. . . . I doubt that you could ever be able to turn it out again. I don't think it could ever be duplicated."

Timberline Lodge project, Oregon Works Progress Administrators and Partners, circa 1938. Left to right: Emerson J. Griffith, William Wechner, Max Lorenz, six young women on the Winter Sports Carnival court, Margery Hoffman Smith, W. I. Turner, Ray Daniels, and an unidentified man. Oregon Historical Society Research Library negative #CN 013026.

Thanksgiving message sent from workers at Timberline Lodge to President Franklin D. Roosevelt, expressing their gratitude for the opportunity to work on the lodge, circa 1937. Oregon Historical Society Research Library negative #39913.

TIMBERLINE ROAD, MT. HOOD—

Road to Timberline Lodge, circa 1938. Oregon Historical Society Research Library negative #78833.

CHAPTER FOUR

EARLY YEARS OF CHAOS, CLOSURE, AND GROWTH: 1938 TO 1975

*It has often been said that Timberline belongs on
Mount Hood, and that is so true, but it is also true that
Timberline fits into the fabric of the Pacific Northwest.
It suits its people so well: fine, and very understated;
real, and not at all flashy; democratic, and very special.
Coming from back East, where things are not the same, I
could appreciate all this at a glance. I had always wanted
a job that was half outdoors and half indoors and intended
to be a camp director when I left college. I wanted to run
a place like Timberline, where my efforts would make a
difference.*

—Richard L. Kohnstamm,
in *Timberline Lodge: A Love Story* (1986)

16-021 Timberline Lodge in Mid-Winter

Hank Lewis and Tom Terry skiing off the roof of Timberline Lodge, circa 1940. Photograph by Sawyers. Courtesy of www.MountHoodHistory.com. Friends of Timberline Archive.

TODAY, visitors to Timberline Lodge dine next to a roaring fire in the award-winning Cascade Dining Room, choosing from a menu that features Northwest specialties such as salmon, trout, berries, hazelnuts, and wines. Day or overnight guests relax in the swimming pool, hot tub, or sauna. More than 1650 acres of terrain draws skiers and snowboarders to Mount Hood's southern slopes.

Recreational options were far fewer and operations more primitive in the early days at Timberline. WPA funding ran out before the ski chalet, swimming pool, and other planned facilities could be built. From the earliest days, the public has loved the lodge building and its museum-quality furnishings, but many visitors spent very little money at the lodge. Even when the Magic Mile ski lift opened in November 1939, opportunities for making money through the lodge operation were limited, and early operators struggled to make a profit.

When Timberline opened in 1938, visitors on a limited budget could sleep in a dormitory room for one dollar and fifty cents to two dollars. These accommodations were often rented to young skiers who were glad to share a room and pay a cheaper rate. Dormitory rooms held four, six, eight, or ten beds. Rooms with double beds rented for three dollars and

Part of Bedroom Suite - Timberline Lodge

fifty cents single occupancy or five dollars double occupancy. Rooms with twin beds cost between six dollars and eight dollars. Deluxe guest rooms were ten dollars. Dinner in the dining room cost one dollar and fifty cents, and one dollar and twenty-five cents in the Ski Grille. To put these rates in perspective, in 1935 the average annual income in Oregon was $394 per capita.

Guest room at Timberline Lodge decorated in Trillium design scheme, circa 1938. Courtesy of McLean Family Collection.

THE GREATEST GOOD

In summer 1936, eighteen months before Timberline Lodge opened, the Forest Service began the search for a lodge operator. The agency was ambivalent about turning Timberline over to a private party. In early 1938, Robert Marshall, chief of the Division of Recreation and Lands for the Forest Service, suggested that the government operate the lodge so it could exercise complete control over services offered. The Forest Service's goal, as Chief Ferdinand Silcox wrote in a January 1938 letter to WPA administrator Harry Hopkins, was to provide the public with recreational opportunities: "The Forest Service will do its best to assure that the Timberline Lodge will always be administered so as to render

Forest Service personnel gathered for the visit of CCC Director Robert Fechner to the CCC Camp, 1933. Left to right: C. J. "Shirley" Buck (District Forester), T. T. Munger, Chester Morse, Robert Fechner, John Bruckart (Supervisor, Columbia National Forest), Ferdinand Silcox (Chief, U.S. Forest Service), Jim Frankland, John Kirkpatrick (ranger, Randle Ranger District). Courtesy of Richard McClure. Archives of Gifford Pinchot National Forest, U.S.D.A.

Archery was a summer activity available to the first guests at Timberline Lodge, circa 1938. Courtesy of Oregon State Library, 2006.001.0332.831.

Horseback riding was another of the first activities offered to summer guests at Timberline Lodge, circa 1938. Courtesy of Oregon State Library, 2006.001.0333.828.

the greatest good to the citizens of the United States as a center for out-door enjoyment."

Some planned facilities, such as a swimming pool, raised the question whether Timberline would become a Sun Valley type of resort or remain a gateway to a wilderness experience. In 1938, after consideration, regional forester C. J. "Shirley" Buck decided against a pool: "The presence of a pool denotes a distinct step away from mountain recreation activities and toward urbanized forms." While the Forest Service would not approve installation of a swimming pool at the lodge in the late 1930s, a pool was built in 1958 and advertised as the highest pool in the Northwest, at 6000 feet elevation. The heated pool is open year-round.

Issues over services and recreational focus led the Forest Service to argue for government control over the operations. In addition, the For-

Outdoor swimming pool at Timberline Lodge, built in 1958.

Brochure advertising Timberline Lodge, circa 1938. This may be the first brochure to promote the lodge. Courtesy of Mount Hood Cultural Center.

Poster to promote Timberline Lodge, by the Illinois Federal Art Project, circa 1938. WPA Negatives Collection (negative #2354), Portland Art Museum, Oregon.

est Service was sensitive to accusations that the lodge was elitist. In an article on September 11, 1938, *Oregonian* columnist Jay Franklin called the lodge "a first-class luxury hotel built by relief labor for the use of the stiff-collar and white-tie classes." Oregon WPA administrator Emerson J. Griffith sought the help of the Federal Art Project to counter these charges. At his request, the Illinois FAP created posters emphasizing that Timberline was a public recreational facility that welcomed everyone.

During the search for an operator, no suitable applicants came forward. Just prior to the 1938 opening, the Mount Hood Development Association, the local booster organization that raised funds for the sponsor contribution to the initial WPA application, formed Timberline Lodge, Inc. The Forest Service issued a ten-year permit to Timberline Lodge, Inc., beginning January 8, 1938, for an annual fee of $250, paid in advance, and, after outstanding Mount Hood Development Association bonds were retired, 80 percent of the profits. In the permit, the Forest Service ignored some parameters suggested by recreation chief

Florence McLean, daughter of Timberline's manager Clarence McLean, and saint bernard dogs outside the main door to the lodge, 1938. Courtesy of McLean Family Collection.

PENDLETON WOOLEN MILLS

Pendleton Woolen Mills and Portland Woolen Mills provided the first blankets for guests at Timberline Lodge. Still an active Oregon company, Pendleton Woolen Mills began in 1889 from a mill opened in Salem by Thomas Kay, whose daughter married C. P. Bishop. In 1909, in Pendleton, Oregon, Bishop reopened a mill that had made wool blankets and robes for Native Americans before it closed. Throughout its history, Pendleton has produced woolen blankets and other products incorporating Indian designs. Pendleton created a special blanket with a decorative border of pinecones for Timberline when the lodge opened in 1938. During the 1970s restoration project, Pendleton donated woolen fabrics for hand-hooked rugs to Friends of Timberline. In 2006, Pendleton produced a blanket designed by Fred Mattila to raise funds for continuing lodge restoration projects. When guest rooms were recently redecorated, Pendleton blankets were selected to be folded across the foot of each bed.

Ski Lounge (now lower lobby) in 1938, with skiers resting on rawhide and iron chairs. WPA Negatives Collection (negative #4557), Portland Art Museum, Oregon.

Robert Marshall, such as having the Forest Service operate the lodge, paying prevailing wages, and including a nondiscrimination clause. The lack of a nondiscrimination clause later chagrined the Forest Service on at least one occasion when a potential guest's chauffeur was refused a room. Marshall continued to recommend that the Forest Service operate the lodge through appropriations from Congress. The funding did not materialize, and the lodge has always been operated by private individuals and companies under a special use permit.

The first manager, Clarence E. McLean, known as "Larry" or "Mac," came from Portland's Multnomah Hotel. He enlisted five family members to help run the lodge, but he soon found the extreme winter weather on the mountain to be a challenge. He left by April 1939, and eventually moved to the milder climate of the Oregon coast, where he operated the Gearhart Hotel. Perhaps his most lasting contribution to Timberline Lodge was the introduction of saint bernard dogs as mascots, first Lady and then Brule, a tradition that continues.

Clarence McLean and his family set up the first procedures for operating the lodge. While beautiful, the building was not designed for efficiency. The dumbwaiter was a source of early complaints as illustrated in a July 27, 1938, report by the Forest Service chief engineer: "This dumb-

Main Lounge - Timberline Lodge

Main lobby (originally called the Main Lounge) in 1938, looking toward the dining room. The wrought-iron ashtrays have since been removed. Courtesy of McLean Family Collection.

waiter has been, and still is, a constant source of trouble and expense. To the best of my knowledge, it has never functioned with any degree of dependability. Just let a crying need for it arise and it is sure to fail." As subsequent lodge operator Richard L. Kohnstamm later remembered, there was no loading dock. All food had to be carried into the building and hauled up to the kitchen by the dumbwaiter. The only storage space was the attic, reached by a narrow winding staircase.

In the first winter, business boomed, but income fell off when the ski season ended. Less than half of the visitors who came to the lodge in June 1938 ate in one of the restaurants and very few rented a room. The lodge operator and the Forest Service soon found that day visitors did not generate enough income to pay for the lodge's upkeep. In addition, the interests of day tourists and overnight guests were sometimes at odds. Curious visitors roamed guest room halls and occasionally startled guests in their rooms. In an attempt to manage the public and generate income, the Forest Service imposed a twenty-five cent charge to those who wanted to go above the ground floor Ski Lounge unless they were overnight guests.

The fee caused a public outcry, including accusations brought by the Portland Industrial Union Council that the publicly funded Timberline

Early recreational opportunities included trail rides and horse-packing trips in the summer, 1950s. R.L.K. and Company Collection, Friends of Timberline Archive.

had become the playground of the elite few who could afford to stay as guests. Forest Service defenders of the fee claimed it was consistent with practices in similar parks and recreation areas. The Forest Service continued to charge the entrance fee through 1940, then abolished it and did not consider it again until 2007, when it was proposed as an income-generating mechanism to raise funds for needed maintenance.

TIMBERLINE'S FIRST CHAIRLIFT

No funding was guaranteed for a chairlift when the lodge opened in February 1938. Skiers skied down to Government Camp and hiked back up or caught a ride to the lodge. In addition, no funding was available for the toboggan runs, ski jump, ice-skating rink, and tennis courts described in the original WPA application. These were never constructed. The Ski Chalet with auditorium facilities adjacent to the lodge was also not built because of lack of funding at the end of the 1930s. Guests complained that the lodge did not provide enough to do.

For summer recreation, the lodge offered horseback riding. Colonel Hartwell Palmer, a retired World War I cavalry officer (not related to Joel Palmer, the Oregon pioneer after whom the Palmer Glacier was named), operated horse stables at Timberline Lodge from 1938 through 1942. He also was credited with laying out hiking and riding trails between the lodge and Government Camp, although most of the trail building was done by CCC workers from Camp Zigzag. Another recreational activity, a skeet-shooting and small-bore rifle range in the Salmon River Canyon, was considered but probably never built.

Some Forest Service employees opposed construction of a chairlift. John Sieker, acting chief, Division of Recreation and Lands, wrote in a July 22, 1938, memo: "The construction of this chairlift is inappropriate from a scenic standpoint and will detract materially from the enjoyment of many people who visit Mt. Hood and who are not guests at the resort. It may also be a dangerous precedent in further developments, not only at this resort but at other points in the national forests."

Sieker was not alone. Others in the Forest Service also wanted to preserve the wilderness and favored using simple ski tows or a vehicle like the Sno-Motor (a predecessor to the snowcat) to transport skiers. Forest Service chief Ferdinand Silcox, however, recognized that the lodge had been built primarily for skiers and overruled his subordinates. Jencks Mason quoted Silcox's statement: "I have decided that since we have carried the development of Mt. Hood and the Timberline Lodge as far as we have, there is no reason for us to draw a fine line of distinction between a ski lift and a ski tow." While the Forest Service debated the

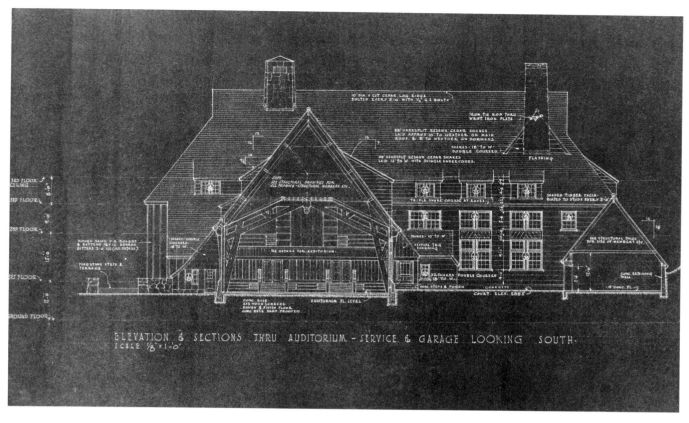

Blueprint for the Ski Chalet planned for an area east of Timberline Lodge, circa 1936. Oregon Historical Society Research Library negative #105737.

Timberline Lodge with chairlift, circa 1939. Oregon Historical Society Research Library negative #26882.

suitability of a chairlift in the national forests, a private developer at Sun Valley had built the world's first ski chairlift in 1936, a feature that would be central at major ski areas in the years to follow.

In fall 1938, construction of the chairlift began, and in May 1939, Crown Prince Olav and Princess Martha of Norway attached chrome-plated nuts and bolts to the first lift tower in a pre-dedication ceremony. In late 1939, the chairlift opened along with a stone and wood warming hut at its upper terminus. When Chief Silcox died unexpectedly in 1939, the hut was named Silcox Hut in appreciation of his support for the chairlift.

The chairlift's name, Magic Mile, was bestowed by Jim Nutter. Nutter promoted a public relations event for the lodge, a ski race parallel to the lift. He adapted the Magic Mile name from a well-known downhill Austrian race, the Flying Kilometer. The term "Magic Mile" later became identified with the lift rather than the race, and the name was retained when a double chairlift replaced the original single chair in 1962. When the lift opened in 1939, tickets cost thirty-five cents for a one-way ride, fifty cents for a round trip, one dollar for three one-way rides, and two dollars for all day. In a 1989 memoir, Norman Wiener remembered preparing the lift for opening: "There were four of us in that first lift crew. . . . Obviously, we all started the job without any prior experience in running a ski lift. In the early fall of 1939, prior to the first snows, we spent our time getting the lift ready to run. This included lifting and installing the cable on the towers, placing numbers on the back of each chair, placing numbers on each tower, practicing with the lift on an operational basis, and planning how we were going to operate with the public. One of the decisions was to sell tickets at the lower terminal of the lift. This meant the construction of a small shack adjacent to the loading area with a ticket-selling window available for the ticket seller."

Wiener later became a prominent Portland attorney and continued his association with Timberline Lodge by representing lodge operator Richard L. Kohnstamm for more than fifty years. The Stormin' Norman ski run is named for Wiener.

MOUNTAIN RESCUE

Prior to construction of the lodge, lost or injured hikers or skiers were rescued by volunteers who were often members of winter sports clubs on Mount Hood. In 1937 as the lodge was nearing completion, members of the Nile River Yacht Club (a ski club, despite its name) and the Wy'East Climbers Club approached the Forest Service about providing first aid for skiers. Wy'Easter Henry (Hank) Lewis, an expert skier, remembered

The Sno-Motor, circa 1937. Friends of Timberline Archive.

THE SNO-MOTOR, THE FIRST SNOWCAT

The first snowcat was developed for use on Mount Hood. According to an unpublished paper by engineer Ward Gano and to George Henderson's 2006 memoir, Ira Davidson, foreman of the WPA stonemasons, designed a primitive snowcat to haul rock to the building site during Timberline's construction in 1937. During construction of the Magic Mile chairlift in 1939, the Forest Service modified the design with a split track and used it to transport materials over the snow from the parking area to the chairlift's tower sites. Monarch Forge & Machine Works of Portland made what was called the Sno-Motor under the direction of Ted Flynn, Forest Service equipment engineer, for use during the chairlift construction. The Forest Service eventually sold the design to Tucker Sno-Cats of Medford, Oregon, and the Sno-Motor became the Sno-Cat, a term now in common use as "snowcat."

Silcox Hut, 1939, the upper terminus for the original Magic Mile chairlift. Friends of Timberline Archive.

SILCOX HUT

Silcox Hut, built in 1939 as the upper terminus for the Magic Mile chairlift, was abandoned in 1962 when the new Magic Mile chairlift was built west of the hut and the lift no longer terminated there. Over the ensuing years, the building was nearly destroyed by vandalism. Climbers Alan Pennington and Jon Smolich had developed a plan to restore the hut, but were killed in a climbing accident. Their plan was adopted by Nancy Randall, a Portland attorney, who organized the nonprofit Friends of Silcox Hut in 1984 and successfully nominated it to the National Register of Historic Places.

Renovations in the 1980s were initially minimal because the plan was to make the hut a haven for climbers and to secure it against vandals and weather. Friends of Silcox Hut soon developed more elaborate plans. Portland architect Jimmy Onstott designed a bunkroom in the former lift terminus area, a row of bathrooms, and a restoration of the eating area and fireplace. When the hut reopened in 1993, it received the People's Choice Award and the Craftsmanship Award from the Portland chapter of the American Institute of Architects. Silcox Hut is now open for group rentals and is so popular that reservations are usually required months in advance. Groups as large as twenty-four can rent the facility for an overnight stay, which includes transportation to the hut by snowcat, dinner next to the fireplace, overnight bunkroom accommodations, and breakfast.

Silcox Hut (1939) at 6950 feet elevation on Mount Hood. Beyond the hut is the upper terminus of the 1962 Magic Mile chairlift. The towers for the Palmer lift are visable above the roof.

Silcox Hut dining area.

that the Forest Service accepted their offer, and members of the new ski patrol received badges that read "Forest Guard" and five dollars for each day of service.

The organization was launched with a meeting between Lewis and Forest District Ranger Harold Engles. When Lewis asked Engles for direction, Engles responded, "You are supposed to know what to do." The Forest Service provided no further guidance or equipment, so Lewis borrowed a toboggan from the Wy'East Climbers cabin and dragged it up to the lodge to transport injured people off the ski slopes.

To recruit members for the ski patrol, the two clubs set up first aid classes in Portland. Lewis recalled that the first fifty members of the organization were drawn by lots to avoid showing preference for anyone, except for the first number, which went to Barney Macnab, who served as president. Though the Forest Service depended on the ski patrol and established a first aid room in the lodge, housing for ski patrol members was not provided. Members occasionally bunked with the horses in the stable below the parking lot.

The Mount Hood Ski Patrol is the oldest volunteer ski patrol in the country. It currently operates out of a building in Government Camp provided through the Forest Service. Its services include a Nordic patrol as well as an alpine ski and snowboarder patrol at all Mount Hood ski areas. It is a nonprofit organization that relies on donations and benefits for funding.

CLOSURE DURING WORLD WAR II (1942–1945)

The financial situation at Timberline Lodge became so critical in 1939–1940 that the board of Timberline Lodge, Inc., began to pressure manager Arthur V. Allen to cut salaries and staff. "Wobbling on the brink of a financial collapse one can only imagine the burning intensity of the Board's hand upon the manager," forest ranger Max E. Becker wrote to the forest supervisor on February 8, 1940. "He [the manager] was forced to take a fifty percent cut in salary which was refused. Then he was forced to fire almost half of his help, followed by a reduction in salaries for the rest." As a result, the staff mutinied in 1939–1940. The lodge's boiler operator became so angry at Allen that he pulled the pin that provided heat and light to the lodge. The management called in the sheriff to start up the boiler.

Opportunities to expand business at the lodge were hampered by a lack of meeting rooms, inadequate ski accommodations, and a dearth of recreational facilities. In the first five years of operation, small profits were realized for two years and losses were incurred the other three years.

Indian head door at the end of a snow tunnel. Courtesy of McLean Family Collection.

Timberline Lodge, Inc., experienced small losses in 1938 ($873.61) and 1940 ($794.74), profits in 1939 ($11.24) and 1941 ($2619.32), and a loss in 1942 ($2315.81) as the country shifted its attention to the war.

Despite America's entry into World War II in December 1941, Timberline's operators hoped to keep the lodge open. During the war, the navy considered using the lodge as a recuperative facility for officers, and even investigated installing a bowling alley for officers' recreation. Eventually these plans were abandoned. When gas rationing was instituted, even fewer tourists traveled up the mountain. It became impractical to continue operations, and the lodge closed in September 1942.

For three years, the Forest Service managed the building through caretakers and watchmen under the direction of ranger Harold Engles. Engineer Arthur A. Mitchell was responsible for keeping the interior temperature above forty degrees to control freezing and dampness. Colonel Hartwell W. Palmer, Ole Lien, and George Lasher assisted Mitchell and served as watchmen. Throughout the war, the road to the lodge was not cleared during winter, so all supplies for those maintaining the lodge were packed in from Government Camp by foot.

GAMBLING, SCANDAL, AND CHAOS IN THE EARLY 1950S

World War II ended in August 1945, and Timberline Lodge reopened on December 2, 1945. Postwar Forest Service inspection reports showed that Timberline's operator earned profits of $2692.09 in 1946 and $24,650.87 in 1947. The success was short-lived, however, and operations suffered from the quick turnover of three managers in seven years. The weather compounded the lodge's managerial problems. In 1949, unusual snowstorms buried and isolated the lodge, and the operation lost $11,135.

The infrastructure was also showing its age and revealing the shortcomings of its Depression-era economies. For example, spare parts were unavailable to repair plumbing and electrical systems that had been cobbled together from World War I surplus. Lodge operations continued to be hampered by the absence of ancillary structures not built through the WPA, particularly a ski chalet, which would have reduced overcrowding in the lodge public areas.

In 1950, the Forest Service allowed lodge management to create the Ram's Head Bar in a section of the mezzanine. Although the Forest Service found the bar to be unsightly and disapproved of the adults-only area on the mezzanine, the bar remained open because it provided profits, according to an October 18, 1951, Forest Service memorandum.

On August 1, 1952, the company that operated the lodge, Timberline Lodge, Inc., was sold to Carl R. McFadden, John McFadden, and Elston Ireland through a $23,559.16 promissory note. In May 1953, the Oregon Liquor Commission issued a license for lodge management to sell liquor by the drink. Until then, the lodge had been dry, although guests could bring their own alcoholic beverages. Although gambling was not prohibited by the Forest Service, the lodge permit required that any new enterprise be approved. The operator never requested a permit to conduct gambling, but by the 1950s it was taking place at the lodge surreptitiously.

In fall 1953, forest ranger Ralph Wiese discovered a blackjack table and portable bar in room 301. He investigated further and found slot

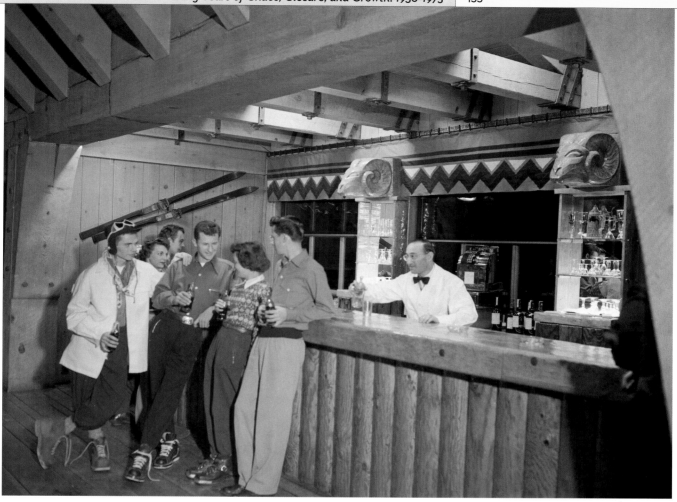

Skiers at Ram's Head Bar, November 8, 1950. Delay photo 0472F. Courtesy of Historic Photo Archive.

Skiers at the soda fountain in the Ski Lounge, November 10, 1951. DeLay photo 0210B. Courtesy of Historic Photo Archive.

The Skiway bus carrying skiers from Government Camp to Timberline Lodge, September 1953. CS00375-01. Courtesy of Historic Photo Archive.

THE SKIWAY TO TIMBERLINE

Although it was not operated by Timberline Lodge, Inc., the aerial Skiway bus has persisted in memory as perhaps the most noteworthy failure associated with Timberline Lodge. For a period of time between 1951 and 1956, the Skiway ferried skiers from Government Camp to Timberline. The cableway, however, was not adequate for the aerial buses attached to it, and it did not function properly. Many skiers remember the trip to Timberline on the Skiway as more expensive and slower than driving Timberline Road. Skier Carol Hardwick, who rode the Skiway as a child, recalled that riders entered a small, two-story hut at Government Camp, walked upstairs, and stepped into the bus. The seats had been removed and skiers stood, holding their skis, for the ride up to a platform west of Timberline, near Pucci's Glade, where they unloaded. After the Skiway stopped operating, the hut at Government Camp became a small hotel and later condominiums.

machines, two on the mezzanine and one in a closet in the manager's room. This discovery precipitated a meeting between the Forest Service and the lodge's board of directors in December 1953. At the meeting, the Forest Service brought up numerous other problems, including the operator's poor credit rating, nonpayment of a Sandy Electric Cooperative utility bill, hiring employees of "doubtful character," alterations to the lodge made without Forest Service approval, and unsubstantiated rumors of other activities that the regional forester preferred not to discuss at the meeting. Afterward, the lodge manager resigned, and the board voted to fire the assistant manager who refused to resign.

In late December 1953, Charles W. Slaney, a Portland movie house owner, became manager, and conditions worsened. Forest Service concerns increased over inadequate maintenance and operation, including major lapses in providing fire protection and failure to file income tax returns or to provide insurance. Throughout 1954, the Forest Service sent repeated memos to Slaney, directing the management to repair chairs and benches that had been left out in the snow, and noting that tourists were complaining about the messy appearance of the lodge grounds. The most serious complaints affected the safety of the ski operation: the operator failed to maintain the main safety brake for the chairlift, to install a guardrail around the lift mechanism, to place adequate rubber liners on the pulleys, and to hire enough employees to operate the lift and tows. According to a 1956 *Sports Illustrated* article, the lodge manager failed to follow the most ordinary operating procedures, such as retrieving the keys for twenty-four of the guestrooms: "Guests who had mistakenly taken them along dropped them in the mail to be returned to the hotel; but Slaney would not pay the two cents due on each key and so they stayed in the post office."

On January 8, 1955, the Forest Service canceled the permit for Timberline Lodge, Inc., citing mismanagement and unsafe operation. Slaney did not leave. Five weeks later, on February 17, 1955, at 1:45 p.m., the Sandy Electric Cooperative turned off power to the lodge because utility bills had not been paid. The lodge was closed until further notice. Without electricity, remaining guests checked out by candlelight. The Forest Service immediately sought a new operator. Slaney's attorney threatened legal action against any new operators, claiming that Timberline Lodge, Inc. had not abandoned its right to operate. Several individuals expressed an interest in operating concessions in the lodge, but the only applicant who met all the criteria for lodge operator was Richard L. Kohnstamm.

Richard L. Kohnstamm at front door of Timberline Lodge, circa 1955. Oregon Historical Society Research Library negative #CN 011808.

THE BEGINNING OF PROSPERITY: RICHARD L. KOHNSTAMM

Richard L. Kohnstamm was the director of Portland's Neighborhood House, a multiservice agency founded in 1905 whose activities since 1920 have included fitness and recreation. Kohnstamm enjoyed skiing and fell in love with the lodge the first time he visited. He had become friendly with Jim Duncan, who in 1955 was the longest tenured employee at Timberline. Duncan encouraged Kohnstamm to apply for the permit to operate the lodge.

Kohnstamm was born in 1926 in New York City, where his family had developed a successful business in food additives called H. Kohnstamm & Co. He grew up attending camp in Maine as a camper, counselor, and supervisor for fourteen years. Kohnstamm served as a gunner in World War II from 1944 to 1946 and was part of the occupation forces in Munich at the end of the war. After the war, Kohnstamm obtained a master's degree in social work from Columbia University. He also visited ski resorts throughout Europe, particularly in Sweden and Switzerland.

In his successful application for the special use permit to operate Timberline Lodge, Kohnstamm proposed adding the facilities that had been included in WPA applications: a ski chalet or day lodge for ski operations, conference facilities, a garage or maintenance building, and additional rooms for guests and employees. Eventually almost all the proposed facilities were provided, but it took over thirty years because of the long and complicated process of obtaining approvals and supporting funding from the government.

Once awarded the permit in April 1955, Kohnstamm organized R.L.K. and Company and set about making improvements. The first priority was to clean up. In 1956 Kohnstamm described the lodge's filthy appearance to *Sports Illustrated*: "We knew things were bad up there . . . but we weren't prepared for what we found at the lodge. It's a work of art, you know, and it's hard to understand how anyone could treat it that way." In addition to layers of grease in the kitchen, Kohnstamm said windows were broken in the guest rooms and original hand-woven draperies had been used to stuff the holes. Original handcrafted furniture had been broken up for firewood.

A DESIGN FOR GROWTH

Almost immediately, Kohnstamm began a significant overhaul of Timberline's ski facilities, which at that time consisted of the Magic Mile chairlift. He focused primarily on alpine skiing and ski racing, but also

EMILIO PUCCI:
OLYMPIC SKIER AND FASHION DESIGNER

Emilio Pucci came to Portland originally in 1934 to study political science at Reed College. A member of the Italian Olympic ski team, he coached Reed's ski team while a student there. The ski team needed a uniform, so Pucci approached Harold Hirsch at White Stag, a Portland outdoor clothing manufacturer, and together they designed white ski uniforms made of cavalry twill, a hard-finished worsted wool material. It was Pucci's first venture into clothing design.

After World War II, his design career began in earnest when *Harper's Bazaar* asked him to design skiwear for an article on winter fashion. He then designed clothing for women, and in 1950 opened an haute couture house. Pucci later designed a Pucci skiwear collection for White Stag, as well as stewardess uniforms for Braniff Airlines from 1954 to 1968. In addition to his success in fashion, Pucci, a member of Italian nobility, also earned a doctorate in political science and was elected to the Italian parliament. Pucci remained fond of the Pacific Northwest and frequently visited. In 1989, he designed a scarf for Friends of Timberline to sell as a fundraiser. He died in 1992.

Italian marchese and fashion designer Emilio Pucci (left) and Timberline operator Richard L. Kohnstamm in the Cascade Dining Room at Timberline Lodge, probably November 1957. Friends of Timberline Archive.

promoted ski jumping and tobogganing. He installed a new rope tow and a double chairlift below the lodge near Pucci's Glade, a run he named in 1957 for fashion designer Emilio Pucci, who returned from Italy for its dedication.

By the late 1950s, the Magic Mile chairlift was nearly two decades old. Its lower terminal was located east of the lodge and was often drifted over by heavy snowfall. To double the lift's capacity and update it, Kohnstamm built a new Magic Mile lift to the 7000-foot level that terminated in a new building west of Silcox Hut in 1962. Above that level, skiers could ride a snowcat to an altitude of 10,000 feet and make an eight-mile run down to Government Camp. The accessibility of skiing at higher elevations enabled Timberline Lodge to advertise itself as the only resort in America to offer skiing year-round.

Kohnstamm retained prominent Austrian ski instructor Pepi Gabl to start a ski school at Timberline in winter 1955. Gabl had recently won the Tyrolean Championship and was a three-time member of the Austrian national ski team. He had also coached teams in Austria (including the women's national team), Czechoslovakia, Hungary, Belgium, and the United States, and had been head instructor at the Sepp Rusch Ski School in Stowe, Vermont. Gabl conducted the First International Summer Racing School at Timberline in 1956.

Skiing films, such as *Skis in the Bamboo Jungle*, *Skis above the Clouds*, and *Pepi Gabl: Maker of Champions*, publicized the lodge. Mount Hood's summer snow attracted ski film-maker Warren Miller, as Richard Kohnstamm recalled in Jean Arthur's book about skiing on Mount Hood: "Warren Miller shot a movie above the lodge my first summer, 1955. He told us how great the skiing was. Warren put a bug in my hat to begin summer skiing. . . . So we went for it." In addition, Kohnstamm wrote to skiers throughout the United States, Canada, and Europe encouraging them to ski at Timberline. Kohnstamm was instrumental not just in the growth of skiing at Timberline, but also in the expansion of the regional and national ski industry. He helped found the Pacific Northwest Ski Areas Association in 1957 to promote Northwest skiing. In 1992, he was inducted into the National Ski Hall of Fame in Ishpeming, Michigan.

Meanwhile, the investment of over $500,000 in the lodge between 1955 and 1966 paid off with increased numbers of skiers. During the 1957 ski season, between 2000 and 4000 people skied at Timberline every weekend. Kohnstamm's successful marketing and strong management helped sustain growth through the next decades. In addition to the Pucci lift and new Magic Mile lift, Kohnstamm built the Victoria Station chairlift and installed a swimming pool. In 1973, 20,000 skiers visited Timberline's slopes on a busy weekend.

Austrian Weekend at Timberline Lodge, circa 1958. This alpine festivity was among the most popular events Kohnstamm initiated to promote the lodge in the 1950s and 1960s. R.L.K. and Company Collection. Friends of Timberline Archive.

The lodge hosted 750,000 visitors in 1973, including many nonskiers. Occupancy at the lodge increased. Rates at Timberline increased with the rising national economy. In 1965, a deluxe fireplace room cost twenty-nine dollars a night, and an all-day lift ticket cost five dollars. Long before daycare became popular, Kohnstamm investigated setting up a nursery at the lodge so that mothers of young children could ski. In contrast to the early 1950s, the 1960s' visitors came to ski and not to gamble. Timberline was again a family-friendly lodge.

Knowing that visitors would be attracted to the mountain for special events, Kohnstamm supported races that had been popular and created new events, dances, and popular music performances, which meant that something happened almost every weekend. In the 1959–1960 season, for example, Timberline hosted a "Pray for Snow Dance," dogsled races, a government-sponsored Snow Survey Institute, a Winter Carnival, an Austrian Weekend, a Canadian Weekend on the queen's birthday, a Golden Rose Race, and the International Summer Racing School. Some of these had taken place for years, and other events became annual favorites. Kohnstamm's promotional events played a large role in Timberline's increasing popularity.

Annual revenues grew to $1.3 million in the early 1970s. The lodge was, however, feeling the strain of large numbers of skiers. The building and its furnishings needed an influx of public funds for improvements and contributions for restoration.

The C. S. Price Wing of Timberline Lodge.

CHAPTER FIVE

A PUBLIC AND PRIVATE PARTNERSHIP PRESERVES A NATIONAL ICON

The Works Progress Administration possibly found its highest expression in the construction of Timberline Lodge for it used the greatest variety of labor found on any project in Oregon, if not in the United States. Skilled workmen and those who benefitted from on-the-job training, representatives of all the arts and many of the professions, found employment. Creative genius, frequently thwarted during the Depression by the necessity of earning a living in other fields, found a medium.

—Nomination to National Register of Historic Places, 1973

Raven's Nest Bar in the C. S. Price Wing of the lodge, with some of the handcrafted furnishings created in the 1990s. Mount Hood is visible through the windows.

MANY SKIERS in the 1960s remember coming into the Ski Lounge for lunch, ice-covered wool ski pants dripping as they warmed up by the fire, the smell of wet wool mingling with orange peels and smoke. Although the Ski Grille was likely to be crowded to overflowing, over 80 percent of Timberline's visitors, winter or summer, spent less than fifty cents per visit at the lodge. To attract more profitable business from conventions and meetings and to ease overcrowding by skiers, lodge operator Richard Kohnstamm developed plans with the Forest Service to expand the facilities with a convention wing and a day lodge for skiers. At the same time, Kohnstamm was negotiating with the Forest Service to execute a renewed permit, since his current permit was due to expire.

In the early 1970s, as a result of Kohnstamm's lobbying and of support by Oregon's congressional delegation, federal funds were made available to build a three-story convention wing and a maintenance building at Timberline. For the convention wing, the architects designed a contemporary structure that echoed the shape of the original building, with a steeply pitched shingled roof and board-and-batten siding. The design earned a 1976 AIA design award for the three firms that collaborated on the project: Farnham, Peck Associates; Fletcher and Finch; and Zaik/Miller. Architect A. P. DiBenedetto was project architect for the Forest Service and consultant on the project. The addition was christened the C. S. Price Wing, to honor the Oregon painter whose two large 1937 murals painted for Timberline hang in the stairwell.

In 1974, R.L.K. and Company received a thirty-year permit to operate Timberline Lodge, a term that allowed for the long-range planning that was needed to complete many of Kohnstamm's goals for the national treasure entrusted to his company. This permit initiated one of the most fruitful eras of Timberline's longstanding partnership of public agencies, private entities and individuals, and nonprofit organizations. This partnership, which continues through the present, has built and furnished the C. S. Price Wing and Wy'East Day Lodge, restored and enhanced handcrafted elements in the lodge, and expanded recreational offerings. Funds for many of the lodge's capital improvements, maintenance, renovations, and repairs come from the 1950 federal Granger-Thye Act, which allows the Forest Service to maintain the lodge by using fees received from the operator.

FRIENDS OF TIMBERLINE

In 1975, the lodge found another significant source of ongoing support when the nonprofit Friends of Timberline was organized. Its mission is "preservation, conservation, and protection of the historical integrity of the lodge and to communicate the spirit of its builders." The idea came from Seattle resident Anne Wright, a regular Timberline guest in the 1960s, one so loyal to the lodge that she took home tattered draperies to repair them. Once, when Wright was chatting with Kohnstamm, he lamented the cost of maintaining the historic structure. Wright recommended that he ask the community for support in refurbishing the lodge. Several years later, Kohnstamm approached his friend John A. Mills, a recently retired banker, and asked him to organize a nonprofit group to raise money for restoring the lodge's furnishings. Soon after, Mills received a $200 check from Kohnstamm with a note asking, "What have you done about organizing our nonprofit?" With this seed money for the

Partners from the U.S. Forest Service, R.L.K. and Company, and Friends of Timberline at the dedication of the amphitheater renovation in 2006. Left to right: Christy Covington, Jon Tullis, Gary Larson, Bob Liddell, John A. Mills, and Jeff Kohnstamm.

yet-unnamed support organization, Mills turned to Rachael Griffin, a Portland sculptor, painter, writer, and collector who had recently retired as curator of the Portland Art Museum. It was she who suggested that the group be called "Friends" with the goal to restore, reproduce, and maintain furnishings at the lodge. Portland attorneys Norman Wiener and David Munro formed the organization and wrote the bylaws.

Once Friends of Timberline had a name and a mission, recruiting board members was surprisingly easy. As with construction of the lodge in the late 1930s, people were honored to participate. Of the first twenty-five people asked to join the board, twenty-two accepted. They included politicians, members of the art community, mountain climbers, and longtime supporters of skiing at Timberline. Senator Mark Hatfield, Senator Bob Packwood, Congressman Wendell Wyatt, photographer Ray Atkeson, artist Tom Hardy, hiker Robert Peirce, and businessman Jack Meier were among the first members. Meier, instrumental in starting Timberline forty years earlier, was chairman of the board.

Mills started raising money in late 1975 by soliciting memberships. In the first year, $3000 came from 300 donors in thirteen states and two foreign countries. One early contributor, a doctor from Boise, Idaho, sent a $100 check with the note, "Timberline Lodge brings to mind memories of some of my fondest indiscretions." Mills raised $24,000 from nine Oregon foundations and trusts, $3000 from Oregon corporations, and $1000 from local organizations, including half from the Portland Junior League. Over $7000 of in-kind contributions included fabrics for textile restoration. Between 1975 and 1979, individuals, cor-

Paul Bunyan opus sectile *murals (1936–1938), by Virginia Darcé, restored in 1976.*
Blue Ox Bar.

Douglas Lynch, one of the original
Timberline Lodge artists, in 2006. Lynch
supervised the restoration and hanging of
three of his l938–1939 linoleum murals
that had been removed and stored in the
attic when the Ski Grille (now the Barlow
Room) had been expanded.

porations, and foundations, mostly from the Northwest, contributed over $50,000 to Friends of Timberline, as well as over $250,000 in labor and materials for restoration of art and craftwork at the lodge. Since that time, Friends has raised about $4 million for restoration.

Rachael Griffin headed the Friends' Restoration Committee. In 1975, she enlisted members of Portland's Junior League to interview the lodge's original builders, craftspeople, and artists about the original artwork and to give direction to restoration efforts. This committee also inventoried the lodge's art and furnishings, which had not been done since 1938. The resulting work was published as a catalog in 1978.

Matching grants of $14,000 from the National Endowment for the Arts and the Oregon Art Commission funded restoration of seven oil paintings by the Northwest Regional Conservation Laboratory at the Portland Art Museum. Ruby Hammill donated $6000 toward the matching funds and later gave additional funds for art restoration and artwork. In addition, Friends of Timberline commissioned rematting of some of the botanical watercolors and cleaning and repainting of the linoleum murals by Douglas Lynch in the Ski Grille.

Some artists restored their own work. Virginia Darcé returned to Timberline to repair the Paul Bunyan glass murals in the Blue Ox Bar

Rachael Griffin, *by Manuel Izquierdo,
circa 1985. Bronze bust in the Rachael
Griffin Historic Exhibition Center.*

in 1976. The mosaic floor compass in the lower lobby, nearly destroyed by being trod on for decades by heavy ski boots, was mended by Mario Ferrarin, son of the original artisan Pete Ferrarin, and by Raymon Re, using Verona yellow marble and Belgian black marble, according to a 1978 article about the restoration in the *Oregon Labor Press*.

Rachael Griffin instituted Timberline's biennial Mountain High exhibition, which celebrates the lodge's ongoing connection to art and craft. Over the years, the Mountain High exhibit has focused on wrought iron, textiles, wood, glass, and, for one exhibit, art of the WPA. An exhibition center to showcase Timberline's history of crafts was also Griffin's idea. When Griffin died in 1983 at seventy-seven, her obituary stated that she was "in large part responsible for the renovation of artistic attributes of Timberline Lodge and the placing of new art there." Three years later, the Rachael Griffin Historic Exhibition Center opened in the lower lobby. It includes a model guest room and a media room that continuously projects film of the history of the construction of the lodge. She is memorialized in a bronze bust (circa 1985) by Portland sculptor Manuel Izquierdo.

TEXTILE RESTORATION

More than any other Timberline furnishings, the original textiles suffered from the passage of time. By 1975, only a few hooked rugs, some woven samples, several faded appliquéd draperies, and a few other pieces of fabric remained. To replace handmade textiles, Portland Mayor Neil Goldschmidt suggested that Friends of Timberline apply to a federal program, the Comprehensive Employment and Training Act (CETA), to fund hiring of workers. The program, enacted in 1973, provided federal funds for employment and training. The application was successful, and in October 1975, with CETA funds, eleven seamstresses and fabric artists began re-creating Timberline's textiles. They worked in two workshops, one for bedspreads and draperies, and the other for hooked rugs.

Between 1975 and 1978, artist and teacher Marlene Gabel directed and taught the rug hookers, seamstresses, and weavers. Many worked in the backyard studio of Gabel's southwest Portland home. Looms also were set up at a northwest Portland yarn store, Wildflower Fibres, and the Oregon School of Arts and Crafts (now Oregon College of Art and Craft) in Portland. Pendleton Woolen Mills provided wool and The Goldsmith Co. provided burlap for hooked rugs. Portland rug merchants and restorers Atiyeh Bros., Inc., and local textile companies Kandel Knitting Mills and White Stag also donated materials. Sailcloth for appliquéd draperies, linen, wool, and chenille for draperies in the main lobby and the Cascade Dining Room, and yarn for woven uphol-

stery fabric were purchased or donated. Using the records of the original designs and remaining samples of original fabrics to guide them, the women created fabrics resembling the original materials for the lodge's public areas and guest rooms.

    The weaving patterns used for upholstery and draperies in public areas were variations of traditional designs and were based on original fabric samples made by WPA workers for Timberline Lodge. Design designations included stripes, "Ms" and "Os," crackle-weave plaid, modified monk's cloth, plain weave, modified "summer-winter," twills, chevron, and a small zigzag variation of "rose path." Colors for the restoration project were similar to those used in the original WPA fabrics, including rich reds and blues for wildflowers such as Indian paintbrush and lupine, and the warm browns and greens of the forest.

Marlene Gabel studio, CETA textile restoration project for Timberline Lodge, 1977. On the far left is Thelma Dull, one of the original WPA weavers. Photograph by Don Normark, Friends of Timberline Archive.

Blue Gentian room, one of eight restored fireplace guest rooms at Timberline Lodge.

Weavers under the CETA project and volunteers wove 461 yards of fabric in that initial funding period. The textiles of the main lobby and mezzanine were re-created with draperies, hand-woven upholstery for chairs and couches, and hand-hooked rugs. Fabric was woven for replacing nine sets (three pieces each) of twelve-foot panels for Cascade Dining Room draperies, a project completed after CETA funding ended. The draperies woven in the 1970s for the main lobby and the Cascade Dining Room have been relined four times. Appliquéd draperies were sewn for the C. S. Price Wing in a zigzag pattern adapted by Linny Adamson and Annin Barrett from new wall sconces in the wing.

The goal for the guest room restoration was to reproduce all the original room schemes. But even Margery Hoffman Smith, who had designed the original room schemes, later declared that having individual room designs was impractical for a hotel. The restoration workers copied or adapted motifs from most of the original schemes, such as Moon over the Mountain, Anemone, Solomon Seal, Trillium, and Blue Gentian. They created hand-appliquéd draperies and woven or appliquéd bedspreads, hand-woven upholstery, and hand-hooked rugs.

Before the CETA project ended in 1978, seven of the guest rooms had been restored, including Blue Gentian, Blue Spruce, Shooting Star, Swamp Lily, Mountain Trail, Field and Stream, and Trillium. Handmade textiles for all guest rooms and for the public areas of the lodge were created in subsequent years. Hand-appliquéd draperies still define the rustic decor of the guest rooms. Over time, worn fabrics that had been hand-woven, appliquéd, and hooked since the 1970s were replaced with different bedding designs and machine-made rugs. Current guest room decor includes hand-appliquéd draperies and some hand-woven upholstery. The beds are adorned with hand-appliquéd pillows (recycled from bedspreads) and Pendleton blankets.

In 1978, Marlene Gabel left the project to become executive director of Portland's Contemporary Crafts Gallery, an education center, gallery, and shop for artists that began in 1937 under the WPA as the Oregon Ceramic Studio, now the Museum of Contemporary Craft. After her departure, textile restoration work continued under the direction of Linny Adamson, a weaver in the CETA workshop. She became Timberline's curator the year after the CETA project ended. Adamson is responsible for the current Timberline selection of art and furnishings. With funding from Friends of Timberline and through the Granger-Thye Act, Adamson continues to coordinate the ongoing fabrication of textiles as well as other projects to renovate, replace, or restore the lodge's furniture, wood carvings, lighting fixtures, art, and metal hardware, and structural repair. She also plans exhibits and serves as a regional resource on craft.

Annin Barrett working on appliquéd draperies in a zigzag pattern adapted for some public areas of the lodge. Barrett has been involved with textile restoration at the lodge since 1975. Photograph by Linny Adamson, Friends of Timberline Archive.

WOOD RESTORATION

Even before Friends of Timberline began projects to restore and refurbish the lodge, the Forest Service and R.L.K. and Company replaced and augmented damaged or missing wood furniture. Starting in 1971, Richard Kohnstamm arranged for dining room chairs to be replicated by inmates at the McNeil Island Penitentiary in southern Puget Sound and hired furniture makers to make more bedside tables for guests' comfort. The pieces of handmade replacement and replica wooden furniture are nearly indistinguishable from the originals.

Original beds in the lodge were twin or double size. A special original design included two twin beds that could be hinged together to make a king-size bed. Replicas have been made of this design. Queen-size bed frames, resembling the original twin and double frames, have replaced the smaller beds to meet guest preferences.

A major furniture restoration project was initiated in 1984. Books of diagrams of original furniture plans created by the WPA were useful

Timberline Lodge's Cascade Dining Room with original and re-created chairs and tables.

to woodworkers creating replicas of designs. *The Oregonian* reported in 1984 that William C. Donald constructed fifty chairs for the mezzanine, five dining room tables, twelve beds, ten dressers, four corner desks, and ten bedside tables. Additional tables for the mezzanine, dressers, mirrors, and copies of the wood armchair used by President Franklin D. Roosevelt in 1937 have also been made.

Through funding by Friends of Timberline and the Granger-Thye Act, wood restoration is continous. Contractor Jerry Gomes and others have also repaired windows, renovated guest rooms, upgraded bathrooms, and improved lighting in public areas, among other efforts. Artists have carved animal heads to replace weathered carvings on exterior beam ends and posts at the front terrace, and have created decoration for the Wy'East Day Lodge, which was dedicated in 1981. After A. P. DiBenedetto retired as U.S. Forest Service architect in 1979, he formed the Portland architectural firm that eventually became DiBenedetto, Thomson and Livingstone. The firm has provided architectural services for several renovation projects at Timberline.

METAL RESTORATION

Restoration and additions to the lodge's distinctive metalwork began in the 1970s. Around 1977, Friends of Timberline commissioned Portland artists Dexter Bacon and Carol Mischler, teachers at the Oregon Arts and Crafts Society (now the Oregon College of Art and Craft) to remake spun copper ashtrays for the public areas, since many had been lost through the years. (In keeping with the current no-smoking policy, ashtrays have since been removed and are in storage except for several on the terrace and at swimming pool areas.)

Not long after Friends of Timberline was organized, Portland businessman Arthur McArthur offered to restore the wood, iron, and rawhide chairs and loveseats found in the lower lobby (then still the Ski Lounge), asking just thirty dollars per chair, the cost of materials. McArthur researched the original treatments used on the metal and wood of the chairs and loveseats by consulting with O. B. Dawson, supervisor of the WPA metalworking shop, and Ray Neufer, supervisor of the WPA woodworking shop. Over the next thirty years, McArthur improved and fine-tuned the process of restoring and re-restoring the chairs and loveseats. He taught the process to his son, Alan Hart-McArthur, who has continued to work on restoration projects with the lodge.

Passing craft traditions from one generation to the next is an extension of the WPA goal that the creation of furnishings for Timberline Lodge should give impetus to revitalizing Oregon's craft industry. The chain of craftsmanship is well exemplified by Timberline's ironwork, which began with Dawson in the 1930s and continues to the present. In the 1970s, Russell Maugans, a professional pilot and amateur blacksmith, visited the lodge and was struck by its beautiful ironwork. Kohnstamm put Maugans in touch with Dawson. After he retired, Maugans devoted himself to replicating wrought-iron lamps for the lodge using techniques and finishes Dawson taught him. Between 1979 and 1985, Maugans made more than 150 pieces of ironwork at his forge on Whidbey Island in Washington, including fireplace tools, kick plates, door

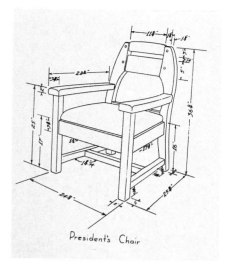

Diagram of President's Chair, from bound volumes of original furniture designs, 1942. Copies of these WPA books are in the John Wilson Special Collection and Oregon State Library. Photograph by Susanna Kuo.

Arthur McArthur restoring rawhide and iron chairs in the 1970s. Photograph by Richard Munro, Friends of Timberline Archive.

latches, hinges, trim for tables and chairs, handrails for stairways, a replica wheelbarrow chair, twelve terrace wood and iron chairs, and two round terrace tables. He also worked on the gates in the Rachael Griffin Historic Exhibition Center in 1985. These gates repeat the coyote head motif on the Cascade Dining Room gates designed in 1937 by Margery Hoffman Smith and Dawson.

In 1980, Maugans told Darryl Nelson, a local blacksmith, "I've got to take you up to this place on Mount Hood. I think you'd really like it." Nelson did. In 1981, he undertook his first project for Timberline Lodge, the fireplace tools for the Wy'East Day Lodge. The oversize tools reflect the scale of the open, two-story day lodge.

Nelson recalled that he and Maugans were installing new wrought-iron handrails on three flights of stairs in the lodge in the 1980s in order to meet safety codes. They heard guests climbing the stairs below them, admiring the rails. One guest exclaimed, "They just don't make things like this anymore!" The guests saw Maugans and Nelson as they

Pelican newel post with new wrought-iron handrails.

Russell Maugans working on a ram's head fireplace tool for Timberline Lodge, circa 1981. Friends of Timberline Archive.

installed another new handrail, and asked the blacksmiths what they were doing. Maugans answered that he and Nelson were just putting the handrails back on the stairway.

Maugans was in the process of planning gates for the Blue Ox Bar in 1985 when he became terminally ill. Nelson and other members of the Northwest Blacksmiths Association made the gates. Nelson asked Maugans's widow to suggest something as a memorial to Maugans that could be incorporated into the design. She went into Maugans's workshop and selected a small bird that Maugans had made as a replica of a piece by the nationally famous blacksmith Samuel Yellin. The bird was put on the cane bolt, the vertical bar that goes into the floor to hold the gate closed. This project drew on the skills of many blacksmiths who worked in what Nelson called "the spirit of Timberline," harking back to Dawson's WPA workshop, where work was not signed by individual craftsmen. Although not officially designated, the gates were named by the blacksmiths as the Russell Maugans Memorial Gates. The gates replaced a wooden door and allow visitors to see the Paul Bunyan murals even when the Blue Ox Bar is closed.

Some new ironwork replicates original pieces, including floor and table lamps. Other projects are new designs such as the wrought-iron rams'

Small bird made by Russell Maugans after a Samuel Yellin design and put on the cane bolt of the Blue Ox Bar gate.

Gates for the Rachael Griffin Historic Exhibition Center, made by members of the Northwest Blacksmith Association in 1986. In Hot Iron News, *a newsletter of the Northwest Blacksmith Association, Darryl Nelson wrote that the gates were the work of Terry Carson, Maria Cristalli, Joe Elliot, Alice James, Japheth Howard, Roger Olsen, and himself. Located in the Rachael Griffin Historic Exhibition Center of the lodge. Photograph by Paul Boyer.*

heads on banner poles in the lower lobby, flagpoles on the Roosevelt Terrace, and iron hardware in guest room areas. Stair and elevator railings and new, easy-to-open door latches are designs that help bring the lodge current with disability and fire codes. New hand-wrought ironwork "in the spirit of Timberline" is found even in the farthest corners of the lodge, such as the wrought-iron door handles, grillwork, and brackets in the lodge's wine vault.

For the Silcox Hut renovation, begun in the late 1980s and completed in 1993, Darryl Nelson used local birds and animals, including a raven's head, a marten (named Marty by the Silcox craftsmen), a ground squirrel, and a bushy-tailed pack rat from around the hut in his wrought-iron designs. In the fireplace are bobcat-head andirons that depict Comedy and Tragedy.

Darryl Nelson and other blacksmiths work on fireplace tools and other wrought-iron pieces for Timberline Lodge, 2006, at Fire Mountain Forge, Eatonville Washington.

"Comedy" bobcat andiron at Silcox Hut, circa 1990.

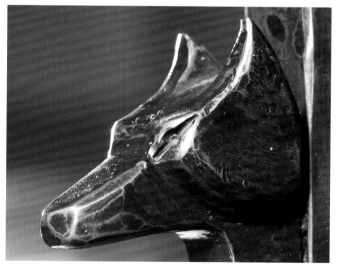

Wolf head on Barlow Room stair railing, by blacksmiths Russell Maugans and Jim Garrett, circa 1985.

LIGHTING ENHANCEMENTS

Over the years, Timberline Lodge's original lighting fixtures have been rewired and refitted or replaced. Original glass diffusers have been replaced with acrylic. Guest room fixtures have been placed in storage and new fixtures have been created in styles compatible with the originals. In the early 1970s, Fred Baker was engaged to rework many fixtures he created when the lodge was built..

The original coverings of the three large globe light fixtures in the main lobby were probably oiled muslin. In 1970, Monica Setziol-Phillips, daughter of Oregon artist LeRoy Setziol, made parchmentlike coverings from paper-backed linen for the light fixtures.

Rawhide was originally used for lampshades on table and floor lamps in the public areas and guest rooms. In 1976, these shades were replaced by Cecil and Helen Snow with leather thongs identical to the originals. In the 1980s, the lampshade project was coordinated through Linny Adamson with Phil and Kristy St. Clair, who had learned to work with leather by making sandals for Portland hippies in the 1970s. The St. Clairs made bell-shaped shades for the table lamps and smaller guest room floor lamps and straight tapered shades for larger lobby floor lamps. Phil St. Clair remembered that when he finished a new shade, he signed it on the inside. He was surprised to learn that the Forest Service objected to the signature. Eventually, he changed the end of the rawhide lacing to a wide piece so that he could sign the piece and hide the signature under the loops. Currently, Denise "Dede" Tuel re-creates and restores lampshades for the lodge.

Restored hexagonal globe light fixture in main lobby of lodge.

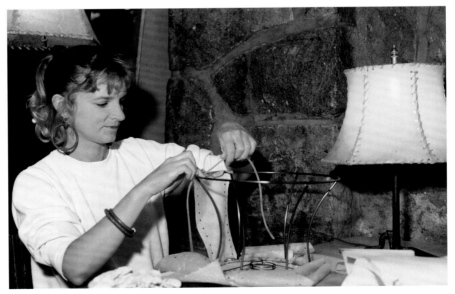

Kristy St. Clair repairing lampshades using rawhide thongs, 1980s. Photograph by Linny Adamson, Friends of Timberline Archive.

Water bug light fixture in main lobby, 1937.

In 1996, Friends of Timberline initiated the ongoing "Light Up the Lodge" project to bring lighting up to current safety standards in the C. S. Price Wing and in hallways and guest room stairways. Led by Friends board member and architect Richard Spies, the project renovated and improved the lighting output of old fixtures. He also added new fixtures designed to be historically compatible with the originals. For example, the original upside-down water bug (also called water-skipper) lights in the main lobby inspired the more recent elongated ceiling lights of similar design in the C. S. Price Wing. The original globe chandeliers of the main lobby inspired a similar globe in the Raven's Nest Bar in the C. S. Price Wing. In stairways and hallways, sixty new square wall sconces, which were decorated with geometric patterns similar to those on original fixtures, along with square ceiling fixtures were installed to improve visibility. A second phase of the project was initiated in 2006 to improve lighting on the headhouse ceiling beams and on paintings in the mezzanine and main lobby.

WY'EAST DAY LODGE IS BUILT

Ski facilities at Timberline Lodge received a boost in 1978 when the Palmer chairlift was built from the upper terminus of the Magic Mile lift, rising 2500 more vertical feet toward the summit, to an elevation of 8545 feet, adding more lifts to Timberline's year-round ski facilities (the lifts are closed for only two weeks after Labor Day). Once the Palmer lift was installed, the regular use of the snowcat to ferry skiers high on Mount Hood stopped.

Increased crowds that the Palmer lift brought to Timberline helped provide the impetus for building a day lodge in 1981 for skiers. Designed by Broome, Oringdulph, O'Toole, Rudolf and Associates, the low, flat-roofed, 44,000-square-foot Wy'East Day Lodge was intended not to compete visually with the main lodge. The pink color of the day lodge's concrete walls blends with the surrounding volcanic soil, and the tall chimney is higher than the greatest recorded snow depth at that spot.

In the early 1980s, Bridget Beattie McCarthy, former director of the Oregon School of Arts and Crafts (now the Oregon College of Art and Craft), spearheaded the funding and creation of handmade furnishings for the day lodge, including cast concrete refuse containers, light fixtures, signs, desks, benches, counters, and chimney grates. As with the main lodge, art in the day lodge was funded through a public and private partnership and showcases pieces by Northwest artists, including glass art, textiles, and enameled steel.

Enameled steel sculpture on the Wy'East Day Lodge, by Bonnie Bronson, 1982.

Wy'East Day Lodge's cafeteria and bar are divided by Paul Marioni's glass mural The Human Spirit, *1983.*

HISTORIC PRESERVATION: AN ONGOING PARTNERSHIP

Timberline has always been a building by the people and for the people. In the Depression, out-of-work craftsmen and builders rejoiced at the opportunity to build a lodge high on one of the Northwest's most beautiful peaks. Visitors revel in the lodge's unique setting, its warm ambience, and its handcrafted furnishings. Ladybird Johnson, well known for her national beautification efforts, recognized the significance of Timberline Lodge. Attorney Norman Wiener remembered that as First Lady, Johnson hosted a reception and dinner in 1968 for U.S. Forest Service administrators at Timberline Lodge.

After a rocky start, when closure during World War II and subsequent poor management threatened its existence, in 1955 Richard Kohnstamm brought vision, managerial expertise, and passion to what was to become his life work. Thirty years after taking over the lodge management, he said, in *Timberline Lodge: A Love Story*: "I feel that I have the best job in the United States. . . . It has allowed me to express myself, to work in a beautiful setting, to see little by little how this 1955 white elephant is being turned into the national treasure it was intended to be."

Beginning in the 1970s, as the lodge neared its fortieth birthday, the public increasingly recognized Timberline's historic and architectural significance. In 1973, Timberline Lodge was placed on the National Register of Historic Places. The National Register, administered by the National Park Service, includes more than 80,000 properties (districts, sites, buildings, structures, and objects) of significance in American history, architecture, archaeology, engineering, and culture.

On December 22, 1977, the U.S. Department of the Interior designated the lodge a National Historic Landmark, one of only about 2500 in the United States, recognizing its exceptional value in interpreting the heritage of the New Deal. Joan Mondale, wife of then Vice President Walter Mondale, came to designate Timberline Lodge a National Historic Landmark—the finest example of WPA "mountain architecture." National Historic Landmark status conveys a higher level of preservation than does the National Register. As a landmark, the lodge structure is preserved and managed with recognition of its historic character. In the case of Timberline Lodge, its landmark status is balanced with its purpose as a lodge. It is both a museum and a hotel. Although several movies had been filmed near Timberline previously, including *Bend of the River* (1952), *All the Young Men* (1960), *Lost Horizon* (1973), and *Hear No Evil* (1993), Timberline was promoted most visibly by the 1980s horror movie *The Shining*, based on a Stephen King novel, which portrayed the exterior of the lodge, and included a notorious scene of actor Jack Nicholson hacking down a guest room door with an ax.

As expectations were raised regarding the lodge's appearance, Friends of Timberline and Richard Kohnstamm, through R.L.K. and Company, continued to work cooperatively to enhance the lodge's historic character while still keeping it an accessible retreat. Beginning in 1999, a Historic Building Preservation Plan (HBPP) has been in effect to help guide this proven partnership of private enterprise, public agencies, and nonprofit entities as future projects are undertaken. Under the auspices of the Forest Service, the Oregon State Historic Preservation Office, and the Advisory Council on Historic Preservation, the HBPP identifies treatment strategies for various elements of the lodge, from "Preservation/Restore" to "No Specified Treatment Required." The HBPP gives the Forest Service the power to assess any given project's potential to affect the lodge's historic qualities, as well as to meet accessibility, safety, and health codes. The plan will help to ensure that the lodge remains an icon of the New Deal.

THE MAN WHO SAVED TIMBERLINE: RICHARD L. KOHNSTAMM

When Richard L. Kohnstamm died in 2006, the news media described him as "the man who saved Timberline." In honor of his contributions to skiing, all ski areas offered free skiing for one day. Oregon Representative Earl Blumenauer's statement, read before the U.S. House of Representatives on April 26, 2006, recognized Kohnstamm's work in preservation through partnership: "Dick was not just a leader in alpine sports, an innovator in year-round skiing, but also a force in recreation and tourism at the national level as well. His passions ranged from historic preservation to, notably, public broadcasting leadership. He was a pioneer in creative ways to fashion public and private partnerships before the buzzword became popular." A tract of land above the Palmer Snowfield has been proposed to be designated the Richard L. Kohnstamm Wilderness Area in his honor.

Richard L. Kohnstamm in 1987.
Photograph by Jeff Becker. Courtesy of Timberline Lodge.

R.L.K. and Company president and area operator Jeff Kohnstamm with his father Richard L. Kohnstamm, circa 2004–2005. Timberline Lodge photograph.

The Kohnstamm family continues to manage the lodge. Jeff, one of Richard Kohnstamm's four sons, has been president and area operator of Timberline since 1992. The management team consists of company directors Mark Vincent, general manager of hotel operations; Steve Kruse, general manager of mountain operations; and Jon Tullis, director of public affairs and planning. In addition to overseeing the operations of the lodge and ski area, the directors are active in the broader cultural and business landscapes of Oregon, including Jeff Kohnstamm's chairmanship of the Oregon Tourism Commission and Tullis's seat on the Oregon Heritage Commission.

Scott Skellenger, assistant general manager of hotel operations, oversees reservations, the front desk, and housekeeping. Skellenger's attention to customer service is one reason that travel writer Gerry Frank has reported that Timberline Lodge is in such fine shape. Skellenger once recovered a guest's heirloom baby blanket from the depths of a dumpster and another time cooked rainbow trout himself when guests returned late from a fishing expedition.

Following the company's fiftieth anniversary in 2005, the management team released a conceptual development plan titled *The Next 50 Years: Our Vision for the Future* and a companion publication titled *Guiding Principles for Our Staff and Guests*. Tullis explained that the vision for Timberline "is guided by its place in history, its beautiful setting, its dedication to quality recreation and hospitality, and its aspiration to continue to be a place for the 'everyman,' rather than to operate and promote itself as an exclusive resort."

In fact, while Timberline is a ski resort, many visitors come to see or stay in the lodge, and guest rooms have been upgraded in response to tourists' needs. Timberline's maintenance and restoration issues are ongoing. In his role as public affairs and planning director, Tullis has expressed recent concerns about the aging infrastructure of the lodge and especially the eventual deterioration of such systems as the original plumbing, fire suppression, heating pumps, electricity, and lighting. Tullis said that "efforts are being made at the highest levels of the Forest Service as well as the United States Congress to address these deferred maintenance issues in the coming years."

Since the turn of the twenty-first century R.L.K. and Company has also focused on the exterior lodge environs and ski operations. In 2007, the Jeff Flood Express quad (four-seat) chairlift was built, opening 220 new acres of the Still Creek Basin to skiers on eight new alpine trails and one new Nordic trail. The Jeff Flood Express is a 1.2-mile ride from 4850 to 6000 feet elevation. In 2008, snowboarders and skiers paid between forty-nine dollars and fifty-four dollars for an all-day lift ticket, which provides access to forty-one trails, five high-speed quad chairlifts, one triple chairlift, one double chairlift, two rope tows, and Nordic trails. During the winter, the Palmer Snowfield is accessed by snowcats taking skiers above the lifts to higher elevations. Altogether, Timberline's lifts and tows can carry 9869 people uphill every hour to ski over approximately 1650 acres. The Jeff Flood Express chairlift is powered by wind. In a partnership with the nonprofit Bonneville Environmental Foundation, Timberline is offering BEF SkiGreen tags to skiers who wish to offset their drives to and from Mount Hood.

Additional projects for the Timberline environs include removing parking from the front of the lodge and revegetating the area with native alpine plants. The planting will build on a project undertaken by Friends of Timberline that featured boulder placement and plantings in front of the main lodge and between the Wy'East Day Lodge and Timberline Lodge. A Cascadian style landmark entrance sign will identify the road to Timberline on Highway 26. Future plans include bus shuttles and a gondola from Government Camp, six miles below the lodge, to relieve parking pressures. Plans also include building a satellite parking lot and basic facilities three miles below the lodge.

Congress appropriated $1.24 million in 2001 to provide barrier-free access and to make the lodge completely compliant with Americans with Disabilities Act requirements. The Forest Service and R.L.K. and Company added a ground-level entrance from the parking lot at the

Architectural rendering of the proposed snow tunnel entrance for Timberline Lodge, 2004. NE Works (now rhiza a+d), Peter Nylen and Ean Eldred architects, Friends of Timberline Archive.

east end of the building, installed an additional elevator, multiple lifts (to provide access to the swimming pool, mezzanine, and C. S. Price Wing), and handrails, and reworked some guest rooms and bathrooms for ADA access. The Portland architectural firm DiBenedetto, Thomson and Livingstone designed the elevator and new entrance that were completed in 2005.

For more than fifty snowy winters, visitors had entered the main lodge through a sheet metal Quonset hut, a piece of World War II surplus, which provided access to the lodge through drifted snow and protected the lower lobby from the elements. In 2004, Friends of Timberline held a design competition to replace the utilitarian metal entrance with something more distinguished and welcoming. From the twenty-three entries, Portland architects Ian Eldred and Peter Nylen of NE Works (now rhiza a+d) won the competition with a translucent tunnel that resembles a snow cave.

Upgrades and improvements have been guided by a plan developed by representatives of R.L.K. and Company and the Forest Service in a series of meetings in 2001. A statement of principles called the Timberline Compact guides their partnership in operating Timberline Lodge and ski area. In 2008, the partnership renegotiated the compact, and R.L.K. and Company received a new thirty-year permit with the Forest Service. In June 2008, the Pacific Northwest Ski Areas Association recognized the success of the partnership in naming Gary Larson, supervisor of the Mount Hood National Forest, as the 2008 Forest Service Partner of the Year.

To a certain extent, the issues that surround the lodge operation today are the same as those that confronted early operators—providing a balance between insuring privacy for guests and enabling access to the public, and maintaining a compromise between the preservation of an historic handmade building and meeting the demands of two million visitors annually. Timberline Lodge depends on the ongoing partnership of public and private interests to preserve the integrity of a landmark that is not only a ski resort, but a living museum with some of the most beautiful and historically significant art and craftwork in the nation.

In "The Old Blacksmiths," O. B. Dawson wrote, "The planners and the architects had one uppermost thought in the planning of that lodge; it must be as beautiful both inside and out as the beautiful surroundings in which it stands, and it truly turned out just that way."

Mount Hood through the octagonal window at Silcox Hut.

INVENTORY OF TIMBERLINE LODGE'S ART AND ARTISTS

This inventory provides information about the art and artists whose work is displayed at Timberline Lodge. When you are visiting Timberline, you can use it as a guide to this National Historic Landmark. The inventory includes all the artworks commissioned under the Works Progress Administration (WPA) for the lodge, additional WPA art loaned or donated for display at the lodge, and more recent artworks donated or commissioned for the lodge. Almost all the original art at Timberline was loaned to the Forest Service by the WPA in 1938 and 1939.

The artwork at Timberline is the most important of some artists' careers. The two murals painted by C. S. Price, for example, were his two largest works. Charles Heaney's *The Mountain* is also one of two of his largest paintings. The linoleum murals by Douglas Lynch and the *opus sectile* murals by Virginia Darcé were also their largest and most publicly visible work.

Several significant paintings have been added to the Timberline collection since the WPA period. In addition, other WPA works by Darrel Austin and Howard Sewall have been loaned for display at the lodge. The largest collection of art at Timberline comprises the more than 150 botanical watercolors and hand-colored lithographs executed under the Federal Art Project (FAP). Another rich collection at Timberline is the group of interesting watercolors and prints sent from FAP projects in other states. Timberline's distinctive woodcarvings, marquetry, and newel posts are also included in the art inventory.

The art inventory is separate from the inventory of Timberline's furnishings, distinguished as utilitarian objects. The furnishings inventory includes furniture, metal fixtures (although some are purely decorative), and textiles for upholstery, draperies, bedspreads, and rugs.

This inventory is organized alphabetically by medium: glass (including ceramics and mosaics), linoleum panels, lithographs and other prints, metalwork, oil paintings, photography, tapestries and fiber art, watercolors and botanical watercolors (including hand-colored lithographs), and wood carvings and marquetry. Within each medium, artists are listed alphabetically. Multiple works by the same artist are listed alphabetically under the artist's name. Information about individual artists includes a biographical sketch, media used, education, selected collections where work can be viewed, and a list of the artworks and their locations at Timberline. Information was lacking for several artists. Listed lodge locations for artworks are current at the writing of this book, but pieces are moved to different locations from time to time. If a location for a major artwork is not listed, the piece may not have been on display at the time this inventory was taken. Measurements of artworks are given first by height, followed by width.

GLASS, MOSAICS, AND CERAMICS

DARCÉ, VIRGINIA CHISM
b. 1910, Portland, Oregon; d.1985, Los Angeles, California

Virginia Darcé worked in W. P. Fuller Glass Company's stained glass window department in Portland, Oregon. Under the WPA, she painted a seventy-foot-long mural for the Oregon City Post Office and a mural for the Naval Station at Tongue Point, Astoria, Oregon. During World War II, she worked as a writer for the Spokane *Spokesman-Review* and painted murals on the dome of Spokane's Greek Orthodox Church. She later worked in Germany as an interior designer, where she directed decoration of the United Service Organization center in Hamburg. She worked as an interior decorator in Los Angeles for many years. Darcé returned to Portland in 1976 to restore her murals in the Blue Ox Bar.

Media: Watercolor, oil, mosaic, writing.
Education: University of Oregon (student of noted art teacher Eugene Steinhof).
Selected Collections: Portland Art Museum (Oregon).
Work at Timberline: For the Timberline Blue Ox Bar glass murals, Darcé employed *opus sectile*, a mosaic technique in which glass, stone, or mother of pearl pieces are cut to the shape of areas in the design. Inspired by murals of Diego Rivera, she used large, simplified forms to illustrate vignettes from the tale of Paul Bunyan, the legendary lumberjack. Charles Haller and Pete Ferrarin assisted her in making the murals.

Blue Ox Bar, 1936–1938:
(1) *Paul Bunyan Carrying Babe the Blue Ox in the Winter of the Blue Snow.* 65¾ × 56¾ inches. Darcé described this mural in a 1979 interview with Linda Paganelli of the Forest Service: "The winter of the blue snow he found Babe, the blue ox, in the water, in a river, almost drowned. And that's . . . the first mural, where he's holding the little ox in his arms, and he has picked him up out of the water, which is at his feet there."

(2) *Paul Bunyan Folding His Arms.* 65¾ × 52 inches. Darcé described Paul Bunyan: "He was a French Canadian on the borderline . . . between Canada and Michigan, where the first lumber camps developed. . . . He had a two-bladed ax, which is part of the illustration in the murals, and he would cut a wide swath across the mountainside with his ax. . . . He could swing it for a couple of miles at a swing."

(3) *Paul Bunyan with his Blue Ox.* 56½ × 150⅜ inches. Part of the collection at Timberline on permanent loan to U.S. Forest Service, January 18, 1939, through a January 18, 1938, per WPA loan form.

Untitled (Paul Bunyan in three panels). 1930s. Watercolor. 11¾ × 45¾ inches. Darcé described the illustration: "And then when Babe grows up, he [Paul] and Babe have all these marvelous exploits, and . . . there are stories about how many pancakes he could eat, and the Chinese cooks fastened hams on their feet and skated on the pancake griddle to grease it for his pancakes."

Untitled (people pursuing recreational activities on the mountain). 1937. Watercolor. 14⅝ × 19½ inches. Signature and date lower right.

FERRARIN, PETE, AND MELVIN KEEGAN
See *Pioneer Scene* under "Wood Carvings and Marquetry" for Keegan's biography.
Media: Mosaic
Education: Training received in Italy.

Floor Compass. 1937–1940. Marble mosaic is brass set in cement. About 98⅜ inches in diameter. Square-on-square design at center. Arrows point to four compass points. The original architectural drawings for the compass depicted a head of Zeus blowing the winds at the center and skiers in bronze inlay around the directional arrows. The design as executed was simplified. Melvin Keegan probably designed the compass. Pete Ferrarin made the original compass and his son, Mario Ferrarin, and Raymon Re repaired the compass in 1979. The compass was further altered when the Barlow Room was remodeled in 1986.

KEE, BUE

b. 1893, Portland, Oregon; d. 1985, Multnomah County, Oregon

Media: Oil, watercolor, pastel, ceramics.

Education: Museum Art School, Portland, Oregon; Oregon Society of Arts and Crafts, Portland, Oregon.

Work at Timberline: Though none of the listed pieces was created for Timberline, according to WPA records Bue Kee made a ceramic piece *Bananas*, which was apparently once displayed at or intended for Timberline although its current location is unknown.

Green ceramic carp. 1937–1938. 6¾ inches high, 13½ inches long, 2¼ inches wide. Signed and imprinted "fired at Oregon Ceramic Studio." Not intended for Timberline, but completed under Federal Art Project and representative of Bue Kee's style. Gift of Gladys Everett, 1977. Display case by Cascade Dining Room.

Fruit. 1937–1938. White ceramic pomegranate. 6 inches high, 5-inch-square base. Probably not intended for Timberline. Gift of Gladys Everett, 1977. Display case by Cascade Dining Room.

Fruit. 1937–1938. Fired and glazed round green fruit with flowers on top. 5½ inches high, base 3¾ × 3½ inches. Probably not intended for Timberline. Gift of Gladys Everett, 1977. Display case by Cascade Dining Room.

LAMAN, THOMAS

b. 1904, Walla Walla, Washington; d. 1964, San Francisco, California

Thomas Laman assisted Robert Stackpole on sculpting granite pylons in front of the San Francisco Stock Exchange. He painted murals in the San Mateo, California, post office and at other locations under the WPA. Laman sculpted the stone Benjamin Franklin sculpture at Franklin High School in Portland, Oregon, and later designed furniture in San Francisco.

Media: Sculpture, oil, various.

Education: California School of Fine Arts (studied sculpture with Robert Stackpole); Museum Art School (now Pacific Northwest College of Art), Portland, Oregon.

Spring on the Mountain, by Thomas Laman, 1938–1940, with water fountain. Glass mosaic, 85⅜ × 102½ inches. The wall mosaic overlooks Melvin Keegan's floor compass in the lower lobby.

Work at Timberline: In 1939, Thomas Laman requested materials for the drinking fountain mosaic and an information sign, including 100 square feet of cathedral glass, evidence that contradicts the popular belief that the mosaic was made from pieces left over from the Blue Ox Bar murals. The mosaic, *Spring on the Mountain,* illustrates in glass tesserae a deer, bear, fish, ruffled grouse, skunk, conifers, skunk cabbage, trilliums, and rhododendron. Virginia Darcé executed at least one drawing for a drinking fountain mosaic with native animals, but Laman is generally credited with the design that resulted in this mosaic at Timberline. Charles Haller and Pete Ferrarin, who worked on the Paul Bunyan murals, also helped with the drinking fountain mosaic.

Spring on the Mountain. 1938–1940. Glass mosaic. 102½ × 85⅜ inches. Part of Timberline Lodge collection on permanent loan to U.S. Forest Service, August 29, 1939. Left of lower lobby entrance around water fountain.

MARIONI, PAUL
b. 1941, Cincinnati, Ohio
A pioneer of the American studio glass movement, Paul Marioni works in many dimensions in glass. His work is often figurative, intellectual, and witty. He is a Fellow of the American Crafts Council and a former member of the board of directors of the Glass Art Society. He has taught at the San Francisco Art Institute, California College of Arts and Crafts, San Francisco State University, Pilchuk Glass School (Stanwood, Washington), and Penland School of Crafts (Penland, North Carolina).
Media: Glass.
Education: University of Cincinnati, Ohio (1964–1967), San Francisco State University (1963–1964).
Selected Collections: Smithsonian's National Museum of American Art (Washington, D.C.), American Craft Museum (New York), Museum of Glass (Tacoma), Washington State Arts Commission Art Collection in Olympia, Oakland Art Museum (California).

The Human Spirit. 1983. Cast glass and silicone mural in four parts, each mounted in an almost square panel of approximately 57 9/16 × 57⅝ inches. Several facial types were created in metal molds. Once the glass bricks were cast, Marioni added individualized details such as clothing textures and facial features including moustaches, crow's-feet, and smiles. The glass panels include a solid crystal ball and a fish-eye lens. *The Human Spirit* is among Marioni's earliest commissioned work. Wy'East Day Lodge cafeteria.

STEELE, EMILY
Emily Steele is a Eugene, Oregon, artist.
Media: Glass.

Skier. Circa 1985. Opaque white leaded glass. Estimated 45 × 38 inches. Wy'East Day Lodge lounge.

LINOLEUM MURALS

LYNCH, DOUGLAS
b. 1913, La Grande, Oregon
Douglas Lynch, a graphic designer and painter, taught design for many years at the Museum Art School in Portland. His designs were published in national magazines and advertising campaigns, and he worked on display windows at Portland's Meier & Frank department store from about 1932 to 1940. Lynch designed the flag for the City of Portland.
Media: Oil, watercolor, linoleum, graphics.
Education: Museum Art School (now the Pacific Northwest College of Art), Portland, Oregon; Chouinard Art Institute, Los Angeles; and Rudolph Schaeffer School for Design, San Francisco.
Work at Timberline: Margery Hoffman Smith saw Meier & Frank display windows featuring carved linoleum panels and hired Lynch to design panels for the Ski Grille (now the Barlow Room).

Calendar of Mountain Sports, Barlow Room, 1938–1939. Two of the twelve murals are signed. The artist's titles for the murals (listed here) are different from those on the WPA loan form. Barlow Room. The first three murals are on the east (left) side of the entry door:
(1) *Toboggan.* 56 × 50 inches.
(2) *Photographer.* 56 × 48 inches.
(3) *Winter.* 56 × 142 inches.

Six murals are on the west (right) side of the entry door:
(4) *Dancers.* 56 × 52 inches.
(5) *Dinner Table.* 56 × 52 inches.
(6) *Cabin & Cooking.* 56 × 130 inches.
(7) *Camping/Artist and Wildflowers.* 56 × 118 inches.
(8) *Family Camping.* 56 × 118 inches.
(9) *Packhorses* (girl pulling horse). 56 × 118 inches. Mural surrounds window.

Three additional murals were stored in the attic at Timberline before they were located under a stack of mattresses in the 1970s or early 1980s. The panels were chipped, cracked, soiled, and missing the color glazing. Lynch said, "Dale Grassman cleaned and repaired them, matching the patching as close as he could get it to the linoleum. Then, after he finally got

(above) Untitled mural, 1939. Oil on plaster, 56 × 116⅛ inches. This mural was painted in the Ski Grille over the doorway that originally led out into the snow. This room is now the Barlow Room.

(below) Family Camping, *by Douglas Lynch, 1938. This work is a study for the eighth panel of the* Calendar of Mountain Sports *murals. Lynch identified the man in the center as regional forester Thomas Sherrard.*

them mounted on plywood panels, I went out to his shop and put a final coat of white shellac on them to hold them stable." These murals are mounted at the back of the Barlow Room in approximately their original positions on the wall opposite the main door:

(10) *Angler and Fly Box*. 56 × 50 inches.

(11) *Fly Fishing*. 56 × 60 inches.

(12) *Spring Walk*. 56 × 60 inches.

Lynch also painted two murals for the arched walls at the back of the Barlow Room over a door that originally led outdoors:

Untitled. 1939. Oil on arched plaster walls. Two murals, each 56 × 116⅛ inches. One mural frames a door that originally led outside on the north side of the lodge, and the other frames a former window. The mural over the window is signed "Douglas Lynch 1939" in the upper left corner.

LITHOGRAPHS AND OTHER PRINTS

The lithographs at Timberline Lodge include a print by Oregon artist Rockwell Carey, made under the Federal Art Project (FAP) and donated for display at Timberline. In addition, eight prints from FAP artists who worked elsewhere in the country were sent from FAP headquarters in Washington, D.C.

CAREY, ROCKWELL W.
b. 1882, Waldo Hills, Oregon; d. 1954, Portland, Oregon
Rockwell Carey painted a mural, *Early Mail Carriers of the West*, for the Newburg, Oregon, post office under the Treasury Relief Art Project. Under the FAP, he produced lithographs of various views of Timberline Lodge. He had moved to Santa Barbara, California, by 1949, and died in Portland five years later.
Media: Watercolor, oil, lithography.
Education: Museum Art School (1910).
Work at Timberline: A photograph may have inspired the composition of Carey's lithograph, *Timberline Lodge*, circa 1937. The piece was in the possession of Oregon WPA administrator Emerson J. Griffith and his wife after the WPA ended, and was donated for display at Timberline.

Timberline Lodge. Circa 1937. Lithograph. 9 × 12 inches. Not hung at the lodge when this inventory was completed.

DWIGHT, MABEL,
NÉE MABEL JACQUE WILLIAMSON
b. 1876, Cincinnati, Ohio; d. 1955, Sellersville, Pennsylvania
Mabel Dwight grew up in New Orleans and married Eugene Higgins, a painter and etcher. They divorced after eleven years, and she changed her last name to Dwight. In 1927, when working as an illustrator in New York, she began producing lithographs. Dwight participated in the Contemporary Print Group in creating two portfolios of Realist prints in 1933, and she worked on lithographs and watercolors for the FAP from 1935 to 1939. One series included more than 100 prints of New York City personalities. Through the FAP, Dwight expressed social concerns in her prints, including anti-Fascist themes. Later, she lived in Pipersville, Pennsylvania.

Media: Watercolor, lithography.
Education: Hopkins Art School (San Francisco, California) and in Paris (1920s).
Selected Collections: Metropolitan Museum of Art, Boston Museum of Fine Arts, Art Institute of Chicago, Whitney Museum of American Art, Berlin Museum, Victoria and Albert Museum (London), and Bibliothèque nationale de France (Paris).
Work at Timberline: The subject matter of the lithograph *Montauk Lighthouse* is unusual for Dwight, whose prints characteristically dealt with the human situation. Built in 1796, the Montauk Lighthouse is the oldest lighthouse in New York.

Montauk Lighthouse. 1936. Lithograph. 12 × 18 inches. Signature lower right. Printed in lower left corner: "Federal Art Project—WPA/NYC." Mezzanine.

GANSO, EMIL
b. 1895, Halberstadt, Germany; d. 1941, Iowa City, Iowa
In his native Germany, Emil Ganso became a baker in Halberstadt. In 1912, he emigrated to the United States, where he continued to work as a baker in Hoboken, New Jersey. About 1924, the Bulgarian/French artist Jules Pascin befriended him and gave Ganso the opportunity to work in his studio. Gallery owner Erhard Weyhe put Ganso on a monthly allowance so that he could devote himself to art. Ganso later joined the Woodstock artists' community in New York. He made prints for the New York FAP.
Media: Painting (various), wood engraving, lithography, etching.
Education: Guggenheim Fellowship (1933) to study art in Europe.
Selected Collections: Metropolitan Museum of Art (New York), Whitney Museum of American Art (New York), Woodstock Artists Association (Woodstock, New York), Butler Institute of American Art (Youngstown, Ohio), Los Angeles County Museum, and Boston Museum of Fine Arts.
Work at Timberline: The print *Summer Evening* is a peaceful scene of a fisherman sitting by a framed wooden dock, across a lake from a cluster of frame buildings and rounded, wooded hills. There is a rowboat down the lake from the fisherman.

Summer Evening, *by Emil Ganso, 1937. Aquatint, 10 × 15 inches. Room 107.*

Summer Evening. 1937. Aquatint. 10 × 15 inches. Signature lower right. Printed in lower left corner: "Federal Art Project—WPA/NYC." Room 107.

JACK, MABEL WELLINGTON
b. 1899, New York?; d. 1975, New York?
Mabel Wellington Jack made prints under the New York FAP, focusing on scenes of contemporary life. Examples are *Doughboy Dynamite* (1938), *Street Excavation* (1938), and *Ramp at West 19th Street* (1939).
Media: Lithography.
Selected Collections: Some of Mabel Jack's work under the WPA is in the Library of Congress, including *Swan Dive,* a lithograph of a diver.
Work at Timberline: In *Speed Boat,* the fast pace made possible by new forms of transportation is illustrated by a speedboat hurtling across the water and a biplane diving in the sky. Both machines contrast with the seagulls, whose domain the boat and plane are invading.

Speed Boat. 1937. Lithograph. 10 × 16 inches. "MWJ" in lower left corner. Signature and date lower right. Printed in lower left corner: "Federal Art Project—WPA/NYC." Room 107.

KLOSS, GENE, NÉE ALICE GENEVA GLASIER
b. 1903, Oakland, California; d.1996, Taos, New Mexico
Gene Kloss split her time between Taos and Berkeley

Speed Boat, *by Mabel Wellington Jack, 1937. Lithograph, 10 × 16 inches. Room 107.*

(1925) and eventually moved entirely to New Mexico. Her husband was poet Phillips Wray Kloss. She produced nine aquatint etchings and 270 other prints under the FAP. Kloss expressed her enthusiasm for the FAP in an interview with author Jacqueline Hoefer published in 2003: "I think [New Deal art projects] stimulated an interest in art. Because people in outlying places who had never seen anything had murals in their post office and received some of the easel pictures or prints to hang in their schools and in public buildings. I think it is one thing that stimulated the public interest in art. [The New Deal] was a very pronounced help to me in my career because the government subsidy alone gave it dignity and importance."
Media: Oil, watercolor, etchings.
Education: University of California at Berkeley (studied etching with Perham Nahl), graduated 1924; California School of Fine Arts and California College of the Arts.
Work at Timberline: Through the FAP, Kloss made three or four etchings under Russell Vernon Hunter that were printed in editions of fifty each. *New Mexican Village* may be one of these. The composition is in a tilted perspective, the town oriented around the large adobe church. People walk in the street around a building that could be a school. Other isolated villages and hills can be seen in the distance.

New Mexican Village. 1937. Etching. 16 × 21 inches. Signature lower right. Title lower left. Room 215.

MARKHAM, KYRA, NÉE ELAINE HYMAN

b. 1891, Chicago, Illinois; d. 1967, Pétionville, Haiti
Kyra Markham was a mural painter, portrait painter, lithographer, etcher, illustrator, lithographer, craftsperson, decorator, and drawing specialist. She also designed book jackets and illustrations while pursuing a theatrical career. In 1916, she joined the Provincetown Players in Massachusetts. She worked in the film industry during World War I. She may have been married to David S. Gaither, who was a theatrical scene designer.
Media: Oil, lithography, etching.
Education: Art Institute of Chicago; Art Students League, New York.
Selected Collections: Smithsonian, Library of Congress, New York Public Library, Metropolitan Museum of Art, and Whitney Museum of American Art.
Work at Timberline: The lithograph *Sweeping the Snows of Petrouchka*, produced under the FAP in New York, depicts the set for a theatrical event, probably the ballet *The Snow Maiden* by Tchaikovsky.

Sweeping the Snows of Petrouchka. 1936. Lithograph. 10 × 12 inches. Signature and date lower right. Printed in lower left corner: "Federal Art Project—WPA/NYC." Room 107.

MURPHY, MINNIE LOIS

b. 1901, Lyons, Kansas; d. 1962, Glendale, California?
Minnie Murphy was a graphic artist, painter, designer, and illustrator active in Colorado and California. In the late 1930s, she spent summers in Glendale, California.
Media: Painting, etching, engraving, block printing, lithography.
Education: Columbia University, New York; Art Students League.
Selected Collections: Metropolitan Museum of Art, Whitney Museum of American Art, Brooklyn Public Library (New York).
Work at Timberline: The engraving *Spring* is filled with pattern that suggests the richness of spring vegetation, an impression reinforced by the tree in the foreground, which is rendered as a tree of life. The geometric stucco buildings, including the square steepled church in the distance, are typical of the Southwest.

Sweeping the Snows of Petrouchka, *by Kyra Markham, 1936. Lithograph, 10 × 12 inches. Room 107.*

Spring. 1937. Wood engraving. 6 × 8 inches. "MLM" printed lower right corner. Signature lower right on mat. Room 212.

SKOLFIELD, RAYMOND WHITE

b. 1909, Portland, Maine; d. 1996, Hallowell, Maine
Raymond Skolfield painted in a representational manner. His subjects were often landscapes.
Media: Painting, lithography.
Education: Student of P. Hale, G. Demetrios, M. Young, G. Picken, and G. Pène du Bois, Art Students League, New York.
Work at Timberline: In the lithograph *The Fog Lifts*, occupants of a rowboat in the foreground gaze at a distant three-masted sailboat. This composition may represent an historical event in the American Revolution.

The Fog Lifts. 1937. Lithograph. 12 × 16 inches. Signature lower right. Printed in lower left "Federal Art Project—NYC/WPA." Mezzanine.

WEBB, ALBERT J.

b. 1891, New York, New York; d. 19??, New York, New York?
Albert Webb worked primarily as a painter, and first exhibited his art at the end of World War I. Under the WPA Graphic Arts Division (1935–1940), he made etchings,

drypoint engravings, and lithographs. He became an established printmaker, who worked in a Social Realist style. His often portrayed themes of the homeless and unemployed of the Depression. He lived in New York City most of his life.

Media: Painting, etching, lithography, drypoint engraving.

Education: Arts Students League, New York.

Selected Collections: Metropolitan Museum of Art, City College of New York, Brooklyn Museum (New York).

Work at Timberline: *Music Lovers* depicts a street musician entertaining a crowd that is rendered only in outlines.

Music Lovers. 1937. Drypoint. 8 × 9 inches. Signature lower right. Printed in lower left corner "Federal Art Project—NYC/WPA." Room 220.

METALWORK

BRONSON, BONNIE
b. 1940, Portland, Oregon; d. 1990, Mount Adams, Washington

Bonnie Bronson received a grant from the Oregon Art Advocates in 1973 to develop an industrial enameling process at a firm in Seattle. She was killed in a mountain climbing accident in August 1990. After her death, family and friends formed the Bonnie Bronson Foundation, an independent fund that provides a grant to an artist each year.

Media: Welded and painted steel, porcelain enamel on steel.

Education: Museum Art School (now Pacific Northwest College of Art), Portland, Oregon.

Selected Collections: Reed College (Portland, Oregon), Justice Center (Portland, Oregon).

Work at Timberline: Bronson wrote an artist's statement about the sculpture she made for the Wy'East Day Lodge: "The idea for the sculpture came from the roof lines of the old lodge. The scale needed to be large enough to place importance on the Wy'East Day Lodge and the color subtle, so as not to take away from the old lodge." She described the importance of light on the steel surface: "The sculpture takes on the mood of the day according to the light. The glass surface becomes reflective with different types of exposures and the relief changes as the sun moves."

Untitled. 1982. Enameled steel sculpture. Estimated 72 inches (at lowest point) and 156 inches (at highest point) × about 276 inches. Wy'East Day Lodge, east façade by parking lot.

FREEDMAN, CARL

Untitled. 1985. Steel mobile. Estimated 48 × 120 inches. Wy'East Day Lodge, main lobby.

HARDY, TOM
b. 1921, Redmond, Oregon

Tom Hardy taught at the University of British Columbia (Vancouver), University of California at Berkeley, California School of Fine Arts, Tulane University, and Reed College. He has executed many significant sculpture commissions for important sites throughout the United States.

Media: Watercolor, oil, metal.

Education: Oregon State University, University of Oregon.

Selected Collections: University of Oregon (Eugene); Portland Art Museum (Oregon); Portland State University (Oregon), west façade of Neuberger Hall.

Work at Timberline: In addition to the metal sculpture *Ravens*, a watercolor painting of Mount Hood (1963) is in the Timberline Lodge collection.

Ravens. 1975. Arc-welded steel depicting a swirl of flying birds. Height approximately 108 inches. Tri-circular base 29½ × 13 inches. Signature on base. On long-term loan from R.L.K. and Company. Raven's Nest Bar in C. S. Price Wing.

IZQUIERDO, MANUEL
b. 1925, Madrid, Spain

Manuel Izquierdo came to the United States in 1942. He was professor of art at Pacific Northwest College of Art in Portland from 1951 to 1997, an instructor at University of California at Davis, Portland State University (Oregon), and Pacific University (Forest Grove, Oregon), and an artist-in-residence at Reed College (Portland, Oregon).

Ravens, *by Tom Hardy, 1975. Steel, height approximately 108 inches, tri-circular base 29½ × 13 inches. Raven's Nest Bar.*

Media: Sculpture (clay, bronze, wood), prints (etching, woodcuts, engravings, silkscreen), painting (watercolor, oil).
Education: Museum Art School (now Pacific Northwest College of Art), Portland, Oregon, BFA in 1951. Studied with William Givler, Louis Bunce, Frederick Littman, and Lloyd Reynolds.
Selected Collections: Pettygrove Park (Portland), Portland Art Museum (Oregon), Seattle Art Museum, Tacoma Art Museum, Metropolitan Museum of Art, Santa Barbara Art Museum.
Work at Timberline: As a member of the Museum Art School faculty, Izquierdo had known Rachael Griffin when she was a curator at the Portland Art Museum.

Rachael Griffin. Circa 1985. Bronze. Approximately 12 × 8 × 8 inches on bronze base. Bust mounted on a wood pedestal. Commissioned by a private bequest for the Rachael Griffin Historic Exhibition Center. Lower lobby.

OIL PAINTINGS

AUSTIN, DARREL
b. 1907, Raymond, Washington; d. 1994, New Fairfield, Connecticut
Darrel Austin became acquainted with Charles Heaney and C. S. Price at Emil Jacques's studio in Portland. He married artist Margot Helser in 1933. After living in Portland, Los Angeles, and New York, he moved to New Fairfield, Connecticut, in 1945.
Media: Oil.
Education: University of Oregon, Emile Jacques School of European Art in Portland through Columbia University (now the University of Portland), University of Notre Dame (circa 1925).
Selected Collections: Portland Art Museum (Oregon), Oregon Historical Society (Portland), Los Angeles County Museum of Art, Metropolitan Museum of Art, Museum of Modern Art (New York), Boston Museum of Fine Arts, Detroit Institute of Arts, Pennsylvania Academy of Fine Arts (Philadelphia).
Work at Timberline: Austin met with Timberline's designers and architects in May 1936, before construction began on the lodge. The paintings he completed for the lodge were among its first artworks, and portrayed outdoor activities on the mountain.

Dishwashers. 1936. Oil on canvas. 45 × 37 inches. No visible signature. Part of the collection at Timberline on permanent loan to U.S. Forest Service, June 23, 1938. Mezzanine.

Musicians. 1936. Oil on canvas. 45 × 37 inches. No visible signature. Part of the collection at Timberline on permanent loan to U.S. Forest Service, June 23, 1938. Mezzanine.

The Skier. 1936. Oil on canvas. 45 × 37 inches. No visible signature. Part of the series of paintings of mountain activities intended for Timberline, but not historically among the paintings at the lodge. On long-term loan from Jefferson High School, Portland Public Schools, Portland, Oregon. Mezzanine.

Woodcutters. 1936. Oil on canvas. 45 × 37 inches. No visible signature. Part of the series of paintings of mountain activities intended for Timberline, but not historically among paintings at the lodge. On loan from the Portland Art Museum. Mezzanine.

GIVLER, WILLIAM

b. 1908, Omaha, Nebraska; d. 2000, Portland, Oregon
William Givler began as an instructor at the Museum Art School in Portland in 1931 and served as its dean from 1944 to 1973.
Media: Oil, tempera, pastels, lithography, etching, aquatint.
Education: Museum Art School (now Pacific Northwest College of Art), Portland, Oregon; Art Students League.
Selected Collections: Portland Art Museum (Oregon), Reed College (Portland, Oregon), Hallie Ford Museum (Salem, Oregon), Seattle Art Museum, Bibliothèque Nationale (Paris), Victoria and Albert Museum (London).

Mount Hood. 1963. Oil on canvas. 14¼ × 20 inches; 20⅛ × 26½ inches framed. Signature lower right. Commissioned by R.L.K. and Company to commemorate the twenty-fifth anniversary of the construction of Timberline Lodge. Mezzanine.

HEANEY, CHARLES EDWARD

b. 1897, Oconto Falls, Wisconsin; d. 1981, Portland, Oregon
While at the Museum Art School in Portland, Charles Heaney studied with Harry Wentz and William Givler. He was a good friend of C. S. Price. One year after he finished *The Mountain* for Timberline Lodge, Heaney painted *Mountains,* a similar composition on canvas of the same size that is in the collection of the Portland Art Museum. Heaney continued to draw and paint landscapes throughout his life, especially the flat, open plateaus of eastern Oregon dotted with lonely box-shaped houses and bisected by rivers or roads.

Mount Hood, *by William Givler, 1963, in an alcove on the mezzanine. Oil on canvas, 14¼ × 20 inches.*

Media: Oil, watercolor, tempera, etching, woodcut, lithography.
Education: Apprenticed to a jewelry engraver, Museum Art School (now Pacific Northwest College of Art), Portland, Oregon; University of Oregon Extension, Portland.
Selected Collections: Portland Art Museum (Oregon), Oregon Historical Society (Portland), Hallie Ford Museum of Art (Salem, Oregon), University of Oregon (Eugene), Seattle Art Museum, National Museum of American Art (Washington, D.C.).
Work at Timberline: According to art historian Roger Hull, Charles Heaney made sixty-four paintings under the WPA (including *The Mountain*) and nine wood-

cuts, described in the WPA Art Project report as "wood engravings." Three woodcuts depict Timberline Lodge, including the weather vane (called *Tower*), the lodge entrance, and the building with Mount Hood as backdrop. Heaney also produced several other paintings in the 1950s that hang at the lodge.

The Mountain. 1937. Oil on canvas. 34¼ × 42½ inches. Signature lower right (under frame). Current frame by Skip Enge. Part of the collection at Timberline Lodge on loan to the Forest Service, December 15, 1938. Main lobby.

Untitled (road in eastern Oregon). 1950s. Oil on board. 21¼ × 46⅜ inches. Signed "Heaney" in lower right.

Road to Shaniko. 1950s. Oil on board. 19 × 64¾ inches. Signed "Heaney" in lower right.

Untitled (mountain). 1950s. Oil on panel. 9½ × 13¾.

MCLARTY, WILLIAM JAMES (JACK)
b. 1919, Seattle

Jack McLarty moved from Seattle to Portland as a child. Starting in 1946, McLarty taught at the Museum Art School, where he remained until retirement in 1981. McLarty and his wife, Barbara, represented many local artists at the Image Gallery, Portland, starting in 1961, which remained open for over thirty years.

Media: Oil, acrylic, lithography, woodcut, engraving, etching, serigraphy.

Education: Museum Art School (now Pacific Northwest College of Art), Portland, with Clara Jane Stephens, American Artists School (New York).

Selected Collections: Portland Art Museum (Oregon), Lewis and Clark College (Portland), Pacific University (Forest Grove, Oregon), Hallie Ford Museum (Salem, Oregon), Oregon Historical Society (Portland), Seattle Art Museum.

Night Swimmers. 1988. Oil on canvas. 51 × 40¾ inches. Signature lower right. Painting was at Kahneeta High Desert Resort and Casino in Warm Springs, Oregon, before it was donated by the artist to Friends of Timberline. Swimming pool hallway.

MORANO, MICHAEL
b. 1950, Boston?; d. 1994, Portland, Oregon

Michael Morano was a preparator for the Boston Museum of Fine Arts before he moved to Portland. He won an award from the Beaverton Arts Commission in 1993. Morano was a mountain climber who frequently ascended the slopes of Mount Hood to draw and paint vistas. He never tired of painting Mount Hood as a subject. He also made frames and integrated them into his paintings by extending the composition into the frame and, often, painting the title on the frame as part of the work.

Media: Oil.

Education: Rhode Island School of Design.

Selected Collections: East Bank Lofts (Portland, Oregon).

Government Camp. Circa 2002. Oil on panel. 37½ × 82½ inches. Donated by Michael Parsons. C. S. Price Wing.

PANDER, HENK
b. 1937, the Netherlands

Henk Pander came to Portland in 1965 and taught at the Museum Art School from 1965 to 1967. His subjects sometimes combine the beauty of nature with manmade disasters, such as the interaction of landscape with twisted metal of a dismantled airplane or wrecked truck. Kitty Harmon quoted Pander in *The Pacific Northwest Landscape: A Painted History*: "My paintings give form to events I have witnessed throughout my life and are an attempt to make visual sense out of contemporary dilemmas." This award-winning painter has done numerous portraits and completed many commissions.

Media: Oil, watercolor.

Education: Rijksakademie van beeldende kunsten, Amsterdam.

Selected Collections: Oregon State Capitol, Oregon Historical Society (Portland), and Oregon Department of Forestry (Tillamook), Heathman Lodge (Vancouver), Heathman Hotel (Portland), Multnomah Athletic Club (Portland), Oregon State Department of Public Safety Standards and Training (Salem), the Rijksmuseum (Amsterdam).

C. S. Price, by Henk Pander, 1976. Oil on canvas, 45 × 51³/₁₆ inches. C. S. Price Wing.

C. S. Price. 1976. Oil on canvas. 45 × 51³/₁₆ inches. Signature lower right. Commissioned by C. S. Price's niece through Friends of Timberline. Before painting the portrait, Pander researched his subject by interviewing Price's friends and studying Price's palette. Since Price was deceased, Pander used a photograph to achieve the likeness of the face and painted half the face in shadow. Pander dressed like Price and wrapped a canvas around his middle like an apron. Pander painted the torso as a self-portrait looking in a mirror. Corridor to C. S. Price Wing.

Richard L. Kohnstamm. 2004. Oil on canvas. 84 × 59 inches, frame 86 × 64 inches. Signature lower right. The painting was commissioned by the Kohnstamm family to commemorate fifty years of the R.L.K.

and Company's operation of Timberline Lodge. The painting includes details emblematic of Kohnstamm's love of the lodge. He wears a ski sweater given to him by his friend, skier Bud Nash (1932–1983). A pin on his sweater represents Kohnstamm's membership on the eighth Winter Olympic Committee. He stands in front of Mount Hood and holds a model of the lodge in his hand. On one side sits a saint bernard, mascot of the lodge, and on the other is a raven in the snow, bird of the mountain. The portrait was painted from life. Lower lobby.

PRICE, CLAYTON SUMNER
b. 1874, Bedford, Iowa; d. 1950, Portland, Oregon
Raised on a cattle ranch, C. S. Price homesteaded and proved up a ranch of his own by the early 1900s. From 1909 to 1910, he worked as an illustrator for *Pacific Monthly* magazine, first in Portland and then in Monterey, California. By 1918, he gave up illustrating and devoted himself to oil painting. He returned to Portland in 1929 and remained there for the rest of his life. Price's good friends, including Charles Heaney and Douglas Lynch, described the meaning Price was searching for in painting as the "Great Reality," and others remembered that he called it the "one big thing," an elusive essence of expression.
Media: Oil.
Education: St. Louis School of Fine Arts, Missouri (1905).
Selected Collections: Portland Art Museum (Oregon), Oregon Historical Society (Portland), Multnomah County Library (Portland), Hallie Ford Museum of Art (Salem, Oregon), Jordan Schnitzer Museum of Art at the University of Oregon (Eugene), Metropolitan Museum of Art, National Museum of American Art (Washington, D.C.).

Huckleberry Pickers. 1937. Oil on canvas. 56 × 136½ inches. Signed "C. S. Price" lower right. Originally painted for the Cascade Dining Room, it was not installed at Timberline until 1975, when it was hung in the C. S. Price Wing.

Pack Train. 1937. Oil on canvas. 57¾ × 139½ inches. Signed "C. S. Price" lower left. Originally painted for the Cascade Dining Room, it was not installed at Tim-

berline until 1975 when it was hung in the C. S. Price Wing.

The Team, or *Plowing.* 1937. Oil on canvas. 41⅝ × 51¹⁄₁₆ inches. Signature lower right. Part of the collection at Timberline on permanent loan to U.S. Forest Service, January 18, 1939. Main lobby.

Mountain Landscape. 1937. Oil on canvas. 35⅞ × 43¾ inches. Signature lower right. Part of the collection at Timberline on permanent loan to U.S. Forest Service, January 18, 1939. Main lobby.

SEWALL, HOWARD STOYELL
b. 1899, Minneapolis; d. 1975, Portland, Oregon
Howard Sewall was a mural painter, musician, and teacher. He came to Portland in 1920. In addition to the two large murals he created for Timberline Lodge, Sewall painted eleven murals for the Imperial Hotel in Portland and sixteen paintings for Oregon City High School under the FAP. He also designed and executed silkscreen draperies for the Naval Station at Tongue Point, Astoria, Oregon. He taught painting at the Salem, Oregon, Art Center in 1940 and in his downtown Portland studio until 1965.
Media: Oil, watercolor, tempera, printmaking.
Education: Washington School of Art (Washington, D.C.), studied under Eliza Barchus (Portland, 1920); University of Oregon.
Selected Collections: Multnomah County Library (Portland), Pacific University (Forest Grove, Oregon).
Work at Timberline: The two murals *Symbolizing Lodge Builders* depict woodworkers and metalworkers stylized as Egyptians in triptychlike compositions. Originally intended for the Ski Lounge, the murals were instead installed in the Cascade Dining Room after the C. S. Price murals were rejected as too large. Since being restored in 1975 and 1976, the murals have hung on the mezzanine. Several other paintings Sewall completed under the FAP were donated for display at Timberline after 1980.

Symbolizing Lodge Builders—Metal Workers. 1937. Oil on wood. 48 × 115⅝ inches. Signature lower left. Part of the collection at Timberline on permanent loan to U.S. Forest Service, July 6, 1938. Mezzanine.

Symbolizing Lodge Builders—Wood Workers. 1937. Oil on canvas. 48 × 117⅛ inches. Signature lower left. Part of the collection at Timberline on permanent loan to U.S. Forest Service, July 6, 1938. Mezzanine.

In the Garden. Circa 1938. Oil with palette knife on wood. 43½ × 38½ inches. "Howard S. Sewall" lower right corner. Plaque on frame: "Oregon WPA Art Project." This painting was not at Timberline until after 1980, when it was donated by the Metropolitan Arts Commission, Portland. Mezzanine.

Untitled (standing Indian woman holding basket, and another figure on a rock). Circa 1938. Oil on panel. 10⅛ × 12 inches. Signature lower right: "H. S. Sewall." Frame made by Erich Lamade. This painting may have been a study for a mural project. Rachael Griffin Historic Exhibition Center, model room.

Timberline Lodge. Circa 1938. Watercolor. 13 × 9 inches. Main lobby.

SMITH, MARGERY HOFFMAN
b. 1888, Portland, d. 1981, San Francisco
Margery Hoffman Smith was an interior designer best known for her work at Timberline Lodge. She was also a benefactor of the arts and a painter.
Education: Bryn Mawr College, Parsons School of Design, Art Students League, New York
Media: Oil
Work at Timberline: Smith was responsible for the original interior decoration of the lodge. Her family later donated an oil painting to the lodge.

Untitled (vase of flowers). Undated. Oil on canvas. 36⅜ × 30¾ inches. Wine cellar.

PHOTOGRAPHY

GILTNER, PETER
b. 1944, Colfax, Washington
Peter Giltner taught drawing at the Oregon School of Arts and Crafts, Portland, when Bridget McCarthy was its director. When McCarthy was searching for a fund-raising concept to furnish the Wy'East Day Lodge, Giltner developed an idea to incorporate photos into a mural.
Media: Mixed media, including photography, oil painting, drawing, sculpture.
Education: University of Central Washington, Ellensburg (BA and MA in Fine Arts and Education).
Selected Collections: Seattle Art Museum, Washington Park Zoo (Seattle).
Work at Timberline: The mural, *The First Snowfall*, was assembled from small photographs of 10,000 contributors who paid ten dollars each to support the Wy'East Day Lodge hand-crafted furnishings project. Giltner sketched a snow-covered mountain with clouds. A photograph of the sketch was greatly enlarged, creating circles where photographs of the contributors could be stripped in. Negative film of the combined image was printed onto photographic paper, air-brushed, and laminated onto a support. Among his assistants was his wife, Margaret Twelves. Giltner also made photographic copies of the handwritten lettering on the mats of the botanical watercolors when the original mats were being replaced.

The First Snowfall. 1982. Mixed media mural. 84 × 120 inches. Wy'East Day Lodge cafeteria.

TAPESTRY AND FIBER ART

BOUSSARD, DANA
b. 1944, Salem, Oregon
In addition to creating visual art, Dana Boussard is also a speaker about art, and has produced a film, *Montana Defined by Images*, which focuses on the relationship of art to the natural world. In 2008, she completed a stained glass work commissioned for the Holy Spirit Church in Great Falls, Montana, which comprises six large window areas containing twenty-three panels, each 4 × 8 feet.
Media: Textiles, glass, paint, graphic art.
Education: University of Chicago; St. Mary's College, South Bend, Indiana; Art Institute of Chicago; BFA and MFA, University of Montana, Missoula.
Selected Collections: Oregon Health and Science University (Portland), Portland State University Educational Facilities (Oregon), Anchorage International Airport (Alaska), Montana State Library (Helena).

The Mountain Holds Its Secret. 1983. Pieced tapestry. 92 × 103⅜ inches, 92 × 120 inches, and 92 × 97¾ inches. The three-panel tapestry comprises an airbrushed silk-screened scene that incorporates American Indian symbols from the original Timberline Lodge decorative scheme. Mount Hood forms a background across the panels. Each of the panels is a piece of uncut cotton stretched over a wooden frame. Margery Hoffman Smith's grandnieces and grandnephews sponsored this work in commemoration of the interior designer of the lodge. Boussard explained, "The faces represent the people of the past along with the cooperative efforts of all who made the area what it is today." Wy'East Day Lodge, lower level by stairway.

GOLDSMITH, LAYNE
b. circa 1950
Layne Goldsmith, a former fiber arts teacher at the Oregon School of Arts and Crafts (now the Oregon College of Art and Craft) and the University of Oregon, Eugene, has participated in many exhibits, lectures, and workshops.
Media: Fiber art.
Education: Cranbrook Academy of Art (MFA, Fiber, 1979); California State University, San Jose (BA 1972 and MA 1975).
Selected Collections: Washington State Arts Commission (Olympia), King County Arts Commission (Seattle), various companies in Seattle and Bellevue, Washington, and elsewhere.

Wy'East. 1982. Felted wool panels. Approximately 120 × 232 inches. Three square, overlapping panels placed asymmetrically on the diagonal. In the artist's statement that accompanies the piece, Goldsmith wrote, "While remaining singular, this peak was one of many of its own kind, as can be seen by looking from its top to those of its sisters and brothers in both directions. This place is a host for all manner of life forms, each with a unique rhythm and cycle and place." Wy'East Day Lodge cafeteria.

WATERCOLORS

Fourteen watercolors were part of a group of about twenty-five watercolors and lithographs and other prints by artists from other areas of the country that were sent to Tim-

berline Lodge in 1938. Sixteen, including the following six watercolors, became part of Timberline's collection on permanent loan to the U.S. Forest Service. Two are missing: Sheffield Kagy's relief *Sugar Bush* and Russell Limbach's colored lithograph *Connecticut Winter.*

BOSA, LOUIS
b. 1905, Codroipo, Italy; d. 1981, Doylestown, Pennsylvania
Louis Bosa came to the United States from a small town near Venice, Italy. After graduating from the Art Students League, Bosa taught there and at the Cape Ann Art School in Rockport, Massachusetts. He later taught at the Cleveland Institute of Art (1949–1979). In the 1930s and 1940s, he primarily portrayed New York City street scenes in his work. He concentrated on figural representational work.
Media: Watercolor.
Education: Accademia delle Belle Arti, Venice; studied with John Sloan at the Art Students League, New York.
Selected Collections: Metropolitan Museum of Art, Whitney Museum of American Art, Philadelphia Museum of Art.
Work at Timberline: *Pennsylvania Landscape* is a colorful scene of shoebox farmhouses and barns in a valley surrounded by mounded hills and feathery trees. The small figure guiding a plow behind a white and black horse engages in a traditional rural activity.

Pennsylvania Landscape. 1937. Gouache. 13⅝ × 18 inches. Signature lower left. Room 208.

COLWELL, ELIZABETH
b. 1881, Bronson, Michigan; d. 1954, Chicago?
Elizabeth Colwell designed the Colwell Hand Letter typeface. In addition to etchings and landscapes, she is known for watercolor still lifes and floral subjects.
Media: Watercolor, etching, crafts, writing.
Education: Art Institute of Chicago (studied with B. T. Olsen and J. J. O. Nordfeldt).
Selected Collections: Los Angeles Museum of Art, Art Institute of Chicago, University of Chicago, Western Illinois University Art Gallery (Macomb, Illinois).
Work at Timberline: *Tulips and Lilacs* features red and gold tulips surrounded by frilly white lilacs in a cylindrical vase that sits just off center on a round doily ringed in the same red and gold as the flowers.

Tulips and Lilacs. 1937. Watercolor. 23¼ × 19⅛ inches. Signature and date lower left. Room 219.

KERRICK, ARTHUR T.
b. 1901, Minneapolis?; d. 1960, Minneapolis?
Although Arthur Kerrick lived and worked primarily in Minneapolis, he also painted Alaskan scenes on the wall of the Anchorage post office and courthouse during the 1940s under a WPA commission.
Media: Oil, watercolor.
Work at Timberline: *Prairie Farm Dam* depicts a snow-covered Minnesota (probably) farm with frame buildings and a pond created by a dam across a creek.

Prairie Farm Dam. 1937. Watercolor. 18 × 28 inches. Signature and date lower left. Room 108.

LEWANDOWSKI, EDMUND D.
b. 1914, Milwaukee; d. 1998, Rock Hill, South Carolina
Edmund Lewandowski painted post office murals in Wisconsin, Illinois, and Minnesota. In World War II, he made maps and concealments for the U.S. Air Force, and later taught at the Layton School of Art (1947) and Florida State University (Tallahassee, 1949–1954), was director at Layton (1950s–1960s), and served as chairman of the art department at Winthrop College in Rock Hill, South Carolina (1972–1983). Lewandowski was identified with Precisionism, an American art movement of the 1920s and 1930s in which objects are depicted realistically but with emphasis on their geometric form. Valerie Ann Leeds quoted Lewandowski: "Our machines are as representative of our culture as temples and sculpture were of the Greeks. They are classically beautiful and represent physically the progress the nation has made." In the 1950s, Lewandowski's work became more abstract before he returned to more realistic marine and industrial scenes.
Media: Oil, watercolor.
Education: Layton School of Art, Milwaukee, Wisconsin (1931–1934).
Selected Collections: Franklin D. Roosevelt Library (Hyde Park, New York), Museum of Modern Art (New York), University of Wisconsin, Milwaukee Art Institute, Boston Museum of Fine Art.
Work at Timberline: *Algoma* is an early marine scene that closely resembles another of his paintings completed

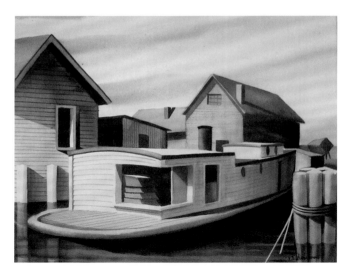

Algoma, by Edmund Lewandowski, 1937. Watercolor, 16½ × 22½ inches. Room 207. Photograph by Leslie Taylor, Friends of Timberline Archive.

at about the same time, *Fishermen's Village* (in the collection of the Franklin D. Roosevelt Library), a watercolor and gouache over pencil, depicting boats and houseboats.

Algoma. 1937. Watercolor. 16½ × 22½ inches. Signature lower right. Room 207.

MODAHL, NANCY
Painter Nancy Modahl Bica is part of the artist community in Monrovia, California. It is not known whether she is the artist who painted *Bowl of Leaves*.

Bowl of Leaves. 1956. Watercolor. 16⅛ × 17¼ inches. On back: "Original by Dora Erickson, Nov. 18–28. Copy by Nancy Modahl, 1956. F-50." Paper is heavily textured. Guest room.

POST, GEORGE BOOTH
b. 1906, Oakland, California; d. 1997, San Francisco, California
George Post worked at the C&H Sugar refinery in Crockett, California. During the Depression, he went to sea to work on an oil tanker. He showed watercolors painted at sea at San Francisco's East-West Gallery with Joseph Danysh, regional director of the FAP. In addition to watercol-

or landscapes of California, Post painted murals in California high schools, Letterman Hospital in the Presidio in San Francisco, and Hartnell College in Salinas, California, under the FAP. He traveled in Mexico and Europe (late 1930s), taught at the California College of Arts and Crafts, and was an art instructor at Stanford University (1940s) and other California institutions. From 1947 to 1973, Post was a professor of painting at California's College of Arts and Crafts in Oakland. Post was considered a master of twentieth-century watercolor painting. He knew that the WPA sent several of his WPA watercolors to Timberline, but he never saw them.

Media: Watercolor.

Education: California School of Fine Arts, San Francisco, now the San Francisco Art Institute (1924–1926).

Selected Collections: Metropolitan Museum of Art, San Francisco Museum of Modern Art, Oakland Museum of Art, M. H. de Young Museum (San Francisco), California Legion of Honor (San Francisco), Seattle Art Museum, Mills College (Oakland, California).

Work at Timberline: The two Post watercolors at Timberline Lodge depict California landscapes, probably painted *en plein air.*

Pine and Oak (at) Shaw's Flat, California. 1936. Watercolor. 21½ × 15¾ inches. Signature and date lower right. Room 208.

Winter at Soulbyville, California. 1937. Watercolor. 15⅜ × 20⅞ inches. Signature lower center. Room 110.

WILDFLOWER WATERCOLORS AND HAND-COLORED LITHOGRAPHS

Botanical watercolors for Timberline Lodge were completed under the Oregon Federal Art Project from 1937 through the spring of 1939. Wildflowers and samples of some trees native to the Mount Hood region were collected and drawn from life with a focus on botanical accuracy. On the reverse of many of the watercolors are comments about the illustration of the plant, sometimes with references to guides to wildflowers and native trees that were in

print when the botanicals were created. Once an original botanical watercolor was completed, several copies were made. All were hand colored.

Imported Castell colored pencils were used to lay in the pigment for the pictures, though WPA superiors in Washington, D.C., had expressed a preference for the use of American-made materials. Then the color was brushed lightly with water, creating a watercolor surface. All the botanicals are original watercolors, some originally drawn in graphite pencil and others are black and white lithographs that were hand colored. Identification in this listing of each composition as a watercolor or a hand-colored lithograph is based on the 2006–2007 conservation assessment and inventory by a professional conservator.

More than 150 botanical watercolors and hand-colored lithographs are in the collection at Timberline, but many others were finished under the project and provided to the Oregon State Library in Salem (OSL), and to John Wilson Special Collections at the Multnomah County Library (MCL) and Jefferson High School (JHS), both in Portland. Identical compositions at one of these other locations are noted in the inventory by the abbreviations OSL, MCL, or JHS.

The attribution of many of the botanical watercolors at Timberline Lodge is problematic. Many of the botanical works appear to have been collaborative efforts while others were by individuals; some appear to be copies of original works done by other artists. The known watercolor artists are listed alphabetically, and the botanicals attributed to that artist are listed alphabetically and then by catalog number. Attribution is based on several kinds of information. On many of the watercolors, the artist is identified on the back or bottom of the work. The work is listed under the name of the copyist, even if another artist is identified as the originator of the composition. The originator's name is identified in the description. In the absence of an artist's name on the artwork, the work is attributed according to the WPA label attached to the frame, if any, or to the artist identified with a WPA negative that corresponds to that composition, if any. Some compositions are attributed to two or three artists who may have completed that work alone or in collaboration, according to information on WPA labels or negatives. Unattributed works are listed at the end. The known artists who contributed work to the lodge under the Oregon FAP include Edward Benedict, Dora Erikson, Karl Feurer, Martina Gangle, George Jeffery, and Elizabeth Hoffman Wood.

Most of the botanical watercolors are framed with mats on which are printed the plants' botanical and common names. Under each artist's name in the inventory listing, each work is identified by the mat label, *retaining the spelling of all plant names (even if incorrect)* on the existing and, in many cases original 1938, labels. Those watercolors with no mat label are identified by the same name that lodge decorators gave to similar compositions, with a note in brackets indicating that there is no mat label. The identification number for each painting is given in brackets at the end of each listing with a cross-listing to identical or similar compositions in other guest rooms and with the names of the artists identified with those compositions in parentheses. The botanical identification written on the reverse or on the WPA label of many of these watercolors is not duplicated in the description unless it differs from the mat label. Spelling of the artist name on the reverse of the artwork or on the WPA label has been retained, *even if incorrect*.

BENEDICT, EDWARD

b. 1870, Gilman, Iowa; d. Portland, Oregon 19??
Media: Watercolor, other?
Education: Unknown.
Work at Timberline: The botanical watercolor listed below is the only one at Timberline Lodge that is identified as painted by Edward Benedict on the back of the work. An identical composition is attributed to either Benedict or Jeffery. He painted wildflower watercolors under the OAP that are in other locations.

Mountain Ash: Pyrus sambucifolia. 1937. Hand-colored lithograph. 16 × 11½ inches. Reverse: "Dec. '37. Benedict." This may be a copy of a composition by Jeffery, since Jeffery is identified on WPA negative #209 jacket and WPA loan receipt, February 23, 1938, acknowledging three *Mountain Ash* watercolors by Jeffery. [USFS.21, identical to USFS.38 (Benedict or Jeffery)]

BENEDICT, EDWARD, OR GEORGE JEFFERY
Biographical information is under individual listings.

Mountain Ash: Pyrus sambucifolia. 1936–1938. Hand-colored lithograph. 15⅜ × 11⅜ inches. Reverse: "Mt. Ash—Pyrus sambucifolia." No attribution on reverse or label, but WPA negative #209 attributes *Mountain Ash* watercolor to Jeffery. WPA loan receipt of February 23, 1938, included three *Mountain Ash* watercolors by Jeffery. [USFS.38, identical to USFS.21 (Benedict)]

ERIKSON, DORIS (DORA)
b. 1905, Orange, Massachusetts; d. 19??, Portland, Oregon?
Dora Erikson may have directed the botanical watercolor project in Portland. Some compositions are identified as a "D. E. original."
Media: Oil, watercolor, sculpture.
Education: Museum Art School, Portland (studied with Harry Wentz and William Givler); Art Students League, New York.
Work at Timberline: Of the listed paintings, eighteen botanical watercolors are identified as Dora Erikson's work from information on the reverse of the artwork. In addition, two botanical watercolors are attributed to Erikson or Feurer; twelve to Erikson, Feurer, or Jeffery; and two to Erikson or Jeffery.

Alpine Fir: Abies lasiooarpa. 1936–1937. Watercolor. 22 × 17 inches. Reverse: "Dora Erikson. September 23–25. Good." [USFS.151, identical to USFS.117 (Jeffery)]

Blue Gentian: Gentiana calycosa. 1936–1938. Watercolor. 10¾ × 13⅞ inches. Reverse: "Dora Erikson. Color very good. Length not more than 3½ or 4⅝ tall at high altitudes, grow very close, buds same size on short stem. Calycosa gentian particularly low growing." "Erikson" is on WPA negative #233 jacket. (Feurer on WPA negative #235a and 235b.) Composition is at MCL, OSL, and JHS. [USFS.132]

Blue Gentron: Gentiana calycosa. 1936–1937. Watercolor. 14¾ × 11⅜ inches. Reverse: "October 19–20. Dora Erikson." Comment on reverse: "Color very good." Blue gentian. "Erikson" is on WPA negative #232

Lupine: Lupinus subalpinus, *by Dora Erikson, 1937–1938. Watercolor, 14½ × 11½ inches. USFS.164.*

jacket. [USFS.156, identical to USFS.124 (not located 2006)]

Bowl of Leaves [no mat label]. 1936–1938. Watercolor. 17¾ × 18¾ inches. Reverse: "A Vase of Leaves." "Erikson" is on WPA negative #269 jacket. [USFS.121]

Columbine: Aquilegia formosa. 1936–1937. Watercolor. 14½ × 11½ inches. Reverse: "November 18–25. Dora Erikson." WPA label: "Dora Erickson." "Erikson" and "Feurer" are on WPA negative #218 jacket. Composition is at OSL, MCL (identified as *Wild Honeysuckle* by Feurer), and JHS. [USFS.176, identical to USFS.14 (Feurer), USFS.28 (Erikson, Feurer, or Jeffery), USFS.145 (Erikson, Feurer, or Jeffery), and USFS.169 (Jeffery)]

Erigeron. 1936–1937. Watercolor. 11¼ × 14⅞ inches. Reverse: "Erigeron: Mountain Daisy. Oct. 1. Dora

Erikson." WPA label: "Dora Erickson. Copy by Jeffrey." Comment on reverse: "More like aster. May be aster. I may not have made blossom large enough from Stevenson's photograph. Strong at base." "Erikson" and "Feurer" are on jackets to WPA negatives #220a, #220b, and #220c. Composition is at MCL (identified as *Aster* by Feurer), OSL, and JHS (copy is signed "Penlock"). [USFS.189, identical to USFS.138 (Jeffery), USFS.165 (Erikson, Feurer, or Jeffery), and USFS.172 (Jeffery)]

Indian Paint Brush: Castilleja augustifolia. 1936–1937. Watercolor. 14⅜ × 11⅜ inches. Reverse: "Dora Erikson. Oct. 21–2. This brighter variety grows lower—at Gov't camp according to Mrs. S." Reference is probably to forester's wife, Mrs. Thomas Sherrard. "Erikson" is on WPA negative #257 jacket. Composition is at MCL, OSL, and JHS. [USFS.700, identical to USFS.113 (Jeffery), USFS.65 (Jeffery), and USFS.107 (Erikson or Jeffery)]

Lupine: Lupinus subalpinus. 1936–1938. Watercolor. 14½ × 11½ inches. Reverse: "Dora Erikson. Good blue. Anatomy of flower not true. This is the mountain blue and they grow quite small." WPA label: "Jeffrey." This single stalk composition varies from other versions. [USFS.164, same composition as USFS.167 and USFS.168 (by Jeffery)]

Lupin: Lupinus subalpinus. 1936–1938. Watercolor. 14½ × 11½ inches. Reverse: "Dora Erikson. Too much purple. Should be blue with white stripes." WPA label: "Jeffrey." [USFS.702, same composition as USFS.164 (Erikson), and USFS.167, USFS.168, USFS.182, and USFS.703 (all by Jeffery)]

Mountain Hemlock: Tsuga mertensiana. 1936–1938. Watercolor. 11⅛ × 14¼ inches. Reverse: "Dora Erikson. Cones more purple when young. Good." Erikson and Feurer identified on WPA negative #247 jacket. Composition is at OSL. [USFS.158]

Mt. Hood Lily: Lilium washingtonianum. 1936–1937. Watercolor. 14½ × 11½ inches. Reverse: "Dora Erikson. Normal size, color good, petals more close. Stephenson photographed. Said to be good." February 28,

White Bark Pine: Pinus albicaulis, *by Dora Erikson, 1937. Watercolor, 22 × 15⅛ inches. USFS.177.*

1938, receipt acknowledged one *Mt. Hood Lily* by Erikson. A different composition was attributed to Feurer and Elizabeth Hoffman Wood. [USFS.39]

Red Monkey Flower: Mimulus lewisi. 1936–1937. Watercolor. 14¼ × 11 inches. Reverse: October 5–6. Dora Erikson. Flower sometimes a deeper red." WPA label: "Erickson." "Erikson" and "Feurer" are on WPA negative #303 jacket. (WPA negative #300 and #303 are similar compositions but the frame of #300 covers more stem.) Composition is at MCL, OSL and JHS. [USFS.42, same composition as USFS.157 (Erikson or Feurer)]

Swamp Laurel: Kalmia polifolia microphylla. 1936–1937. Watercolor. 11 × 13⅝ inches. Reverse: "October 28. Dora Erikson." WPA label: "Feurer (Carl)." "Erikson" and "Feurer" are on jackets to WPA negative #220a, #220b, and #220c. [USFS.192]

Tiger Lily, Honeysuckle, Oregon Sunshine, Mimiulus. 1937. Watercolor. 14½ × 11½ inches. Reverse: "November 18–25. Dora Erikson copy." WPA label: "Jeffrey (copy Carl Feurer). November 1, 1937." Composition is at MCL, OSL, and JHS (identified as negative #279-14). WPA negative #353 is the same composition with no attribution. [USFS.160, identical to USFS.8 (Feurer) and USFS.184 (Jeffery)]

Western Anemone: Anemone occidentalis. 1936–1937. Watercolor. 11⅜ × 14½ inches. Reverse: "Dora Erikson. Sept. 30. More creamy, lemon yellow, leaves deeper green." "Erikson" is on WPA negative #202 jacket. Composition is at OSL, MCL (with additional flower, more foreground and unattributed), and JHS (attributed to Erikson and marked #202-19). [USFS.141, identical to USFS.123 (Jeffery) and USFS.188 (Erikson)]

Western Anemone: Anemone occidentalis. 1936–1938. Watercolor. 11½ × 14½ inches. Reverse: "Dora Erikson. Anemone occidentalis. Stamens too orange. Leaves deeper—not so gray. Vancouver. Mrs. Wood." WPA label: "Erickson. Copy by Jeffrey." "Erikson" is on WPA negative #202 jacket. Composition is at OSL and MCL (without attribution, and including an additional flower and more foreground), and JHS (lithograph, attributed to Erikson and marked #202-19). [USFS.188, identical to USFS.123 (Jeffery) and USFS.141 (Erikson)]

White Bark Pine: Pinus albicaulis. 1936–1937. Watercolor. 22 × 15⅛ inches. Reverse: "September 25–29. Dora Erikson. Very good—best of firs." [USFS.177, identical to USFS.120 (Erikson, Feurer, or Jeffery)]

Willows. 1936–1937. Watercolor. 15½ × 17¼ inches. Reverse: "October 25–28. Dora Erikson." Erikson's name is also on WPA negative #347 jacket. [USFS.148, identical to USFS.35 (Jeffery) and USFS.152 (Feurer)]

ERIKSON, DORA, OR KARL FEURER

The two botanicals listed here are hand-colored lithographs that were not attributed to any artist on the artwork. These compositions are attributed to Erikson and Feurer because these artists are identified on WPA negative jackets for identical compositions and because botanical names on loan receipts were identified as Erikson or Feurer's. Biographical information is under other listings.

Blue Gentian: Gentiana calycosa. 1936–1938. Hand-colored lithograph. Estimated 11 × 15 inches. Reverse: "Blue Gentian." No attribution on reverse or label, but composition is identical to those depicted in WPA negatives #233, #235a, and #235b. WPA negative #233 is attributed to Erikson on negative sleeve and #235 to Feurer. Another example is almost identical, but contains an additional stem. Composition is at MCL, OSL, and JHS. [USFS.3]

Red Monkey Flower: Mimulus lewisi. 1936–1937. Hand-colored lithograph. 15½ × 10 inches. No attribution on reverse or label, but "Erikson" and "Feurer" are on WPA negative #303 jacket (WPA negative #300 and #303 are similar compositions but the frame of #300 covers more of the stem.) February 28, 1938, WPA loan receipt acknowledged three *Monkey Flower* watercolors by Erikson. Composition is also at MCL, OSL, and JHS. [USFS.157, identical to USFS.42 (Erikson)]

ERIKSON, DORA, KARL FEURER, OR GEORGE JEFFERY

The following twelve botanicals have no identification on the artwork. Erikson, Feurer, and Jeffery were identified on WPA negative jackets, loan receipts, and other copies of these compositions. Biographical information is under individual listings.

Astor flonders. 1936–1937. Hand-colored lithograph. 15½ × 10 inches. No attribution on reverse or label. Earlier mat label identified flower as *Erigeron salsuginosus.* The aster composition is attributed to Erikson, Feurer, and Jeffery because it forms the left half of a composition of asters and daisies by Feurer (USFS.46) and Jeffery (USFS.140). In addition, a similar composition by Erikson is at JHS. [USFS.13, identical to USFS.22 and USFS.56 (Erikson, Feurer, or Jeffery).]

Astor flonderis. 1936–1938. Hand-colored lithograph. 19½ × 16 inches. No attribution on reverse label. The aster composition is attributed to Erikson, Feurer, and Jeffery because it forms the left half of a composition of asters and daisies by Feurer (USFS.46) and Jeffery (USFS.140). In addition, a similar composition by Erikson is at JHS. [USFS.22, identical to USFS.13 and USFS.56 (Erikson, Feurer, or Jeffery).]

Blue Lupin: Lupinus subalpinus. 1936–1938. Hand-colored lithograph. 15⅜ × 11¼ inches. No attribution on reverse or label, but WPA loan receipt of February 23, 1938, identified one "double" lupine by Dora Erikson. This composition of a double-stalk lupine is also at MCL (attributed to Feurer) and JHS. Other similar compositions were attributed to Jeffery. [USFS.61]

Columbine: Aquilegia formosa. 1937. Hand-colored lithograph. 15⅞ × 11⅝ inches. Reverse: "Oct. 37." No attribution on reverse or label, but "Erikson" and "Feurer" are on WPA negative #218 jacket, and a WPA receipt of February 28, 1938, includes two *Columbine* watercolors by Erikson. Composition is at MCL (identified as *Wild Honeysuckle* by Feurer), OSL, and JHS. [USFS.28, identical to USFS.14 (Feurer), USFS.145 (Erikson, Feurer, or Jeffery), USFS.169 (Jeffery), and USFS.176 (Erikson)]

Columbine: Aquilejia formosa. 1936–1938. Hand-colored lithograph. 19 × 16 inches. No attribution on reverse or label, but "Erikson" and "Feurer" are on WPA negative #218 jacket. WPA receipt dated February 28, 1938, included two *Columbine* watercolors by Erikson. Composition is at MCL (identified as *Wild Honeysuckle* by Feurer), OSL, and JHS. [USFS.145, similar to USFS.14 (Feurer), USFS.28 (Erikson, Feurer, or Jeffery), USFS.169 (Jeffery), and USFS.176 (Erikson)]

Dark Pine. 1936–1938. Hand-colored lithograph. 15⅝ × 9⅝ inches. Reverse: "White Bark Pine, Pinus albicaulus." No attribution, but WPA negative #312 jacket identified composition as Dora Erikson's and WPA receipt dated February 23, 1938, includes a small *White Bark Pine* watercolor by Erikson. [USFS.12, identical to USFS.29 (Feurer) and USFS.43 (Erikson, Feurer, or Jeffery)]

Lupin: Lupinus subalpinus. 1936–1938. Hand-colored lithograph. 14¼ × 11¼ inches. No attribution on reverse or label. Certain wildflower watercolors were reproduced in different combinations. This composition has three stalks. It is otherwise identical to a "double-stalk" composition. Five lupine compositions at the lodge have one stalk, three are identical to the left stalk in this composition. The two WPA loan receipts dated February 23, 1938, collectively identified three lupine compositions, one "double" by Erikson. Double-stalk lupine composition is at MCL (attributed to Feurer) and JHS. Other similar compositions were attributed to Jeffery. [USFS.23]

Lupine [no mat label]. 1936–1938. Watercolor. 24¾ × 18⅞ inches. Composition identical to WPA negative #285 identified as Feurer's. WPA loan receipt of February 23, 1938, included one large lupine watercolor by Erikson; another form dated February 28, 1938, acknowledged loan of a large lupine watercolor by Feurer. [USFS.66, similar to USFS.31 (Feurer) and USFS.34 (Jeffery)]

Mountain Daisy: Erigeron salsuginosus. 1936–1938. Hand-colored lithograph. 15⅜ × 10 inches. No attribution. The aster composition is attributed to Erikson, Feurer, and Jeffery because it forms the left half of a composition of asters and daisies by Feurer (USFS.46) and Jeffery (USFS.140). In addition, a similar composition by Erikson is at JHS. [USFS.56, identical to USFS.13 and USFS.22 (Erikson, Feurer, or Jeffery)]

Mountain Daisy: Erigeron salsuginosus. 1936–1938. Hand-colored lithograph. 11⅜ × 15 inches. No attribution on reverse or label, but "Erikson" and "Feurer" are on jackets to WPA negatives #220a, #220b, and #220c, and WPA loan receipt of February 28, 1938, included three *Erigeron* watercolors by Erikson. Composition is at MCL (identified as *Aster* by Feurer), OSL, and JHS (copy is signed "Penlock"). [USFS.165, identical to USFS.138 (Jeffery), USFS.172 (Jeffery), and USFS.189 (Erikson)]

White Bark Pine: Pinus albicaulis. 1936–1938. Watercolor. 22 × 14⅜ inches. No attribution on reverse or label, but one WPA loan receipt, February 23, 1938, acknowledged loan of a small *White Bark Pine* by Erikson, and another receipt of the same date also included a *White Bark Pine* watercolor by Feurer and three *White Bark Pine* watercolors by Jeffery. [USFS.120, identical to USFS.177 (Erikson)]

White Bark Pine: Pinus albicaulis. 1936–1938. Hand-colored lithograph. 15½ × 9⅞ inches. No attribution. Reverse: "*Dark pine,*" but WPA loan receipt of February 23, 1938, acknowledged loan of a small *White Bark Pine* by Erikson. Another receipt of the same date included a *White Bark Pine* watercolor by Feurer and three *White Bark Pine* watercolors by Jeffery. [USFS.43]

ERIKSON, DORA, OR GEORGE JEFFERY

Biographical information is under individual listings. Two botanicals are attributed to Erikson or Jeffery on the basis of identification on negative jackets and similar attributed compositions:

Amabolis Fir: Abies amabolis. 1936–1938. Watercolor with graphite. 14 × 19⅝ inches. No signature or artist attribution. "Erikson" is on WPA negative #227 jacket. [USFS.16, identical to USFS.63 (Jeffery)]

Indian Paint Brush: Castilleja augustifolia. 1936–1938. Watercolor. 14½ × 11½ inches. No attribution on reverse or label, but "Erikson" is on WPA negative #257 jacket showing identical composition. Composition is at MCL, OSL, and JHS. [USFS.107, identical to USFS.65 (Jeffery) and USFS.700 (Jeffery)]

FEURER, KARL

b. 18??, Portland, Oregon, Austria, or Germany?; d. 1945, Portland, Oregon

Karl Feurer studied in Germany, lived in Seattle in the early 1920s, and was back in Portland by 1927. Allen and Klevit reported that Feurer's obituary stated that he was born in Portland, but some think he was born in Austria. Margery Hoffman Smith referred to him as a German who had spent his early life in Europe copying the works of old masters in museums and selling the copies. Although Smith did not refer to him by name, she probably meant Feurer, when she described one worker who was living in a piano box eating beans soaked in cold water when he came on the Oregon Art Project, in an interview for Oregon Public Broadcasting *Doorways to the Past*.

Media: Oil, watercolor, lithography.

Education: Dresden Academy, Germany.

Work at Timberline: Of the sixty-seven botanical works attributed to Feurer, fifty are signed on the artwork, and several are identical to WPA negatives attributed to Feurer or were inferred from loan receipts.

Anemone occidentalis (in seed). 1936–1937. Watercolor. 14½ × 11½ inches. Reverse: "Karl Feurer. 4–6 Sept. Very good." Identical to WPA negative #207 attributed to Feurer. [USFS.55]

Anemone occidentalis and Seed Pods. 1936–1937. Watercolor. 11⅜ × 14½ inches. Reverse: "Feurer. Sept. 27." Identical to WPA negative #208, attributed to Feurer on the negative jacket. WPA loan receipt of February 28, 1938, included *Anemone* and *Seed Pod* by Feurer. [USFS.150]

Beard Tongue: Native Penstamen. 1936. Watercolor. 11½ × 14½ inches. Reverse: "Carl Feurer. July 1936. Refer to Gilbert for identification." Composition is identical to WPA negative #212, identified on the negative jacket as by Karl Feurer. WPA loan receipt of February 28, 1938, included a *Beard Tongue* watercolor by Feurer. [USFS.58, identical to USFS.171 (Feurer)]

Beard Tongue: Native Penstamen. 1936–1938. Watercolor. 11¼ × 14½ inches. Reverse: "Feurer." Composition varies from WPA negative #212. WPA loan receipt dated February 28, 1938, included a *Beard Tongue* watercolor by Feurer. [USFS.171, identical to USFS.58 (Feurer)]

Blue Gentian: Gentiana calycosa. 1938. Watercolor. 11⅜ × 15½ inches. Reverse: "Feurer. February 1938. *Gentiana macaunii*." [USFS.10]

Columbine: Aquilejia formosa. 1937. Hand-colored lithograph. 15⅞ × 11½ inches. Reverse: "Feurer. Oct. 37."

The composition is identical to WPA negative #218 identified as by Erikson and Feurer. A WPA receipt dated February 28, 1938, acknowledged loan of two *Columbine* watercolors by Erikson. Composition is at MCL (identified as *Wild Honeysuckle* by Feurer), OSL, and JHS. [USFS.14, identical to USFS.28 (Erikson, Feurer, or Jeffery), USFS.145 (Erikson, Feurer or Jeffery), USFS.169 (Jeffery), and USFS.176 (Erikson)]

Erigeron, Daisy, and other Field Flowers [no mat label]. 1937. Watercolor? 11½ × 14½ inches. Reverse: "Carl Feurer. August 1, 1937. Erigeron and daisy and other field flowers. Do not label." (The writer probably meant to not make a mat label because the flowers depicted were not botanically identified.) [USFS.46]

Fairy Slipper: Calypso borealis. 1936–1938. Hand-colored lithograph. 14¾ × 10 inches. No attribution on artwork, but composition is identical to WPA negative #265 identified on the negative jacket as Feurer's. WPA loan receipt of February 28, 1938, included three *Lady Slipper* watercolors by Feurer. Copy at MCL is identified as #265-6 by Feurer. Copy at JHS is identified as #265-11 by Feurer and dated May 1939. Composition is at OSL. [USFS.125, identical to USFS.48, USFS.68, and USFS.106 (all attributed to Feurer)]

Fern Leaved Lovage: Ligusticum apiifolium. 1936–1938. Hand-colored lithograph. 15⅝ × 11¼ inches. Reverse: *Wild Parsley: Ligusticum apiifolium*. No attribution, but composition is identical to WPA negative #307 by Feurer. WPA loan receipt of February 23, 1938, acknowledged loan of a *Fern Leaved Lovage* by Feurer and another form of February 28, 1938, included three *Wild Parsley* watercolors by Feurer. Composition is at MCL (attributed to Feurer and numbered #307-23) and OSL. [USFS.147, identical to USFS.181 (Feurer) and USFS.186 (Feurer)]

Fern Leaved Lovage: Ligusticum appifolium. 1936–1938. Watercolor. 14½ × 11½ inches. Reverse: "Karl Feurer." Composition is identical to WPA negative #307 by Feurer. WPA loan receipt dated February 23, 1938, acknowledged loan of a *Fern Leaved Lovage* by Feurer and another form dated February 28, 1938, acknowledged loan to U.S. Forest Service of three *Wild Parsley* watercolors by Feurer. Composition is at MCL (attributed to Feurer and numbered 307-23) and OSL. [USFS.186, identical to USFS.147 (Feurer) and USFS.181 (Feurer)]

(Flox) Diffusa. 1936–1937. Watercolor. 11½ × 14½ inches. Reverse: "Feurer. 28 Oct." WPA label: "Carl Feurer." Composition identical to WPA negative #308 identified as by Karl Feurer and almost identical to WPA negative #309. Also at MCL (identified as Feurer's and marked #308-10), OSL, and JHS (identified as #308-2). [USFS.187, similar to USFS.19, USFS.37, and USFS.49 (all by Feurer)]

Honeysuckle, Tiger Lily, Mimulus, Oregon Sunshine. 1937. Watercolor. 14½ × 11½ inches. Reverse: "Feurer. August 18, 1937." WPA loan receipt dated February 23, 1938, acknowledged receipt of a "combination" watercolor of *Honeysuckle, Tiger Lily, Mimulus, and Oregon Sunshine* by Jeffery. Composition is at OSL, MCL, and JHS (as negative #279-14). WPA negative #353 in Friends of Timberline Archive is same composition. [USFS.8, identical to USFS.160 (Erikson) and USFS.184 (Jeffery)]

Indian Hellebore: Veratrum viride. 1937. Watercolor. 14½ × 11½ inches. Reverse: "Feurer. March 19, 1937." Four watercolors are identical compositions to WPA negative 243, identified as Karl Feurer's on the negative jacket. Composition is at MCL (attributed to Benedict and numbered #243-19), OSL, and JHS (attributed to Berndorf and numbered #243-17). [USFS.44, identical to USFS.17 (Feurer or Benedict), USFS.146 (Feurer), and USFS.166 (Feurer)]

Indian Hellebore: Veratrum viride. 1936–1937. Watercolor. 14½ × 11½ inches. Reverse: "Feurer." Four watercolors are identical compositions to WPA negative #243, identified as Feurer's on the negative jacket. Composition is at MCL (attributed to Benedict and numbered #243-19), OSL, and JHS (attributed to Berndorf, perhaps Benedict, and numbered #243-17). [USFS.146, identical to USFS.17 (Feurer or Benedict), USFS.44 (Feurer), and USFS.166 (Feurer)]

Indian Hellebore: Veratrum viridi. 1937–1938. Watercolor. 14¼ × 11⅜ inches. Reverse: "Karl Feurer. March 7th? Very good." WPA label: "Carl Feurer." Four watercolors are identical compositions to WPA negative #243, identified as Karl Feurer's on the negative jacket. Composition is at MCL (attributed to Benedict and numbered #243-19), OSL, and JHS (attributed to Berndorf and numbered #243-17). [USFS.166, identical to USFS.17 (Feurer or Benedict), USFS.44 (Feurer), and USFS.146 (Feurer)]

Lady Slipper: Calypso borealis. 1936–1938. Hand-colored lithograph? 14½ × 11¼ inches. Reverse: "Feurer." Composition identical to WPA negative #265 identified on the negative jacket as Feurer's. WPA loan receipt of February 28, 1938, included three *Lady Slipper* watercolors by Feurer. Copy at MCL is identified as #265-6 by Feurer. Copy at JHS is identified as #265-11 by Feurer and dated May 1939. Composition is at OSL. [USFS.48, identical to USFS.68, USFS.106, and USFS.125 (all attributed to Feurer)]

Lady Slipper: Calypso borealis. 1936–1937. Watercolor. 14⅜ × 11⅝ inches. Reverse: "Feurer." Composition identical to WPA negative #265 identified as Feurer's. WPA loan receipt of February 28, 1938, included three *Lady Slipper* watercolors by Feurer. Copy at MCL is identified as #265-6 by Feurer. Copy at JHS is identified as #265-11 by Feurer and dated May 1939. Composition is at OSL. [USFS.68, identical to USFS.48, USFS.106, and USFS.125 (all attributed to Feurer)]

Lady Slipper: Calypso borealis. 1937. Hand-colored lithograph? 14⅜ × 11⅜ inches. Reverse: "Carl Feurer. Sept. 1937." Composition identical to WPA negative #265 identified on the negative jacket as Feurer's. WPA loan receipt of February 28, 1938, included three *Lady Slipper* watercolors by Feurer. Copy at MCL is identified as #265-6 by Feurer. Copy at JHS is identified as #265-11 by Feurer and dated May 1939. Composition is at OSL. [USFS.106. identical to USFS.48, USFS.68, and USFS.125 (all attributed to Feurer)]

Lady Slipper: Calypso borealis. 1936–1938. Watercolor. 14⅜ × 11¼ inches. Reverse: "Carl Feurer." Composition is identical to WPA negative #264a identified as Feurer's. WPA loan receipt of February 28, 1938, included three *Lady Slipper* watercolors by Feurer. [USFS.143]

Lupine [no mat label]. 1937–1938. Watercolor. 24⅞ × 18⅝ inches. Reverse: "Feurer, 8–12 March." Composition identical to WPA negative #285 identified as Feurer's. WPA loan receipt of February 23, 1938, included one large lupine watercolor by Erikson; another form dated February 28, 1938, included a large lupine watercolor by Feurer. [USFS.31, similar to USFS.34 (Jeffery) and USFS.66 (Erikson, Feurer, or Jeffery)]

Maple Leaves [no mat label]. 1936–1938. Watercolor. 29 × 22½ inches. No attribution on reverse or label, but WPA loan receipt of February 23, 1938, included *Maple Leaves* watercolor by Feurer. *Maple Leaves* is written on dust cover on reverse. Composition is different from WPA negative #407 illustrating maple leaves that is also attributed to Feurer. [USFS.144]

Mountain Ash: Pyrus sitchensis. 1936–1938. Watercolor. 14½ × 11½ inches. Reverse: "Feurer." WPA label: "Jeffrey. Copy by Feurer." WPA negative #209 attributed *Mountain Ash* watercolor to Jeffery. WPA loan receipt dated February 23, 1938, acknowledged receipt of three *Mountain Ash* watercolors by Jeffery. [USFS.6, identical to USFS.21 (Benedict)]

Mountain Hemlock: Tsuga mertensiana. 1938. Hand-colored lithograph. 11 × 15⅞ inches. Reverse: "Feurer. Feb. 1–15 '38." The composition is identical to WPA negative #247 identified as by Erikson and Feurer. The WPA loan receipt of February 28, 1938, acknowledged loan of a *Mountain Hemlock* watercolor by Erikson. The same composition is at the OSL. [USFS.9, identical to USFS.20 (Feurer)]

Mountain Hemlock: Tsuga mertensiana. 1937. Watercolor. 11½ × 15⅝ inches. Reverse: "Carl Feurer. Aug. 1937." The composition is identical to WPA negative #247 identified as by Erikson and Feurer. The WPA loan re-

ceipt of February 28, 1938, included a *Mountain Hemlock* watercolor by Erikson. Also at OSL. [USFS.20, identical to USFS.9 (Feurer)]

Mountain Huckelberry: Vaccinium macrophyllum. 1936–1937. Watercolor. 14½ × 11½ inches. Reverse: "Karl Feurer. Nov 11." WPA label: "Martina Gangle." Composition is identical to WPA negatives #251 and #252 identified as by Martina Gangle. WPA loan receipt of February 23, 1938, included three *Mountain Huckleberry* watercolors by Gangle. Also at JHS in uncolored version identified as #257-11. [USFS.114, identical to USFS.108, USFS.163, and USFS.175 (all attributed to Gangle)]

Mountain Phlox: Phlox diffusa. 1938. Hand-colored lithograph. 11½ × 18⅞ inches. Reverse: "Karl Feurer. Jan. '38." Composition identical to WPA negative #308 identified as by Karl Feurer and almost identical to WPA negative #309. Composition is at MCL (identified as Feurer's and marked 308-10), OSL, and JHS (identified as #308-2). [USFS.19, similar to USFS.37, USFS.49, and USFS.187 (all by Feurer)]

Mountain Rhododendron: Rhododendron albiflorum. 1937. Watercolor. 14¾ × 11½ inches. Reverse: "Feurer. Oct. 1937." Composition may be same as WPA negative 324, identified as Jeffery's. WPA loan receipts in February 1938, acknowledged *Mountain Rhododendron* compositions by Feurer and Jeffery. One *Rhododendron albiflorum* at lodge is identified as by Feurer, 1937. [USFS.18, same as USFS.109 (Jeffery) and USFS.185 (Feurer)]

Mountain Rhododendron: Rhododendron albiflorum. 1936–1938. Watercolor. 14¼ × 11¼ inches. Mat includes common name "Mountain Rhododendron." Reverse: "Original Karl Feurer. Very good." WPA label: "Jeffrey." Composition may be same as WPA negative #324, identified as Jeffery's. WPA loan receipts in February 1938 acknowledged receipt at Timberline of *Mountain Rhododendron* compositions by Feurer and Jeffery. One *Rhododendron albiflorum* at lodge is identified as by Feurer, 1937. [USFS.185, identical to USFS.18 (Feurer) and USFS.109 (Jeffery)]

Mountain Rhododendron: Rhododendron albiflorium, *by Karl Feurer, 1937. Watercolor, 14¾ × 11½ inches. USFS.18.*

Mountain Rhododendron: Rhododendron californicum. 1936–1938. Watercolor. Estimated 13¹¹⁄₁₆ × 11 inches. Reverse: "Feurer." WPA label: "Feurer." Uncolored version, unattributed, at JHS (#323-18). Similar composition at MCL is identified as Benedict's (#323-1). [USFS.116, identical to USFS.25 (Feurer and Benedict)]

Mount Hood Lily: Lilium washingtonianum. 1937. Hand-colored lithograph. 17½ × 14 inches. Reverse: "Feurer. Oct. '37." The composition in these two examples includes two stalks of lilies. A WPA loan receipt of February 23, 1938, included a *Mount Hood Lily* by Feurer. A WPA loan receipt dated February 28, 1938, acknowledged receipt of one *Mount Hood Lily* by Erikson and one by Feurer. [USFS.27, identical to USFS.162 (Jeffery)]

Mount Hood Lily: Lilium washingtonianum. 1937–1938. Watercolor. 14½ × 11⅜ inches. Reverse: "Karl Feurer. Date 15 of March." The same composition is identified as by [Elizabeth Hoffman] Wood and Karl Feurer on WPA negative jacket #273. This composition is found at MCL (identified only as negative 273-1) and JHS. [USFS.180, identical to USFS.54 (Feurer and Wood), USFS.104 (Feurer), and USFS.111 (Feurer)]

Mt. Hood Lily: Lilium washingtonianum. 1936. Watercolor. 16½ × 11⅜ inches. Reverse: "Karl Feurer. Oct. 36. This lily is too large. See Armstrong 3–4 [inches in height]. Color good—more crimson." [USFS.701]

Mt. Hood Lily: Lilium washingtonianum. 1936–1937. Watercolor. 14½ × 11⅜ inches. WPA label: "Elizabeth Hoffman Wood, copy by Feurer." Reverse: "Sept. 16–23." The same composition is identified as by [Elizabeth Hoffman] Wood and Karl Feurer on WPA negative jacket #273. Composition is at MCL (identified only as negative #273-1) and JHS. [USFS.104, identical to USFS.54 (Feurer and Wood), USFS.111 (Feurer), and USFS.180 (Feurer)]

Mt. Hood Lily: Lilium washingtonianum. 1937–1938. Watercolor. 14⅜ × 11⅜ inches. Reverse: "Karl Feurer. Date—16 of March." WPA label: "Elizabeth Hoffman Wood. Copy by Carl Feurer." The same composition is identified as by [Elizabeth Hoffman] Wood and Karl Feurer on WPA negative jacket #273. This composition is found at MCL (identified only as negative #273-1) and JHS. [USFS.111, identical to USFS.54 (Feurer and Wood), USFS.104 (Feurer), and USFS.180 (Feurer)]

Noble Fir: Abies nobilis. 1936–1937. Watercolor. 12¼ × 14⅝ inches. Reverse: "Karl Feurer, week 23–29 Sept. Good—cones not as good." This is the same composition that is in WPA negative #229, but different from another WPA negative also numbered #229 that is identified as Feurer's on the jacket. A WPA loan receipt of February 23, 1938, lists a "large" *Noble Fir* watercolor by Feurer. [USFS.128]

Noble Fir: Abies nobilis. 1937. Watercolor. 11¼ × 15⅜ inches. Reverse: "Carl Feurer. August 27, 1937." Feurer is on WPA negative #229 jacket and image is identical. Composition is at MCL (identified as by Feurer, negative #504), OSL, and JHS. [USFS.4, identical to USFS.11 (Feurer) and USFS.178 (Feurer)]

Noble Fir: Abies nobilis. 1936–1938. Hand-colored lithograph. Estimated 10½ × 14¼ inches. No attribution on work, but WPA negative #229 is identical and jacket attributes it to Feurer. Composition is at MCL (identified as by Feurer, negative #504), OSL, and JHS. [USFS.11, identical to USFS.4 (Feurer) and USFS.178 (Feurer)]

Noble Fir: Abies nobilis. 1936–1937. Watercolor. 15 × 11⅝ inches. Reverse: "Karl Feurer. Week 23–29 September. Very good—the best sample of the nobil fir." WPA negative #229 is identical and also attributed to Feurer. Composition is at MCL (identified as by Feurer, negative #504), OSL, and JHS. [USFS.178, identical to USFS.4 (Feurer) and USFS.11 (Feurer)]

Nodding Bluebells: Mertensia laevigata. 1936–1938. Hand-colored lithograph. 15¾ × 11½ inches. Unattributed, but composition identical to WPA negative #298a identified as Feurer's. Slightly different are negatives #385 and #298b, both identical to each other and attributed to Feurer. Copies of this second composition are at MCL and OSL. [USFS.53]

Phlox diffusa. 1937. Watercolor. 11 × 14 inches. Reverse: "Carl Feurer. August 24, 1937." Composition identical to WPA negative #308 identified as by Karl Feurer and almost identical to WPA negative #309. Composition is at MCL (identified as Feurer's and marked #308-10), OSL, and JHS (identified as #308-2). [USFS.37, similar to USFS.19, USFS.49, and USFS.187 (all by Feurer)]

Phlox diffusa. 1936–1937. Watercolor. 11½ × 14½ inches. Reverse: "*Phlox diffusa.* Karl Feurer. 28 Oct." Composition identical to WPA negative #308 identified as by Karl Feurer and almost identical to WPA negative #309. Composition is at MCL (identified as Feurer's and marked #308-10), OSL, and JHS (identified as #308-2). [USFS.49, similar to USFS.19, USFS.37, and USFS.187 (all by Feurer)]

Red Heather: Phyllodoce empetriformis. 1937. Watercolor? 11⅝ × 14⅝ inches. Reverse: "Carl Feurer. November 1937. Orig. Gangle." WPA Negative #238 attributes the composition to Gangle. WPA receipt from February 23, 1938, confirms loan of Gangle's *Red Heather.* [USFS.1, identical to USFS.70 (Gangle)]

Rhododendron californicum. 1936–1938. Hand-colored lithograph. 15¾ × 11⅜ inches. No attribution, but the composition is identified as by Feurer on WPA negative #317 jacket. One WPA loan receipt dated February 23, 1938, acknowledged loan of two *Rhododendron californicum* watercolors by Feurer and another receipt of the same day referred to two similar watercolors by Jeffery. [USFS.47]

Rhododendron californicum. 1936–1938. Watercolor. 14½ × 11½ inches. Reverse: "Mountain Rhododendron, Rhododendron californicum." No attribution. WPA label: "Feurer. Oregon Water Color. *Rhododendron californicum.*" This composition resembles WPA negative #321. A WPA loan receipt of February 23, 1938, included two *Rhododendron californicum* watercolors by Feurer and another receipt of the same day referred to two rhododendron watercolors by Jeffery. [USFS.112]

Shooting Star. 1936–1938. Hand-colored lithograph. 15⅝ × 10⅜ inches. No attribution on artwork, but composition is identical to WPA negative #329a by Feurer. WPA loan receipt of February 23, 1938, included two *Shooting Star* watercolors by Feurer. Composition is at MCL, OSL, and JHS, in an uncolored version. [USFS.119, identical to USFS.130 (Feurer)]

Shooting Star: Dodecatheon jeffrey. 1936–1937. Hand-colored lithograph. 14½ × 11½ inches. Reverse: "Karl Feurer. Nov. 18." WPA label: "Carl Feurer." The composition is identical to WPA negative #329a by Karl Feurer. WPA loan receipt of February 23, 1938, included two *Shooting Star* watercolors by Feurer. Composition is at MCL, OSL, and JHS in an uncolored version. [USFS.130, identical to USFS.119 (Feurer)]

Shooting Star: Dodecatheon jeffreyi. 1936–1937. Hand-colored lithograph. 14⅜ × 11¼ inches. Reverse: "Feurer. Nov. 4. Try doing leaves with a broader wash to give

Skunk Cabbage: Lysichiton kamtschatcense, *no attribution but probably by Karl Feurer, 1936–1938. Hand-colored lithograph, 15½ × 10½ inches. USFS.64.*

the idea that they are glossy and moist looking." Composition identical to WPA negative #329b identified on negative jacket as by Feurer. WPA loan receipt of February 23, 1938, included two *Shooting Star* watercolors by Feurer. [USFS.142]

Skunk Cabbage: Lysichiton kamtschatcense. 1936–1938. Hand-colored lithograph. 15½ × 10½ inches. No attribution. Composition is identical to WPA negative #332 identified as Feurer's. WPA loan receipt of February 23, 1938, included two *Skunk Cabbage* watercolors by Feurer. Composition is at MCL (not attributed, but numbered #332-3). See the two examples of *Skunk Cabbage: Spathyema foetida.* [USFS.64]

Skunk Cabbage: Lysichiton kamtschatcense. 1938. Watercolor. 14¼ × 11½ inches. Reverse: "Carl Feurer. 1938." Composition is similar in style, but includes more flowers than WPA negative #332. WPA loan receipt dated February 23, 1938, acknowledged loan to U.S. Forest Service of two *Skunk Cabbage* watercolors by Feurer. See the two examples of *Skunk Cabbage: Spathyema foetida.* [USFS.62]

Skunk Cabbage: Spathyema foetida. 1937–1938. Watercolor. 14½ × 10⅝ inches. No attribution, but WPA loan receipt of February 23, 1938, included two *Skunk Cabbage* watercolors by Feurer. See also *Skunk Cabbage: Lysichiton kamtschatcense.* [USFS.149]

Spathyema foetida. 1936–1938. Watercolor. 14⅜ × 11¼ inches. Reverse: "Karl Feurer." WPA loan receipt dated February 23, 1938, acknowledged loan of two *Skunk Cabbage* watercolors by Feurer. See also *Skunk Cabbage: Lysichiton kamtschatcense.* [USFS.115]

Squaw Grass: Xerophyllum tenex. 1937. Watercolor. 14⅜ × 11½ inches. Reverse: "Carl Feurer. 1937." WPA label: "Carl Feurer." Composition is at MCL (unattributed, but numbered #336-7), OSL, and JHS (numbered #336-25). WPA loan receipt of February 23, 1938, included two *Squaw Grass* watercolors by Feurer. [USFS.24, identical to USFS.67, USFS.183, and USFS.196 (all by Feurer)]

Squaw Grass: Xerophyllum tenex. 1936–1938. Hand-colored lithograph. 15½ × 11½ inches. Reverse: "Feurer." Composition is also at MCL (unattributed, but numbered #336-7), OSL, and JHS (numbered #336-25). WPA loan receipt of February 23, 1938, included two *Squaw Grass* watercolors by Feurer. [USFS.67, identical to USFS.24, USFS.183, and USFS.196 (all by Feurer)]

Squaw Grass: Xerophyllum tenex. 1937. Watercolor. 14⅝ × 11¼ inches. Reverse: "Carl Feurer. Sept. 1937." The same composition is at the MCL (unattributed, but numbered #336-7), OSL, and JHS (numbered #336-25). WPA loan receipt of February 23, 1938, included two *Squaw Grass* watercolors by Feurer. [USFS.183, identical to USFS.24, USFS.67, and USFS.196 (all by Feurer)]

Squaw Grass [no mat label]. 1936–1938. Hand-colored lithograph. 15½ × 11 inches. Signed bottom right "Karl Feurer, Timberline Lodge." The same composition is at MCL (unattributed, but numbered #336-7), OSL, and JHS (numbered #336-25). WPA loan receipt dated February 23, 1938, acknowledged loan of two *Squaw Grass* watercolors by Feurer. This example was given to Friends of Timberline from Margery Hoffman Smith's estate. [USFS.196, identical to USFS.24, USFS.67, and USFS.183 (all by Feurer)]

Trillium. 1936–1938. Watercolor. 14⅜ × 22¾ inches. No signature located. The largest of three different *Trillium* compositions, this watercolor is similar but not identical to Feurer's composition of trilliums in WPA negative #388. [USFS.154]

Twin Flower: Linnaea borealis var. americana. 1937. Watercolor. 11⅜ × 14¼ inches. Reverse: "Carl Feurer Sept. 1937 (original by Jeffrey)." Completion of this copy preceded Jeffery's copy (USFS.2) by two months. [USFS.50, identical to USFS.2 (Jeffery)]

White Bark Pine: Pinus albicaulus. 1936–1938. Watercolor. 14⅜ × 11⅜ inches. Reverse: "Karl Feurer. Sept. 1–2." The composition was identified as Dora Erikson's on the WPA negative jacket, negative #312. A WPA receipt of loan of a small *White Bark Pine* watercolor by Erikson dated February 23, 1938. [USFS.29, identical to USFS.12 (Erikson, Feurer, or Jeffery) and USFS.43 (Erikson, Feurer, or Jeffery)]

Wild Heleotrope: Valeciana sitchensis. 1936–1938. Watercolor. 14½ × 11½ inches. Reverse: "Karl Feurer. A little too heavy in feeling." This composition is identical to WPA negative #240, identified as by Karl Feurer. [USFS.69, identical to USFS.122 (Feurer)]

Wild Heliotrope: Valeriana sitchensis. 1936–1938. Watercolor. 14⅜ × 11½ inches. Reverse: "Carl Feurer." This composition is identical to WPA negative #240, identified on the negative jacket as by Feurer. [USFS.122, identical to USFS.69 (Feurer)]

Wild Heliotrope: Valeriana sitchensis. 1936–1938. Hand-colored lithograph.16 × 11⅜ inches. No attribution, but composition is identical to unnumbered and unattributed negative in Friends of Timberline Archive and identical to watercolor attributed to Feurer. Composition is at MCL, OSL, and JHS. [USFS.40, identical to USFS.52 (Feurer)]

Wild Heliotrope: Valeriana sitchensis. 1937. Hand-colored lithograph.15½ × 11⅝ inches. Reverse top left: "Feurer. Oct. '37." Composition is identical to unnumbered and unattributed negative in Friends of Timberline Archive. Composition is at MCL, OSL, and JHS. [USFS.52, identical to USFS.40 (Feurer)]

Wild Parsley: Ligusticum apiifolium. 1936–1938. Watercolor. 14½ × 11½ inches. Reverse: "Karl Feurer. This is best sample. Good color." WPA label: "Carl Feurer." Composition is identical to WPA negative #307 by Feurer. WPA loan receipt dated February 23, 1938, acknowledged loan of a *Fern Leaved Lovage* by Feurer and another form dated February 28, 1938, acknowledged loan to U.S. Forest Service of three *Wild Parsley* watercolors by Feurer. Composition is at MCL (attributed to Feurer and numbered #307-23) and OSL. [USFS.181, identical to USFS.147 (Feurer) and USFS.186 (Feurer)]

Willows. 1936–1938. Watercolor. 15½ × 17¼ inches. WPA label: "Erickson—Copy by Feurer." The composition was also identified as Erikson's on the jacket of WPA negative #347. A WPA receipt dated February 28, 1938, acknowledged loan of a watercolor of *Willows* by Erikson. [USFS.152, identical to USFS.35 (Jeffery) and USFS.148 (Erikson)]

Yellow Daisy. 1936–1938. Hand-colored lithograph. 15½ × 9⅞ inches. No attribution. Composition is identical to WPA negative #214, identified on the negative jacket as *Buttercup* by Feurer. Composition is at MCL (called *Wild Radish* and not attributed) and OSL. The ajuga is combined with aster to make a composition with both wildflowers. [USFS.57]

Yellow Daisy: Arjuca. 1936–1938. Hand-colored lithograph. 15⅝ × 10¼ inches. No attribution on reverse or label. Composition is identical to WPA negative #214, identified on the negative jacket as *Buttercup* by

Feurer. Composition is at MCL (called *Wild Radish* and not attributed to any artist) and OSL. The ajuga is combined with aster to make a composition with both wildflowers. [USFS.5]

FEURER, KARL, OR EDWARD BENEDICT

The two unsigned, hand-colored lithographs that follow were attributed to Feurer or Benedict on the basis of similarity to attributed compositions at Timberline Lodge and MCL. Biographical information is under other listings.

Indian Hellebore: Veratrum viride. 1936–1938. Hand-colored lithograph. 15⅞ × 11⅜ inches. No attribution, but watercolors with identical composition to WPA negative #243 are identified as Feurer's on the negative jacket. Composition is at MCL (attributed to Benedict and numbered #243-19), OSL, and JHS (attributed to Berndorf and numbered #243-17). [USFS.17, identical to USFS.44, USFS.146, and USFS.166 (all by Feurer)]

Rhododendron californicum. 1936–1938. Hand-colored lithograph. 15½ × 10½ inches. No attribution on reverse or label, but composition may be identical to WPA negative #323. Uncolored version, unattributed, at JHS (#323-18). Similar composition at MCL is identified as Benedict's (#323-1). [USFS.25, identical to USFS.116 (Feurer)]

FEURER, KARL, OR GEORGE JEFFERY

The unsigned botanicals listed below were attributable to Feurer or Jeffery by loan receipts and WPA negative jackets. Biographical information is under individual listings.

Mountain Rhododendron: Rhododendron albiflorum. 1936–1938. Hand-colored lithograph. 17 × 13½ inches. No attribution, but WPA loan receipt dated February 23, 1938, includes a *Mountain Rhododendron* composition by Jeffery. Feurer signed several *Mountain Rhododendron* watercolors. This composition differs slightly from USFS.18, USFS.109, and USFS.185, which are in the Timberline Lodge collection. Similar composition is at JHS. [USFS.15]

Rhododendron californicum. 1936–1938. Watercolor. 14½ × 11½ inches. No attribution. This composition re-
sembles WPA negative #321. A WPA loan receipt of February 23, 1938, included two *Rhododendron californicum* watercolors by Feurer and another receipt of the same day referred to two *Rhododendron* watercolors by Jeffery. [USFS.179]

Trillium. 1936–1938. Hand-colored lithograph. 14 × 10⅝ inches. No attribution on reverse or label, but composition is identical to MCL composition identified as *Trillium sessile* by Jeffery (#340-2). WPA loan receipt of February 28, 1938, included three large *Trillium* watercolors by Feurer. [USFS.59]

GANGLE, MARTINA
(GANGL, MARTINA, OR CURL, MARTINA)
b. 1906, Woodland, Washington; d. 1994, Portland, Oregon

Martina Gangle loved nature and included native birds and plants in two tempera murals at Portland's Rose City Park elementary school. She remembered as a child going barefoot and dressing in overalls without a shirt in the spring. Biographer David Horowitz quoted Gangle as saying: "I looked for the first blooms of trilliums, Johnny jump ups, lady slippers, spring beauties and roses." She sometimes spelled her name Gangl. She was married to Hank Curl and known as Martina Curl toward the end of her life.

Media: Oil, tempera, watercolor, woodcuts, lithography.
Education: Museum Art School (now Pacific Northwest College of Art), Portland, Western Oregon State College (Monmouth).
Selected Collections: Portland Art Museum (Oregon), University of Oregon (Eugene), People's Museum (Bay City, Oregon).
Work at Timberline: Six wildflower watercolors are attributed to Gangle, including one of *Anemone*, one of *Caltha*, one of *Red Heather*, and three of *Mountain Huckleberry*. Her name appears on WPA negatives for other *Red Heather* watercolors. Feurer may have hand-colored lithograph copies of Gangle's heather composition. In addition to the wildflower watercolors, some of Gangle's woodcuts were included in a WPA publication, *The Builders of Timberline Lodge.*

Several Gangle sketches donated to Friends of Timberline do not relate to the lodge. They include two intaglio prints, one of a mother with a sick child, prob-

Red Heather: Phyllodoce empetriformis, *by Martina Gangle, 1936–1937. Watercolor, 11½ × 14½ inches. USFS.70.*

ably circa 1940, 7 × 8¾ inches; and another, *Children of the Poor*, a mother and child standing by a trash can, undated, 9¾ × 6¾ inches. A Communist Party member, Gangle often illustrated scenes of social injustice in her artwork, particularly the suffering of destitute mothers and their children. Although socially provocative themes such as labor unrest and economic injustice were common among New Deal artists, the art at Timberline Lodge does not include these subjects. The themes for the work at Timberline were assigned by the administrators as appropriate for specific spots in the lodge, such as guest rooms.

Caltha palustris—Marsh Marigold. 1936–1937. Watercolor. 14½ × 11⅝ inches. Reverse: "Martina Gangle—Marsh Marigold. Week ending Nov. 18." WPA receipt of February 28, 1938, included one *Caltha* watercolor by Erikson. [USFS.159]

Mountain Huckleberry: Vaccinium macrophyllum. 1936–1938. Watercolor. 14⅛ × 11⅜ inches. No attribution on reverse or label, but composition is identical to WPA negatives #251 and #252 identified as by Martina Gangle. WPA loan receipt dated February 23, 1938, included three *Mountain Huckleberry* watercolors by Gangle. Composition is at JHS in uncolored version identified as #257-11. [USFS.163, identical to USFS.108 (Gangle), USFS.114 (Feurer), and USFS.175 (Gangle)]

Mountain Huckleberry: Vaccinium macrophyllum. 1936–1937. Watercolor. 14⅛ × 11⅜ inches. Reverse: "Martina Gangle. October 26–27." Composition is identical to WPA negatives #251 and #252 identified as by Martina Gangle. WPA loan receipt dated February 23, 1938, acknowledged loan of three *Mountain Huckleberry* watercolors by Gangle. Same composition at JHS is an uncolored version identified as #257-11. [USFS.108, identical to USFS.114 (Feurer), USFS.163 (Gangle), and USFS.175 (Gangle)]

Mountain Huckleberry: Vaccinum macrophyllum. 1936–1937. Watercolor. 15½ × 12⅜ inches. No attribution on reverse or label, but composition is identical to WPA negatives #251 and #252 identified as by Martina Gangle. WPA loan receipt, February 23, 1938, included three *Mountain Huckleberry* watercolors by Gangle. Composition is at JHS in uncolored version identified as #257-11. [USFS.175, identical to USFS.108 (Gangle), USFS.114 (Feurer), and USFS.163 (Gangle)]

Red Heather: Phyllodoce empetriformis. 1936–1937. Watercolor. 11½ × 14½ inches. Reverse: "M. Gangle, week ending Nov. 11." WPA label: "Martina Gangle." Gangle identified as artist on WPA negative #238 which is an identical composition. WPA loan receipt, February 23, 1938, included one *Red Heather* watercolor by Gangle. [USFS.70, identical to USFS.1 (Feurer)]

Wind Flower: Anemone deltoidea. 1936–1937. Watercolor. 14½ × 11⅜ inches. Bottom right: "M.G." Reverse: "Martina Gangle. Oct. 28—week ending Nov. 11. Stems should be green & not so thick. Stamens should be a clearer yellow. Centers should be a clearer pale green." WPA loan receipt dated February 23, 1938, acknowledged loan of one *Wind Flower* watercolor by Gangle. [USFS.7]

JEFFERY, GEORGE
b. 1864, Derbyshire, England; d. 1940, Portland, Oregon
Jeffery was trained in china painting at Crown Derby China Works, England. He painted a dinnerware set that was presented to England's Prime Minister William Gladstone. He taught art in Chesterfield (England) and New York, before moving to Portland where he lived after 1890.

Media: Oil, watercolor.
Education: George Stephenson Memorial Hall, Chesterfield, England.
Selected Collections: Nottingham Castle (England), Oregon Historical Society (Portland).
Work at Timberline: Thirty-three botanical watercolors are attributed to Jeffery. Thirty-one of these are signed by the artist.

Alpine Fir: Abies lasciocapa. 1936–1937. Watercolor. 22¾ × 14½ inches. Bottom right: "Jeffery." Reverse: "George Jeffery. Oct. 7. A little fuzzy." A WPA loan receipt of February 23, 1938, included two *Alpine Fir* watercolors by Jeffery. [USFS.117, identical to USFS.151 (Erikson)]

Amabolis Fir: Abies amabolis. 1937. Watercolor. 25¾ × 21 inches. Reverse: "George Jeffery. Sept. 37." [USFS.63, identical to USFS.16 (Erikson and Jeffery)]

Blue Lupine: Lupinus subalpinus. 1937? Watercolor. 14¾ × 11⅝ inches. Reverse: "Geo. Jeffery. Lupine more blue at higher altitude and smaller, more like other sample—blue with white stripes." WPA label: "Jeffrey. Timberline Lodge Nov. 1937?" Single-stalk lupine. [USFS.33, similar to USFS.45 and USFS.182 (both by Jeffery)]

Blue Lupine: Lupinus subalpinus. 1936–1938. Watercolor. Estimated 14½ × 11½ inches. Reverse: "Geo. Jeffery." WPA label: "Jeffrey." Single-stalk lupine. [USFS.703, identical to USFS.182 and USFS.702 (both Jeffery)]

Columbine: Aquilegia formosa. 1936–1937. Watercolor. 14¾ × 11⅞ inches. Reverse: "George Jeffery. Dec. 2nd. Red & yellow & green." WPA label: "Dora Erickson." Composition is at MCL (identified as *Wild Honeysuckle* by Feurer), OSL, and JHS. [USFS.169, identical to USFS.14 (Feurer), USFS.28 (Erikson, Feurer, or Jeffery), USFS.145 (Erikson, Feurer, or Jeffery), and USFS.176 (Erikson)]

Erigeron. 1936–1938. Watercolor. 11⅜ × 14⅝ inches. Reverse or WPA label: "George Jeffery." Composition identical to WPA negatives 220a, 220b, and 220c as by Dora Erikson and Karl Feurer. [USFS.138, identical to USFS.165 (Erikson, Feurer, or Jeffery), USFS.172 (Jeffery), and USFS.189 (Erikson)]

Erigeron. 1936–1938. Watercolor. 11½ × 14⅜ inches. WPA label: "Dora Erickson. Copy by Jeffrey." Composition identical to WPA negatives 220a, 220b, and 220c as by Dora Erikson and Karl Feurer. [USFS.172, identical to USFS.138 (Jeffery), USFS.165 (Erikson, Feurer and Jeffery), and USFS.189 (Erikson)]

Erigeron and Daisy. 1936–1937. Hand-colored lithograph. Estimated 11 × 14 inches. Reverse: "George Jeffery. Dec. 15." This composition combines depictions of asters and yellow daisies included in watercolors by Feurer and Jeffery. [USFS.140, identical to USFS.46 (Feurer). See also: USFS.13, USFS.22, and USFS.56 for asters and USFS.5 and USFS.57 for yellow daisy.]

Indian Paint Brush: Castilleja augustifolia. 1936–1937. Watercolor. 15½ × 11½ inches. Bottom right: "Jeff." Reverse: "Nov. 4." Composition is at MCL, OSL, and JHS. [USFS.65, identical to USFS.107 (Erikson or Jeffery) and USFS.113 (Jeffery)]

Indian Paint Brush: Castilleja augustifolia. 1936–1938. Watercolor. 14½ × 11½ inches. Bottom right: "Jeff." Reverse: "George Jeffery. Use crayon on mat, 1 red line, 1 green line." Composition is at MCL, OSL, and JHS. [USFS.113, identical to USFS.65 (Jeffery) and USFS.107 (Erikson or Jeffery)]

Lupin: Lupinus subalpinus. 1936–1937. Watercolor. 14½ × 11½ inches. Bottom left: "D. E." and bottom right: "Copy by Jeff." Reverse: "Sept. 18–23. George Jeffery." The initials "D. E." refer to Dora Erikson, who probably created the original composition. Two-stalk composition. [USFS.45, similar to USFS.33 and USFS.182 (both by Jeffery)]

Lupine [no mat label]. 1936–1937. Watercolor. 24¾ × 18⅞ inches. Reverse: "George Jeffery. Dec. 8." WPA label: "Carl Feurer." [USFS.34, similar to USFS.31 (Feurer) and USFS.66]

Lupine: Lupinus subalpinus. 1937. Watercolor. 14½ × 11⅜ inches. Reverse: "Sept. 29. Mr. Geo. Jeffery. This one is more the size of mountain lupine and color too." WPA label: "Jeffrey. Nov. 1, 1937." Single-stalk composition. [USFS.167, similar to USFS.164 (Erikson) and USFS.168 (Jeffery)]

Lupine: Lupinus subalpinus. 1936–1937. Watercolor. 14⅝ × 11½ inches. Reverse: "George Jeffery. Sept. 29." WPA label: "Carl Feurer." Single-stalk composition. [USFS.168, identical to USFS.164 (Erikson) and USFS.167 (Jeffery)]

Lupine: Lupinus subalpinus. 1936–1938. Watercolor. 14½ × 11½ inches. Reverse: "Mr. Geo. Jeffery." WPA label: "Dora Ericson." Single-stalk composition. [USFS.182, similar to USFS.33 and USFS.45 (both by Jeffery)]

Mount Hood Lily: Lilium washingtonianum. 1937–1938. Watercolor. 14¼ × 11⅛ inches. Bottom Right: "Jeff." Reverse: "Copy from Mrs. Erskine Wood's sketch. George Jeffery. Jan'y 2nd." Two compositions of *Mount Hood Lily* are attributed to Wood. [USFS.162, identical to USFS.27 (Feurer)]

Mountain Ash: Pyrus sitchensis. 1936–1937. Watercolor. Estimated 14 × 11 inches. Bottom right: "Jeff." Reverse: "Nov. 18. George Jeffery. Original. Pyrus sambucifolia? Pyrus sitchensis? Mrs. Sherrard advises using common name only as exact variety is uncertain." WPA negative #209 attributed *Mountain Ash* watercolor to Jeffery. WPA loan receipt dated February 23, 1938, included three *Mountain Ash* watercolors by Jeffery. [USFS.704]

Mountain Hemlock: Tsuga mertensiana. 1936–1938. Hand-colored lithograph. 11 × 14⅛ inches. Bottom left: "D.E." Bottom right: "Copy by Jeff." Reverse: "18–23 Geo. Jeffery." WPA label: "Dora Ericson." The original is attributed to Erikson (D. E.) and is identical to WPA negative #247 identified as by Erikson and Feurer. The WPA loan receipt dated February 28, 1938, included a *Mountain Hemlock* watercolor by Erikson. Composition is also at OSL. [USFS.129]

Mountain Hemlock: Tsuga mertensiana. 1936–1937. Watercolor. 11 × 14⅜ inches. Front: "Original by D. E. Copy by Jeff." Reverse: "George Jeffery Sept. 18–23." WPA label: "Jeffrey." The original is attributed to Erikson (D. E.) and is identical to WPA negative #247 identified as by Erikson and Feurer. The WPA loan receipt dated February 28, 1938, included a *Mountain Hemlock* watercolor by Erikson. Also at OSL. [USFS.173]

Mountain Hemlock: Tsuga mertensiana. 1936–1937. Watercolor. 11¼ × 14¼ inches. Reverse: "George Jeffery. Nov. 4." The composition is attributed to Erikson and is identical to WPA negative #247 identified as by Erikson and Feurer. The WPA loan receipt dated February 28, 1938, included a *Mountain Hemlock* watercolor by Erikson. Also at OSL. [USFS.174]

Mountain Rhododendron: Rhododendron albiflorum. 1936–1937. Watercolor. 14½ × 11⅝ inches. Reverse: "George Jeffery. Oct. 21st." WPA label: "Jeffrey." Composition may be same as WPA negative #324, identified as Jeffery's. WPA loan receipts dated February 1938 acknowledged *Mountain Rhododendron* compositions by Feurer and Jeffery. [USFS.109, identical to USFS.18 (Feurer) and USFS.185 (Feurer)]

Red Monkey Flower: Mimulus lewissie. 1936–1937. Watercolor. 14¾ × 11⅛ inches. Reverse: "October 13. George Jeffery." [USFS.105]

Red Monkey Flower: Mimulus lewissie. 1936–1937. Watercolor. 14⅜ × 11¼ inches. Reverse: "George Jeffery. Dec. 15." WPA label: "Dora Erickson; copy by Jeffrey." This composition is similar to USFS.105 but contains additional flowers. [USFS.126]

Red Monkey Flower: Nimilus lewisii. 1936–1937. Watercolor. 14⅞ × 11½ inches. Reverse: "George Jeffery. Dec. 2nd. For detail look up Henshaw p. 241, also Harkin p. 328." [USFS.26]

Rhododendron californicum. 1936–1937. Watercolor. 14⅜ × 11⅜ inches. Reverse top right: "Oct. George Jeffery." WPA label: "Jeffrey." This composition is similar, but not quite identical to WPA negative #317, identified as by Feurer. A WPA loan receipt dated February 23, 1938, included two *Rhododendron californicum* watercolors by Jeffery. [USFS.30]

Rhododendron californicum, *by George Jeffery, 1936–1937.*
Watercolor, 14⅝ × 11¼ inches. USFS.32.

Rhododendron californicum. 1936–1937. Watercolor. 14⅝
× 11¼ inches. Reverse: George Jeffery. Oct. 21." Composition is similar but not identical to WPA negative
#321. A WPA loan receipt dated February 23, 1938,
included two *Rhododendron californicum* watercolors by
Jeffery. [USFS.32]

Rhododendron californicum. 1936–1937. Watercolor.14½
× 11½ inches. Reverse: "George Jeffery. Oct. 28th."
This composition resembles WPA negative #321. A
WPA loan receipt dated February 23, 1938, included
two *Rhododendron californicum* watercolors by Jeffery.
[USFS.131]

Tiger Lily, Honeysuckle, Oregon Sunshine, and Mimiulus.
1936–1937. Watercolor. 15¼ × 12½ inches. Reverse:
"George Jeffery? Dec. 9th." WPA label: "Jeffrey."
WPA loan receipt dated February 23, 1938, acknowl-

edged receipt of a "combination" watercolor of *Tiger
Lily, Honeysuckle, Oregon Sunshine and Mimulus* by
Jeffery. Composition is at MCL, OSL, and JHS (as
negative #279-14). WPA negative #353 in Friends of
Timberline Archive is same composition with no attribution. [USFS.184, identical to USFS.8 (Feurer) and
USFS.160 (Erikson)]

Trillium. 1936–1938. Watercolor. 14½ × 11½ inches.
WPA label: "Jeffrey." WPA loan receipt dated February 28, 1938, acknowledged loan of three large *Trillium* watercolors by Feurer. [USFS.161]

Twin Flower: Linnaea borealis var americana. 1936–1937.
Watercolor. 11¼ × 14⅜ inches. Bottom right: "Jeff."
Reverse top right: "Nov. 4." WPA loan receipt dated
February 23, 1938, indicated two *Twin Flower* watercolors by Jeffery were delivered to Timberline. WPA label: "Jeffrey." [USFS.2, identical to USFS.50 (Feurer)]

Twin Flower: Linnaea borealis var americana. 1936–1937.
Watercolor. 13½ × 10¾ inches. Reverse: "George
Jeffery Nov. 11th." [USFS.193 (varies slightly from
USFS.2 and USFS.50)]

Western Anemone: Anemone occidentalis. 1936–1937. Watercolor. 11½ × 14 inches. Reverse: "George Jeffery.
Oct. 7th. Not creamy enough." Composition is at
MCL (without attribution) and OSL with an additional flower and more foreground, and as a lithograph
at JHS (identified as by Erikson and as #202-19).
[USFS.123, identical to USFS.141 and USFS.188
(both by Erikson)]

Willows. 1936–1937. Watercolor. 15½ × 17 inches. Reverse: "George Jeffery. Nov. 18." The composition was
identified as Erikson's on the envelope to WPA negative #347. [USFS.35, identical to USFS.148 (Erikson)
and USFS.152 (Feurer)]

WOOD, ELIZABETH HOFFMAN (LATER ELIZABETH DASCH), AND KARL FEURER

Elizabeth Hoffman Wood (b. 1912, Portland) was interior
designer Margery Hoffman Smith's niece. She loved wildflowers. When her children were young, she would take

them for walks along the Metolius River in Central Oregon to paint wildflowers. She enjoyed lapidary work and later made jewelry that was popular among her friends. Wood was an avid gardener and active supporter of the Portland Art Museum. Biographical information for Karl Feurer is under his individual entry.

Media: Watercolor, enamels, silver and enamel jewelry.

Education: Smith College (Northampton, Massachusetts).

Work at Timberline: She is credited with creating the two compositions of the *Mount Hood Lily* watercolors. The lithograph copy listed here may also be Feurer's copy of Wood's composition. The WPA labels on two other compositions (USFS.104 and USFS.111) identical to the one listed here identify Wood as the artist and Feurer as the copyist. See George Jeffery, *Mount Hood Lily* (USFS.162) for a different composition identified as based on a sketch by Wood.

Mt. Hood Lily: Lilium washingtonianum. 1936–1938. Hand-colored lithograph. Unattributed. 15¾ × 11⅛ inches. The same composition is identified as by [Elizabeth Hoffman] Wood and Karl Feurer on WPA negative jacket #273. Composition is at MCL (identified only as negative #273-1) and JHS. [USFS.54, identical to USFS.104 (Feurer), USFS.111 (Feurer), and USFS.180 (Feurer)]

UNATTRIBUTED

Blue Gentian. 1936-1938. Watercolor? 11½ × 14½. [USFS.124]

Squaw Grass: Xerophyllum tenex. 1936–1938. Watercolor. 14½ × 11½ inches. No attribution. This composition is unlike other examples of *Squaw Grass* at Timberline Lodge. [USFS.110]

Wind Flower [no mat label]. 1936–1938. Watercolor. 11½ × 14½ inches. No attribution. Reverse: "Ask Mrs. Sherrard what this is and if native to Mt. Hood district. Cannot identify—R.B.W." Mrs. Sherrard was the wife of the regional forester, Thomas H. Sherrard. [USFS.190]

WOOD CARVINGS AND MARQUETRY

AMIOTTE, GEORGE

b. 1947, Pine Ridge, South Dakota

George Amiotte is an Oglala Lakota (Sioux) who has been active in film making and preserving traditional Native American culture. Amiotte worked as an art instructor at Lakota Community College, Pine Ridge, South Dakota. He has had numerous shows of his paintings and sculptures, and has given programs on Native American culture, including drum making as a traditional art, in Portland, 1992–1993. Amiotte has coproduced several award-winning documentaries on the cultural revival of Indian communities. In addition to the buffalo head for the Wy'East Day Lodge, Amiotte carved pedestals for the Paul Buckner sculptures in the main lobby.

Media: Oil, wood, mixed media.

Education: University of North Dakota (mid-level medical practitioner, 1993).

Buffalo Head. Circa 1993. Carved wood. Estimated 14 × 15 × 19 inches. Wy'East Day Lodge, lounge.

BUCKNER, PAUL E.

b. 1933, Seattle, Washington

Beginning in 1962, following a Fulbright scholarship, Buckner taught figure studies at the University of Oregon's School of Architecture and Allied Arts, retiring in 1995 as professor emeritus of fine art. Buckner told art historian and printmaker Mary Balcomb, "In my sculpture, I share with all who have reflected with wonder upon the figure—on the continuing celebration of that most basic language."

Media: Wood, bronze, ceramic and stone.

Education: University of Washington (MA 1959); Claremont (California) Graduate University (MFA 1961); Slade School, University College, London (Fulbright 1961–1962).

Selected Collections: South Seattle Community College; Oregon Public Library (Salem); St. Cecilia's Catholic Church (Beaverton, Oregon); Eastern Oregon Correctional Institution (Pendleton); Albany General Hospital (Oregon); Mount Angel Abbey (Oregon); Sacred Heart General Hospital (Eugene, Oregon); United (Congregational) Church of Christ (Forest Grove,

Oregon); Lincoln Center, Washington Square (Portland, Oregon); University of Oregon Museum of Art (Eugene); University of Oregon President's Centennial Medallion (the president's badge of office is a myrtlewood disk edged with bronze).

Work at Timberline: Two sculptures, one depicting an Indian woman and child and the other a pioneer woman and child, were originally designed for Timberline Lodge by Florence Thomas but not completed. In the late 1980s, former Portland Art Museum director Francis Newton promoted the idea to commission the sculptures through Friends of Timberline, and the sculptures were funded through an anonymous donation. Although the subjects are the same, Buckner's depictions are completely original designs.

Pioneer Woman and Child. 1990. Alaska yellow cedar. Height 42½ inches. Main lobby on plinths attached to large columns until 2008. Moved to stair landing in C. S. Price Wing.

Indian Woman and Child. 1990. Alaska yellow cedar. Height 43¾ inches. Main lobby on plinths attached to large columns until 2008. Moved to stair landing in C. S. Price Wing.

DUNCAN, JAMES

James Duncan was among the Timberline builders, and he worked at the lodge after its construction and into the 1950s. He was an expert on the stains and polishes used for wood. He encouraged Richard L. Kohnstamm to become area operator in 1955.
Media: Wood.
Work at Timberline: Duncan also may have carved the Mail Box Post in the lodge (unconfirmed), listed in this inventory.

Indian Head. 1937. Carved wood panel. 27⅛ × 27⅛ inches. Entrance door to lower lobby. Head of Indian chief in headdress, twenty-six feathers, two braids on sides of face, collar under chin. Originally in natural wood color, the Indian head was later painted, either by James Duncan or another employee.

ESPINOSA, LARRY

b. 1893?, La Barca, Jalisco, Mexico; d. 1974, Portland, Oregon
Espinosa was a Forest Service employee.
Media: Wood.

Pony Express Mail Box. October 1938. Wood. 14⅛ × 13⅜ inches, 7¹¹⁄₁₆ inches deep. Carving depicts horse and rider reminiscent of a Pony Express rider. The mailbox was built in the Forest Service Zigzag Ranger Station sign shop. Attached to west wall of lower lobby.

GORHAM, AIMEE SPENCER

b. 1883, St. Paul, Minnesota; d. 1974, Portland, Oregon
Using similar techniques as for her Timberline marquetry work, Aimee Gorham created marquetry panels at Oregon State University (Corvallis), United States National Bank (Klamath Falls, Oregon), and the State Dining Room of the United States Building at the 1939 New York World's Fair. Gorham also used the technique for panels for Alameda, Chapman, Gregory Heights, and Irvington schools in Portland (Oregon). One at Irvington, *International Cooperation*, is a reproduction of marquetry she designed for the 1939 New York World's Fair completed under the Oregon Federal Art Project.
Media: Wood (marquetry).
Education: Pratt Institute, Brooklyn, New York; University of Oregon, Eugene (Carnegie Scholarship).
Work at Timberline: Gorham made two marquetry panels assigned to Timberline Lodge. Lodge interior decorator Margery Hoffman Smith stated that Gorham was not commissioned specifically to the Timberline project and that her work was under the FAP generally. Jerome Seliger, a marquetry craftsman who studied interior design at the University of Oregon, assisted and worked with Gorham for years. Seliger refined a press that placed five tons of pressure on the marquetry pieces glued to plywood. Later, he went into teaching and electronics.

Coyotes. 1937. Wood marquetry. 39½ × 57 inches. Framed in wood with natural finish. Signature lower left. "WPA Federal Art Project" printed along middle of bottom frame. Gorham's cartoon of the design was used to determine shapes of the wood sections. The wood pieces were cut out with an inlay knife and taped

Coyotes, by Aimee Gorham, 1937. Wood marquetry, 39½ × 57 inches. Main lobby.

together. The wood pieces were glued to a piece of plywood, put into a press, and left for twenty-four hours under five tons of pressure. The tape was removed and the wood sections scraped with a hard steel scraper. A specially developed resin was applied to seal the wood. The surface was lightly sanded and twenty coats of wax were applied, using a special white wax formula. Part of collection at Timberline Lodge through WPA loan recorded February 26, 1938. Main lobby, northeast foyer.

Mountain Lions. 1937. Wood. 39 × 56⅞ inches. Signature lower center. Produced with *Coyotes*. Part of collection at Timberline Lodge through WPA loan recorded February 26, 1938. Main lobby, northeast foyer.

KEEGAN, MELVIN AURELIUS
b. 1903, Olequa, Washington; d. before 1986?
Media: Wood, metal, and paint.
Education: Museum Art School (now Pacific Northwest College of Art), Portland.
Work at Timberline: Melvin Keegan carved the three pioneer panels on the front stairway of Timberline Lodge under the FAP. He carved the rams' heads that form the

two bases of the ram's head table now in the main lobby, and he made a copy that was kept by his family. He also is credited with the design of the mosaic compass in the floor at the lower lobby entrance, simplfied from the architectural drawings.

Pioneer Scene. 1937–1938. Carved wood panels, possibly red cedar or redwood. Top panel 40½ × 63⅜ inches, middle panel 37⅜ × 63⅜ inches, lower panel 33 1/16 × 63⅜ inches. The three panels depict pioneers traveling over rugged terrain as they moved west. Natural wood finish. South stairway, first landing. Architect Howard Gifford made drawings of the panels that he intended to be sandblasted wood. In 1937, regional FAP director Joseph Danysh recommended that the panels be designed by one of the artists and sandblasted or carved. The Oregon project report for March 1938 indicated that Valentine M. Weise was carving his second panel and Melvin Keegan was carving the remaining panel.

LAMADE, ERICH
b. 1894, Braunsweig, Germany; d. 1969, Portland, Oregon
Erich Lamade was a well-known painter as well as sculptor. Lamade painted murals at Abernethy Elementary School, Portland, under the FAP. Through the Treasury Department, he was commissioned to paint the murals *Early and Contemporary Industries* (1938) in the post office at Grants Pass, Oregon, and worked with several other artists on the post office murals *Development of St. Johns* (1936) at St. Johns, Oregon.
Media: Oil, tempera, watercolor, and wood.
Education: John Herron Art Institute, Indianapolis; Grand Central School of Art, New York; Museum Art School (now Pacific Northwest College of Art), Portland, Oregon; Art Students League, New York.
Work at Timberline: He carved the *Forest Scene* panel over the fireplace in the Cascade Dining Room under the Federal Art Project.

Forest Scene or *Native Animals*. 1938. Carved wood panel with natural wood finish. 30 11/16 × 131 3/16 inches. Commissioned by Margery Hoffman Smith. Part of collection at Timberline Lodge since March 30, 1938. Cascade Dining Room, over fireplace.

Forest Scene *or* Native Animals, *by Erich Lamade, 1938. Carved wood panel with natural wood finish, 30^{11}/$_{16}$ × 131^{3}/$_{16}$ inches. Cascade Dining Room.*

Untitled (green hills, pink clouds, and blue sky). 1943. Tempera on pastel with wash on paper or board. 9¾ × 13½ inches.

Dry Grass, Eastern Oregon. 1935. Drawing with wash. 12¼ × 15¼ inches. Signature lower left, "Erich Lamade 1935."

Untitled (sawmill). 1933. Oil on panel or canvas? 10 × 11⅝ inches. Signature lower left. Main lobby.

KRAMER, TED

Ted Kramer worked for the federal government for twenty-four years, thirteen years with the Forest Service as a fire suppression crew foreman and the remainder with the U.S. Fish and Wildlife Service. He retired to St. Ignatius, Montana, in 1976, where he made Howard Hill long bows. He carved replacements for the original exterior animal heads in the 1960s.

Ram's Head. Each about 14¾ inches in height, on posts attached to the doorway of the exterior of the front door. These carvings are replacements of the original carvings.

Buffalo Head. Approximately 17¾ inches in circumference. Ends of four logs carved as buffalo heads at the eaves on the exterior west end of the building near the swimming pool. This carving is a replacement.

NITANI, MASAMICHI

b. 1952, Nibutani, Hidaka prefecture, Hokkaido, Japan
Masamichi Nitani is Ezo, a member of the Ainu people, and draws inspiration from traditional Ainu designs. His uncle was a carver, and Nitani learned basic carving in the traditional way, by watching and imitating, before he apprenticed to Kaizawa. Nitani makes his carving tools by hand from wood and metal. A frequent subject is the black bear, an animal revered among Ainu people. Mountain lions and beavers are also favorite subjects. Nitani's exquisite bowls and baskets are inspired by traditional designs. His sculpted pieces are made from a single piece of wood. When a knot or hole is discovered, he works the "flaw" into the design.

Media: Wood, particularly black walnut.

Education: Masamichi Nitani spent three years apprenticed to master woodcarver Moriyuki Kaizawa, in Nibutani, Biratori, Japan.

Selected Collections: World Forestry Center, Portland, Oregon.

Work for Timberline: Nitani was commissioned to carve a bear that was installed in the Wy'East Day Lodge lounge. He also carved a bear head for the exterior of the main lodge to replace a weathered one. When the weathered original carvings were replaced, they were cut off the ends of the log and new carvings attached. The bear head carved by Nitani is the third bear head to be placed on the eave.

Bear's Head. Circa 1993. Carved Douglas fir corbel. Estimated 14 × 15 × 19 inches. Wy'East Day Lodge lounge.

Bear's Head. 1990s. Carved Douglas fir corbel. Estimated 14 × 15 × 19 inches. Exterior at roofline of Timberline Lodge on eave.

SETZIOL, LEROY

b. 1915, near Philadelphia; d. 2005, Sheridan, Oregon
Leroy Setziol grew up in Buffalo, New York, and became a minister in Bennington, New York. During World War II, he served as a chaplain in the South Pacific. Setziol's wife, Ruth, moved to Portland, where she was a teacher. He joined her and began to work there as a wood carver. A self-taught carver, Setziol became one of Oregon's most distinguished artists. He developed a grid system

when carving a piece for Menucha Conference Center in the Columbia River Gorge, which he used in subsequent work. Writer Janet Goetz recounted in his obituary that Setziol believed that "art should be for everyone."

Media: Wood.

Education: Elmhurst College, Elmhurst, Illinois (graduating in 1938), Eden Theological Seminary, St. Louis, Missouri.

Selected Collections: Fourteen panels (1964) at Salishan Lodge, Gleneden Beach, Oregon, St. James Evangelical Church, Portland (Oregon), and Lake Oswego (Oregon) City Hall. More Setziol woodcarvings are in public places than any other Oregon woodcarver.

Untitled carving of organic, geometric shapes (including triangles and circles) in a horizontal grid. 2004. Alaska yellow cedar. 12⅝ inches × 119⅜ inches. Donated by Friends of Timberline board member Joachim Grube. Located on the back patio, attached to the exterior wall of the C. S. Price Wing.

THOMAS, FLORENCE

b. 1906, Chicago, Illinois; d. 19??, Portland, Oregon
Florence Thomas worked in ceramics in Vienna, Austria, and later apprenticed to her father in the Ernest Thomas Cast Stone Company in Portland, Oregon. She worked for Sawyers Photographic Services View-Master Division, which made reels of animated stories.

Media: Ceramics, wood, graphite, various.

Education: Chicago Art Institute, Museum Art School (now Pacific Northwest College of Art), Portland, Oregon. Thomas also studied with Emile Jacques, who taught the University of Portland, formerly known as Columbia University.

Work at Timberline: Thomas carved the *Cougar Resting in Forest* panel in the main lobby. She also made drawings for light fixtures, wood sculptures, and newel posts for the lodge that were published in a book about the lodge written by Claire Warner Churchill under the Federal Writers Project, circa 1936. Thomas also created plaster models of animals and birds that were then carved into various stairway newel posts by the WPA woodworking shop under Ray Neufer.

Cougar Resting in Forest. 1936–1937. Carved wood panel with natural wood finish. 131¹/₁₆ × 31¹/₁₆ inches. Low-relief carving. It was moved from the lintel over the fireplace in the Cascade Dining Room to its present location in the main lobby over doors exiting to the vestibule in 1938–1939.

Newel Post Designs. 1936-1937. Thomas made plaster of Paris castings of animal forms and sent them to the WPA woodworking shop. There, carvers used the castings as patterns for carving newel posts from old telephone poles. The newel post carvings are:

Badger. Post height 59 inches, circumference 44¹³⁄₁₆ inches, depth of carving 6⁵⁄₁₆ inches. Main stairway, mezzanine.

Beaver. Post height 56⁵⁄₁₆ inches, circumference 44¹⁄₁₆ inches, depth of carving 6¹⁄₁₆ inches. Main stairway, between ground floor and first floor landing.

Black Bear. Post height 64³⁄₁₆ inches, circumference 44¹⁄₁₆ inches, depth of carving 9³⁄₈ inches. Main stairway, ground floor.

Eagle. Post height 65¾ inches, circumference 46 inches, depth of carving 17⁵⁄₁₆ inches. South stairway, landing to main lobby.

Fawn. Post height 48¹³⁄₁₆ inches, circumference 43¾ inches, depth of carving 7¹³⁄₁₆ inches. South stairway, ground floor to right of door to lower lobby.

Fox. Post height 58¹¹⁄₁₆ inches, circumference 43 inches, depth of carving 6¹⁄₁₆ inches. Main stairway, second floor.

Lynx. Post height 51⅜ inches, circumference 44¹³⁄₁₆ inches, depth of carving 7¹³⁄₁₆ inches. Main stairway, by main lobby.

Mallard with Broken Wing. Post height 58¼ inches, circumference 37¹³⁄₁₆ inches, depth of carving 8¼ inches. Main stairway, landing to third floor.

Mole. Post height 50⅜ inches, circumference 45¹¹⁄₁₆ inches, depth of carving 8¼ inches. Main stairway, by main lobby.

Owl. Post height 51⅜ inches, circumference 44¹³⁄₁₆ inches, depth of carving 7¹³⁄₁₆ inches. Main stairway, second landing.

Pelican. Post height 48 inches high, circumference 50⅜ inches, depth of carving 11¹³⁄₁₆ inches. South stairway, first floor, off main lobby.

Western Kingfisher. Post height 61 inches, circumference 45⁵⁄₁₆ inches, depth of carving 7½ inches. Main stairway, third floor.

WEISS, VALENTINE M.
Media: Wood.
Work at Timberline: *Pioneer Scene* panels. See Melvin Keegan for description.

ZIPPRICH, JOHN
b. 1951, Los Gatos, California
John Zipprich has competed in world championship ice and snow sculpture competitions in Savonlina, Finland; Moscow, Russian Federation; Sapporo, Japan; and Breckenridge, Colorado.
Media: Wood (carving, intarsia, and mosaic), ice and snow sculpture.
Education: John Zipprich is self-taught and said he has been carving since he was "old enough to hold a pocket knife."
Selected Collections: Charlie's Mountain Place, Mount Hood Cultural Center, I-Fax Grill and Ratskeller (all at Government Camp, Oregon); Imperial River Company (Maupin, Oregon).
Work at Timberline: In 1975, Zipprich began his association with Timberline Lodge as a furniture refinisher. He subsequently was employed by the lodge as an independent contractor to repair and refinish original furniture. He restored the carved Indian Head panel on a lower lobby door in 1976. He has carved signs for the lodge.

Bison's Head. Circa 1993. Carved ponderosa pine. Estimated 14 × 15 × 19 inches. Wy'East Day Lodge lounge.

Ram's Head. Circa 1993. Carved ponderosa pine. Estimated 14 × 15 × 19 inches. Wy'East Day Lodge lounge.

UNKNOWN ARTISTS OR CRAFTSMEN

Other wood architectural decorations at Timberline include carved lintels, panels, and newel posts. These were designed by the architects of the lodge and some, perhaps all, were completed by workers in the WPA woodshop. The decorative painting on lintels was completed on site.

Double Newel Posts. Two, height 51 and 58 inches, circumference 56 inches. Zigzag patterns. Back stairway in west wing. Architect Howard Gifford may have designed posts; carver unknown.

Geometric Carved Newel Posts. Six, heights: 42, 48, 49, 50, 53, and 54 inches, circumference about 45 inches. Designs include zigzag, mountain shapes, rising sun carving. Architect Howard Gifford may have designed posts; carver unknown. Stairway at west end of west wing.

Lintel Carving and Detail on Columns over Front Doorway. About 170¾ inches wide. Lintel carved with chevron, eagle shape, and chevron. Designed by Howard Gifford; carver unknown. Front doorway.

Lintel Carvings over Back Terrace Doorway. Approximately 36 × 55 inches. Carved in a modified chevron on a semicircle. Designed by Howard Gifford; carver unknown. North side of lodge.

Lintel Decorations in Ski Lounge. Eight, about 7¹³⁄₁₆ inches × 17¾ inches. The carved symbols were drawn from the Camp Fire Girls handbook page "The Year in Moons," and are carved into the doorway lintels in the Ski Lounge (now the lower lobby). Designed by Howard Gifford; carver unknown.

Mail Box Post. 50 × 14⅝ inches. Vertical log hollowed out and carved with a pinecone decoration, with a wrought-iron door that allows retrieval of mail. Built in WPA woodworking shop. Metal door made in WPA metal shop. James Duncan may have been carver. Main lobby.

Painted Ram's Heads in Ski Lounge. Three panels, each about 17¾ inches square. Lower lobby.

Stone chimney ornament. 1937. Basalt. Estimated 6 x 8 inches. Three sandblasted figures resembling Northwest Indian petroglyphs:
(1) a circular wheel with four cogs
(2) a flying bird over three triangles (mountain peaks), and
(3) a figure holding a staff and standing next to an elaborate X pattern.

The figures have been named by members of the Confederated Tribes of Warm Springs and recorded by curator Linny Adamson: (1) "working hands" or "red hands, white hands shaking" (a reference to a treaty between tribes and the U.S. government), (2) "return of the hummingbird, return of the spirit" (over mountains, possibly the Cascade Range), and (3) "medicine man with a pipe and thunderbird." Forest Service architect Howard Gifford designed the intaglio figures, according to the Historic American Building Survey, OR-161. Architectural drawings show the third figure as ornamentation on either side of the door to a guest room. The designs may have been inspired by petroglyphs made by local Northwest Indians. Chimney in main lounge.

ORIGINAL FURNITURE, FIXTURES, AND FURNISHINGS FOR TIMBERLINE LODGE

Timberline Lodge's handmade furniture and fixtures are either original to the building or re-creations in original styles. Together, the old and new furnishings make the lodge a living museum.

This inventory identifies original wood furniture, metal furnishings, and light fixtures where at least one example remains in use at the lodge. The inventory is partly based on a 1938 inventory of furnishings that the WPA provided to Timberline upon completion of the project. The number accompanying each item indicates the original quantity of that item according to the 1938 inventory and a location within the lodge where the item may still be found. The few types of original furniture no longer found at the lodge, such as the counter stools originally in the Ski Grille, are not in this inventory. Production dates of 1937–1938 are based on a WPA proposal for furniture production for the lodge, noted in a 1936 Forest Service log.

Over the years, broken or missing wood and metal furnishings have been replaced with handmade replicas or adaptations, many since 1975 through Friends of Timberline. Replicas are not marked to distinguish them from originals. If known, replicas are identified.

FURNITURE

Original furniture at the lodge was constructed in the Portland WPA woodworking shop in the 1930s. Many pieces, such as the dining room chairs, were reproduced many times. Others are one of a kind, such as the lounge chair with strap found in the main lobby. These "odd" items may have been designs that were rejected by the lodge's interior designer, Margery Hoffman Smith, perhaps as incompatible in design or too complex to replicate quickly.

BEDS

Fence rail twin bed. 1937–1938. Twenty-six Douglas fir frame beds, with fence rails in double-bar headboard. Some originally had a luggage shelf at the foot; all shelves have been removed. Some beds have headboards and footboards of the same height, originally used as bunk beds in the lodge's dormitory section. 34¼ to 35⁷⁄₁₆ inches high at head, 24¼ to 35⁷⁄₁₆ inches high at foot, 82⅜ to 85 inches long, and 43¾ inches wide. No replicas. Guest rooms.

Hinged twin bed. 1937–1938. Two pairs of Douglas fir frame beds. Iron hinges connected two twin beds at the head and foot to make a king-size bed. Each bed 29⅞ inches high at head, 23¼ inches high at foot,

Hinged twin bed, circa 1937. Douglas fir frame, iron hinges, each twin bed 29⅞ × 78¾ × 41¾ inches. WPA Negatives Collection (negative #4474), Portland Art Museum, Oregon.

78¾ inches long, and 41¾ inches wide. Replicas. Guest rooms.

Wood and iron double bed. 1937–1938. Ten Douglas fir frame beds, iron strap across headboard and footboard. Some carved with blue gentian, zigzag, or trillium motifs from room designs. 27½ inches high at head and foot, 78¾ inches long, 57⅛ inches wide. New beds in this style are in queen size. Guest rooms.

Wood and iron twin bed. 1937–1938. Thirty-six Douglas fir frame beds, iron strap across headboard and footboard. 34⅝ inches high at head, 27½ inches high at foot, 80⅞ inches long, 43½ inches wide. No replicas. Guest rooms.

CABINETS, CUPBOARDS, AND DESKS

Alcove desk. 1937–1938. Four knotty pine desks, four cubbyholes and rosette decoration carved at each end, massive legs notched around the base. 42⅛ inches high, 35 inches wide, 29⅛ inches deep, 28⅜ inches to desktop. No replicas. Mezzanine.

Bookcase. 1937–1938. Two Douglas fir bookcases, three shelves and two glass doors, iron straps diagonally across doors, iron hinges, and iron door pulls. 42⅛ inches high, 59¹⁄₁₆ inches wide, and 14¾ inches deep. No replicas. Mezzanine.

Corner writing desk. 1937–1938. Ten Douglas fir desks, two drawers and three legs. Drawers and slant top have iron pulls and iron hinges. 40 inches high, 28¾ inches wide, 19¼ to 13 inches deep. No replicas. Guest rooms.

Cupboard (also called wine cabinet). 1937–1938. Nine Douglas fir cupboards, two shelves and two doors, iron hinges and door pulls. Some doors are carved with blue gentian or trillium flowers from room scheme designs. 30⅛ inches high, 32¼ inches wide, and 14 inches deep. No replicas. Cascade Dining Room.

Dining room sideboard. 1937–1938. Two fir cupboards, three shelves and two doors, wrought-iron hinges and door pulls. Coyote heads carved on the ends. 40 inches high, 39¾ inches wide, and 19⅜ inches deep. No replicas. Cascade Dining Room.

Display case. 1937–1938. One Douglas fir–framed glass case, carved legs. 39½ inches high, 62⁷⁄₁₆ inches wide, and 31 inches deep. No replicas. Main lobby.

Highboy. 1937–1938. Thirty Douglas fir dressers, five drawers, and iron drawer pulls. 45 inches high, 30 inches wide, and 17 inches deep. No replicas. Guest rooms.

Lowboy. 1937–1938. Eleven Douglas fir dressers, three drawers, and iron drawer pulls. Seven dressers, 42 inches wide; four dressers, 36 inches wide. An additional half-drawer was put on the left side of the shorter ones. 29 inches high and from 17 to 18⅜ inches deep. No replicas. Guest rooms.

CHAIRS

Balcony desk chair. 1937–1938. Four knotty pine chairs, low back, hand-hold in center back. Legs carved to match desk design. 29¼ inches high, 22⅞ inches wide, 22⅞ inches deep, 17½ inches high to seat. No replicas. Main lobby and mezzanine.

Blue Ox Bar chair. 1937–1938. Twenty Douglas fir fiddle-back chairs. 34 inches high, 15 inches wide, 20⅞ inches deep, 17 inches high to seat. No replicas. Blue Ox Bar.

Card table chair. 1937–1938. Forty-eight Douglas fir straight-backed chairs, upholstered seat and two-slat back. 29½ inches high, 15⅜ inches wide, 19⅛ inches deep, 16⅛ inches high to seat. Replicas. Guest rooms.

Dining room chair. 1937–1938. One hundred-fourteen Douglas fir chairs, haystack arch (or Timberline arch) back chairs. 32¼ inches high, 16⅜ inches wide, 20½ inches deep, 18 inches high to seat. Replicas. Cascade Dining Room.

Fireside easy chair. 1937–1938. One Douglas fir frame chair, wood crosspiece on back and upholstered seat. 27⅜ inches high, 29½ inches wide, 29½ inches deep, 15⅛ inches high to seat. No replicas. Guest room 107.

Lounge chair. 1937–1938. Fourteen Oregon white oak and iron chairs, upholstered seat and back. 30 inches high, 26¾ inches wide, 30⁵⁄₁₆ inches deep, 18¼ inches high to seat. No replicas. Main lobby.

Lounge chair with strap. 1937–1938. One Oregon white oak and iron chair, upholstered seat and back. 30 inches high, 26¾ inches wide, 30⁵⁄₁₆ inches deep, 18¼ inches high to seat. No replicas. Main lobby.

President's chair. 1937. Douglas fir armchair, upholstered seat. 36¼ inches high, 24⅞ inches wide, 22¼ inches deep, 17 inches high to seat. A plaque on the back states the chair was built for President Franklin D. Roosevelt when he dedicated Timberline Lodge on September 28, 1937. Replicas made since 1975. Rachael Griffin Historic Exhibition Center.

Rawhide and iron chair. 1937–1938. Twelve iron frame chairs, Douglas fir back and rawhide seat and arms. 30⁵⁄₁₆ inches high, 23½ inches wide, 31¹⁄₁₆ inches deep, 14⅛ inches high to seat. After 1976, the rawhide strips were replaced by Arthur McArthur and Alan Hart-McArthur of Versatile Sash. No replicas. Lower lobby.

Ski Grille chair. 1937–1938. Thirty-six Douglas fir straight-backed chairs, hollowed seat and partially sol-

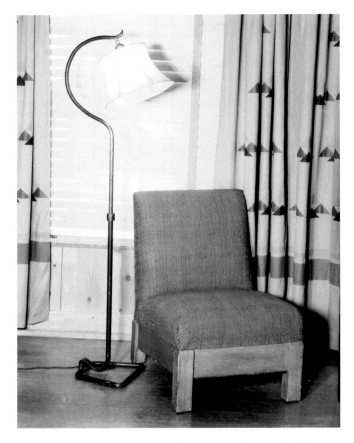

Small easy chair and "Bo Peep" floor lamp, circa 1937. Chair, with Douglas fir frame, is 31¾ × 21 × 25 inches. WPA Negatives Collection (negative #4470), Portland Art Museum, Oregon.

id back, crosspiece at center top of back. 32¾ inches high, 15⅝ inches wide, 20¾ inches deep, 17¾ inches high to seat. No replicas. Mezzanine.

Small easy chair. 1937–1938. Forty-eight Douglas fir chairs, upholstered back and seat. 31¾ inches high, 21 inches wide, 25 inches deep, 16 inches high to seat. No replicas. Guest rooms.

Terrace chair. 1937–1938. Thirty-two Douglas fir and iron chairs; iron frame, seat and back slats of painted wood. 30¾ inches high, 15 inches deep at base, 17 inches high to seat, 16¼ inches wide at top. No replicas. Roosevelt Terrace.

COUCHES, LOVE SEATS, AND WALL SEATS

Built-in corner seat. 1937–1938. Two Douglas fir frame seats, upright back, five angles, upholstered seat and back. 39 inches high, 34⁷⁄₁₆ inches long each side, 17⁵⁄₁₆ inches long on each corner, 71⅞ inches long along back, 16⅛ inches deep, 17¾ inches high to seat. No replicas. Alcove of main lobby.

Fence rail couch. 1937–1938. Nine Douglas fir couches, fence rail back and sides. Originally made with shelf ends. 29 inches high, 94½ inches long from arm rest to arm rest, 34⅜ inches deep, 18⅛ inches high to seat. No replicas. Guest rooms.

Hexagonal lounge couch. 1937–1938. Eight angled Oregon white oak and iron couches, upholstered seat and three back cushions. 30⁵⁄₁₆ inches high, 98⁷⁄₁₆ inches long, 30 inches deep at arm, 15¾ inches high at seat. No replicas. Main lobby.

Lounge loveseat. 1937–1938. Eight loveseats, Oregon white oak arms and back on iron frame. Two each upholstered seat and back cushions. 31¾ inches high, 69⁵⁄₁₆ inches long from arm rest to arm rest, 27½ inches deep, 15⅜ inches high to the seat. No replicas. Mezzanine.

Small alcove seat. 1937–1938. Two five-sided Douglas fir benches, upholstered seat and back. 34⅜ inches high, 29¾ inches long on each side, 12¹³⁄₁₆ inches long at each corner, 43⁵⁄₁₆ inches along back, 15 inches deep, 16½ inches high to seat. No replicas. Mezzanine.

Straight-back bench. 1937–1938. Two Douglas fir benches, upholstered seat and back, divided into three sections. 37¹³⁄₁₆ inches high, 115 inches long, 24⅜ inches deep, 16⅝ inches high to seat. No replicas. Mezzanine.

Straight lounge couch. 1937–1938. Four Oregon white oak and iron frame couches, three seat cushions and three back cushions. 31½ inches high, 72 inches long, 94½ inches long to ends of arms, 22⅜ inches deep, 16½ inches high to seat. No replicas. Mezzanine.

Terrace loveseat. 1937–1938. Four loveseats, iron frame and Douglas fir slat back and seat. 28¾ inches high,

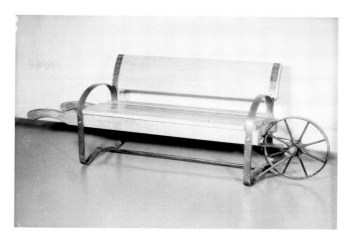

Terrace wheelbarrow, circa 1937. Wood planks and iron, 28⅛ × 82¼ × 19¼ inches. WPA Negatives Collection (negative #4495), Portland Art Museum, Oregon.

45¼ inches long, 24¹⁄₁₆ inches deep, 14⅛ inches high to seat. No replicas. Silcox Hut and lodge exterior.

Terrace wheelbarrow seat. 1937–1938. Three, iron frame, plank back, and seat. Iron wagon wheel at one end, wood handlebars at other end. 28⅛ inches high, 82¼ inches long including handlebars and wheel, 19¼ inches deep, 16⅛ inches high to seat. Replicas. Indian Head door entrance.

STANDS AND STOOLS

Bedroom coffee table. 1937–1938. Nine rectangular tables, fir top and iron legs, iron crosspiece between two ends. These are wider than the suitcase stands. 16¹⁵⁄₁₆ inches high, 29⅞ inches long, 21⅝ inches wide. Guest rooms.

Dressing table stool. 1937–1938. Thirty rectangular Douglas fir stools, upholstered seat. 15½ inches high, 23 inches long, 15½ inches wide. Guest rooms.

Long bench. 1937–1938. Six (of each length) rectangular Douglas fir seats cut to resemble split logs, strap iron legs. Bench was made in 42-inch and 72-inch lengths. 16¾ inches high and 16½ inches wide. Lower lobby.

Round stool. 1937–1938. Twenty-four 15-inch stools and twenty-two 18-inch stools, circular Douglas fir seats

Game table (white oak), card tables, bookcase, and dining room chairs on mezzanine. Timberline Lodge photograph.

and two strips of iron formed into four legs, seat 16¾ inches diameter. Guest rooms.

Suitcase stand. 1937–1938. Thirty-two rectangular stands, Douglas fir seat and iron legs, iron crosspiece between two ends. 18½ inches high, 30 inches long, 15½ inches wide. Guest rooms.

TABLES

Bedside table. 1937–1938. Thirty-two Douglas fir tables, shelf, wood back, and hand-hold on each side. 27 inches high, 18⅜ inches wide, and 13½ inches deep. Replicas. Guest rooms.

Blue Ox Bar table. 1937–1938. Heavy Douglas fir tables, notched legs angled out from tabletop. All are 29½ inches in height. In 1938, four tables 29⅞ inches long and 23⅝ inches wide and one table 71⅝ inches long and 23¼ inches wide. No replicas. Blue Ox Bar.

Card table, tea table, dining room table, and banquet table. 1937–1938. Douglas fir tables joined with wood pins. Five sizes, some square, others rectangular, all about 29½ inches high. Originally, nine card tables 30 inches square, two card tables 35 inches square, five tea tables 41 inches long and 25 inches wide, twenty-eight dining room tables 42 inches long and 28½ inches wide, and one banquet table 84 inches long and 34½ inches wide. No replicas. Cascade Dining Room and mezzanine.

Desk or dressing table. 1937–1938. Ten Douglas fir desks, four drawers on each side, one central drawer under desktop. 29 inches high, 44 wide, and 18⅝ inches deep. No replicas. Guest rooms.

Dressing table. 1937–1938. Twenty Douglas fir dressing tables, three drawers on right side of leg space and one drawer and a cupboard on left side. Iron drawer pulls. 28 inches high, 45 inches wide, and 17 inches deep. No replicas. Guest rooms.

Game table. 1937–1938. Two rectangular Oregon white oak game tables, four legs set at a 45-degree angle from the top corners. 27⅜ inches high, 47¹⁄₁₆ inches long, and 34⅝ inches wide. No replicas. Mezzanine.

Hexagonal coffee table. 1937–1938. Three Oregon white oak tables, six sides and legs. 17 inches high, 37⅜ inches in diameter, 21⅜ inches long on each of six sides. Replicas. Main lobby.

Long coffee table. 1937–1938. Six rectangular Oregon white oak tables. 16 inches high, 59 inches long, 19½ inches wide. No replicas. Mezzanine.

Ram's head table. 1937–1938. One massive Douglas fir table, two pedestal legs of yellow cedar carved in shape of a ram's head at each end. 29 inches high, 72 inches long, and 32 inches wide. Melvin Keegan carved the ram's head without a specific piece of furniture in mind. Ray Neufer and Margery Hoffman Smith decided to use the carving as one of two bases for a table, and asked Keegan to carve the second base. No replicas. Main lobby.

Serving table. 1937–1938. Ten Douglas fir tables, two shelves open at front and back, coyote heads carved in each end. 33½ inches high, 23⅜ inches long, 17¼ inches deep. No replicas. Cascade Dining Room.

Ski Grille or Coffee Shop table. 1937–1938. Twelve Douglas fir tables, heavy legs, notched near base of leg. Six tables 30 inches by 34 inches, and six tables 30 inches by 48 inches. Both sizes about 27⅞ inches high. No replicas. Mezzanine.

Terrace table. 1937–1938. Eight circular tables, top of Douglas fir strips, with iron frame and legs. 38 inches in diameter, 29 inches high. No replicas. Roosevelt Terrace or back terrace.

MISCELLANEOUS

Barlow Room gates. After 1938. Four-part, hinged Douglas fir gate held by iron strap hinges. The gates were added later than 1938. Two outer sections 71⅞ inches high, two center sections 36 inches, total opening 120⅞ inches wide. No replicas. Barlow Room.

Cloak rack. 1938. Four Douglas fir racks, pegs for coats, and shelf; two with open backs, two with paneled backs. 72½ inches high, 66 inches long, and 29 inches deep. No replicas. Main lobby.

Barlow Room gates bordered by hand-appliquéd draperies, built after 1938. Douglas fir, iron strap hinges, four sections, total 71⅞ × 120⅞ inches.

Mirror. 1937–1938. Fifty-nine Douglas fir framed mirrors to be hung over dressing tables. 35¾ inches high, 12⅝ inches wide at base. Replicas. Guest rooms.

Telephone bracket. 1937–1938. Ten Douglas fir boards attached to wall and supported by a triangular piece below. 10⅜ inches high, 15 inches wide, 7½ inches deep. Guest rooms.

LIGHT FIXTURES

The varied designs of the original wood and metal light fixtures reflect the pioneer, Indian, and wildlife themes used throughout the lodge. Geometric lines of many chandeliers also reflect the influence of Art Deco design. Original fixtures as well as repairs and upgrades were made in Fred Baker's lighting shop. Except for the large circular wood fixture for Silcox Hut, there are few replicas of light fixtures in the lodge, although new fixtures improve lighting in the public spaces.

CEILING FIXTURES

Barlow Room chandeliers. 1937. Douglas fir, iron, and glass. Two long carved wood fixtures resembling a stylized Indian war canoe; each suspended by an iron rod attached to hammered iron canopy sunflower, square-on-square, ceiling plate. Each has three lights with glass bowls. 106⁵⁄₁₆ inches long, 13³⁄₈ inches wide, 36¼ inches suspension to ceiling.

Chandelier in main lobby. 1937. Iron and fabric. Three hexagonal chandeliers, each a globe encased by a cast iron band. Six wrought-iron bars attach band to ceiling suspension bars and chain. 128 inches long; globe is 46 inches high and 42 inches in diameter. The iron band was cast in a local foundry; the remaining ironwork was made in the WPA Metalwork Shop.

Cylinder lights—Barlow Room, entry, and hall to lower lobby exhibition area. 1937–1938. Douglas fir, iron, and glass. There are five variations of cylinder lights:
(1) Barlow Room fixture has top and bottom carved wood bands connected with six iron rods. 21⁵⁄₈ inches high and 16½ inches in diameter. Eight fixtures: six in the Barlow Room (three original, three reproductions), and two in the main lobby.
(2) Entry chandelier has an iron cap and one wood ring connected by four iron bars. This chandelier is 22⁷⁄₈ inches high and 15 inches in diameter. Two chandeliers.
(3) Light in lower lobby hallway has six vertical bars that connect top and bottom iron bands and is encircled by an additional iron ring. This fixture resembles a pioneer lantern. 18½ inches high, 14½ inches in diameter, and 14½ inches suspension to ceiling. Nine fixtures.
(4) Light in lower lobby hallway is a cylinder with six iron rods connecting top and bottom iron bands. 13¾ inches high and 8 inches in diameter. One fixture.
(5) Lower lobby ceiling light is an iron cage made of six rods connected to iron rings at the top and bottom with iron band at center. Diffuser is an acrylic cylinder in the center. 17⁵⁄₁₆ inches high × 14⅛ inches wide at center. Two fixtures.

Hall lights. 1937–1938. Iron, acrylic diffuser. Square iron plate mounting to ceiling. Two bands from ceiling join circle at base. Three bands extend horizontally around the fixture. 7⅞ inches square. Twenty fixtures; most in storage.

Main lobby basket light fixtures. 1937. Wrought iron, acrylic diffusers. Five basket-shaped fixtures. Geometric

Light in entrance to main lobby, 1937. Douglas fir, iron, and acrylic diffusers that replaced original glass, 22⁷⁄₈ × 15 inches.

iron bands suggest Art Deco influence. 26 inches high, 36⅝ inches long, and 18¹⁄₁₆ inches wide; suspension is 10¼ inches from fixture to ceiling. Main lobby.

Ox yoke light fixture. 1936–1937. Vine maple, Douglas fir, and iron chain. Four fixtures. WPA wood workshop supervisor Ray Neufer described the process of preparing the wood: cut vine maple was buried in the ground, and a fire built over it and allowed to burn for several days. When the wood was dug up, it was soft and pliable. The design was by architect Gilbert Stanley Underwood. 24³⁄₈ inches high, 57¹⁄₁₆ inches long, and 41⁵⁄₁₆-inch suspension height. Lower lobby, west hall and gift shop.

Silcox Hut circular wood light fixture. 1938–1939. Wood. Large carved circular Douglas fir fixture, reproduction of the original fixture carved with zigzag decoration. 11 inches deep and 31 inches in diameter. The original is sometimes on view in the Rachael Griffin Historic Exhibition Center. Reproductions are at Silcox Hut.

Spun copper fixtures. 1937–1938. Copper and iron spun bowl, iron suspension, and scalloped design on canopy. 4 inches deep and 16⅛ inches in diameter. About eighty fixtures, many in storage.

Water bug chandeliers. 1937. Wrought iron, acrylic diffusers. Three fixtures, each with eight legs leading to

Basket light fixture, 1937. Iron frame with acrylic diffusers that replaced original glass, 26 × 36⅝ × 18¹/₁₆ inches.

ceiling fastenings. Margery Hoffman Smith's design, inspired by water bugs (or water skippers) she saw as a child on Oregon's McKenzie River. Geometric lines suggest Art Deco influence. 10¼ inches high, 84¼ inches long, 16⅛ inches wide, and 24⅜ inches to suspension height. Original diffusers were replaced with acrylic ones in the 1970s. Main lobby.

Zigzag fixtures in Cascade Dining Room. 1937. Iron, acrylic diffusers. Fourteen cylindrical fixtures resembling Indian drums painted burnt red and yellow ochre in a zigzag fashion and suspended from the ceiling by an iron rod. 6¼ inches high and 24⅜ inches in diameter. Cascade Dining Room.

LAMPS

"Bo Peep" floor lamps. 1937–1938. Wrought iron, rawhide shades. Sixty-eight lamps. Each is an iron pole bent into a vertical semicircle in which the princess-line shade hangs. Shade coverings and wire frames have been replaced on many. Iron base shaped into a trapezoid. 58¼ inches high; semicircle is 13¾ inches in diameter; and base is 9⅞ inches. Guest rooms.

Lounge floor lamps. 1937–1938. Wrought iron, rawhide shades. Sixteen lamps. Each is an iron pole bent at base to form trapezoid, resembling branding iron. Original cylindrical parchment shades have been replaced. Wire shade of frame replaced on many. 59⅞ inches high, 13 inches wide, and shade 17¾ inches wide. Main lobby.

Table lamps. 1937–1938. Wrought iron, rawhide shades. Thirty-eight lamps, each with two light bulbs and pull chains, iron pole bent into trapezoid base, resembling a branding iron. Parchment shades were shaped in a princess-line, laced together with rawhide. Original shade covering replaced, and wire frame replaced on many. 21⅜ inches high, 7⅞ inches wide at base; shade is 13 inches high and 13¾ inches wide at bottom. Guest rooms.

WALL FIXTURES

Wall sconces. 1937–1938. Iron. Four lantern-shaped fixtures. Each has a pierced conical iron cap and five iron bars extending to the bottom iron band. 14½ inches high, 7⅞ inches in diameter, 7⅛ inches out from wall, 8⅝ inch wall plate. Mezzanine alcoves.

METAL FIXTURES

Timberline's distinctive ironwork fixtures, such as wall sconces that resemble lanterns or table and floor lamps whose bases resemble branding irons, carry out the pioneer theme. Door handles shaped like arrows accentuate the Indian theme and the animal-shaped andirons are in the wildlife decorative theme.

EXTERIOR METALWORK

Arrow on chimney. 1937–1938. Wrought iron. Arrow with bow formed by a cross and circle. Approximately 39⅜ inches long and 23⅝ inches wide. Attached to north side of headhouse chimney.

Foot scrapers. 1937–1938. One double and three single foot scrapers. Iron. Recycled from railroad rails. Rail wound into a scroll design at one end, and at the other flattened and cut into a cloverleaf pattern with holes to attach scraper to a stone or cement base. Designed by Forest Service architect Dean Wright, double scrapers are 41 inches long and 12¼ inches in diameter; single scrapers are 21⅝ inches long. Replicas. Rachael Griffin Historic Exhibition Center or storage.

Ram's head door knocker, top plates, kick plate, push plates, door latches, and handles. 1937. Wrought iron and cast iron. Hardware and ornament on front door of lodge. Iron door handles (height 29½ inches) end in a curl; ram's head door knocker (height 16¾ inches) anchored to door by sunburst medallion. Door and iron-work weigh about 1000 pounds.

Indian head door. 1937. Wrought and cast iron. Hinges, kick plate, top plate, and door handles. Designs on the kick plates and top plates resemble the letter "J," alternated with curving arrows, and bolts in a pattern of three rows around the inside edges of the plates. Door hinges are rectangular scallops. A carved wood panel of an Indian in full headdress is on the top half. Other doors in the lodge have similar hand-wrought metal decoration including kick plates, push plates, and hinges. In many instances, damaged or missing door decorations have been replaced. Lower lobby entrance.

Silcox Hut dedication sign. 1938–1940. Wrought iron. 36 × 61 inches. Wording: "This building is dedicated to Ferdinand A. Silcox, Chief of the Forest Service, U.S. Department of Agriculture, November 1933–December 1939. He made possible the development of the Timberline Lodge Recreation Area." Silcox Hut over fireplace.

Weather vane. 1936–1937. Brass and bronze. Modification of the Wild Goose Moon symbol from the Camp Fire Girl handbook. 750 pounds, about 29½ feet tall, and almost 8 feet across at its widest point. Roof apex, main chimney.

Window grilles, rectangular and circular to fit hexagonal windows. 1937–1938. Wrought iron. Modified chevron and arrow design forms abstracted human shape. Each is 65 inches in length and 21⅝ inches wide. Four windows on either side of the front door.

INTERIOR METALWORK

Andirons in guest rooms. 1937–1938. Thick iron plate, recycled from railroad rails. Animal shapes, including squirrels, woodchucks (or marmots), rabbits, and beavers in guest room fireplaces. Blacksmith O. B. Dawson designed the animal andirons in the WPA metal shop. The animal outline was burned on the iron and edges were filed. Details were applied on heated forms. Replicas. Drawing of squirrel andiron is dated 1937.

Beaver andirons. 12⅞ inches high and 10¼ inches wide at base.

Arrow on headhouse chimney, 1937–1938. Iron, 39⅜ × 23⅝ inches. Photograph by Susanna Kuo, Friends of Timberline Archive.

Rabbit andirons. 12⅝ inches high and 11 inches wide at base.

Squirrel andirons. 11⅝ inches high and 9⅞ inches wide at base.

Woodchuck (marmot) andirons. 13 inches high and 9⅞ inches wide at base.

Andirons in lobbies. 1937–1938. Iron. Spiral andirons recycled from railroad rails. Seven sets throughout public areas of the lodge, made from rails pulled into a curl. 19¹¹⁄₁₆ inches high, 54 inches long, and 14½ inches wide at feet. Main lobby and lower lobby.

Cheese plate. 1937–1938. One brass tray with incised pinecone pattern on both handles. 25⅝ inches at widest point, 21¼ inches in diameter. Henry Harth made the plate at the Oregon Arts and Crafts Society (now Oregon College of Art and Craft). Display case outside Cascade Dining Room.

Coyote head gates. 1937. Wrought iron. 81⅛ × 63 inches. 1100 pounds. Design features coyote heads repeated in a horizontal band across the gates. Other elements include vertical and horizontal panels of zigzags, semicircles, and stair steps. The bolt is a rattlesnake shape. Where horizontal and vertical bars meet or cross, one bar is passed through the other rather than being welded. Upper hinge on each gate is topped by an iron pinecone finial. The finish is a mixture of linseed oil,

Circular window grille, 1937–1938. Iron, 65 × 21⅝ inches. Beside front door.

Spiral andirons in fireplaces of main lobby and lower lobby. Iron shaped from recycled railroad rails, 19¹¹⁄₁₆ × 54 × 14½ inches.

turpentine, and beeswax that was heated and rubbed into the heated iron with a soft cloth. Cascade Dining Room. Adaptations of the coyote head gates have been made for the Rachael Griffin Historic Exhibition Center and the entrance to the Blue Ox Bar.

Drapery rods. 1937–1938. Wrought iron. Bars have matching iron drapery rings. Rods about ⅜ inches thick and 2 inches wide, running the length of large windows in public areas and guest rooms. Replicas.

Drinking fountain. 1937–1938. Nickel. Estimated about 12 inches high, 8 inches deep, and 18 inches wide. Entrance to lower lobby by mosaic mural.

Fireplace forks. 1937–1938. Wrought iron. Large three-pronged forks. 53½ inches long and 3⅛ inches wide at prong. Two forks for the main lobby were noted in a 1938 inventory. Smaller forks for guest room fireplaces are 35 inches long and are two-pronged. O. B. Dawson designed the original fireplace forks. Most if not all fireplace forks now at the lodge are replicas.

Fireplace screens. 1937–1938. Iron. Fifteen screens hung from iron frames that extend the width of the fireplace opening. The frame is hinged in the middle; the screen is made of hanging strands of linked chains. O. B. Dawson designed the original fireplace screens.

Some screens have been replaced. Three pairs in main lobby, three pairs in lower lobby, one pair in Cascade Dining Room, and one pair in each of the eight fireplace guest rooms.

Fixtures. 1937–1938 and after 1975. Wrought iron and cast iron. In main lobby, forty-eight iron straps with medallions on supporting beams, six horizontal iron straps across intersections between columns and mezzanine floor, strap iron on posts, and iron door handle on exterior door in west alcove of main lobby. Hardware in guest room areas includes hinges, door latches, and push plates. Most original lodge hardware was designed by Forest Service architect Dean Wright. O. B. Dawson stated in a 1975 article in the *Oregon Historical Quarterly* that the guest room door hardware was purchased cast iron and not made in the WPA metal shop.

Information sign. 1939. Wrought iron. 50¾ × 58½ inches. Henry Harth made the sign in the WPA metal shop. "Snow depth average at Timberline" was originally given as 12 feet, but the numbers now list the average snow depth as 21 feet. The 12-foot depth was suggested by forest supervisor A. O. Waha in an August 1939 memo as an average of the snow depth from the previous three years. Lower lobby.

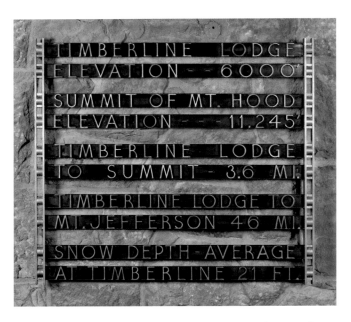

Timberline metal information sign, by Henry Harth, 1939. Iron, 50¾ × 58½ inches. Lower lobby.

Punch bowl. 1937–1938. One footed brass bowl hammered into scalloped edge. 4⅛ inches high, 12⅝ inches diameter at rim. Henry Harth created the bowl at the Oregon Arts and Crafts Society, Portland, Oregon. Display case outside Cascade Dining Room.

Warming oven in chimney. 1937. Wrought iron. Frame and door bolted to stone fireplace in Cascade Dining Room. 31⅛ inches high and 23⅞ inches wide. Decorative detail includes rams' heads on strap hinges.

New wrought-iron hardware in public areas of the ground floor includes standards for banners and easels, gates on the Rachael Griffin Historic Exhibition Center model room, the gate at the entrance to the Blue Ox Bar, kick plates, push plates, door handles, a cashier's screen, and handrails on stairways.

MISCELLANEOUS
Bronze plaque. 1937. Bronze. President Franklin D. Roosevelt read aloud when he dedicated Timberline Lodge: "Timberline Lodge, Mount Hood National Forest, dedicated September 28, 1937, by the President of the United States as a monument to the skill and faithful performance of workers on the rolls of the Works Progress Administration." Coping on Roosevelt Terrace.

First aid room glass window. 1937–1938. Glass. A red cross in leaded glass in a square window, about eight inches square. On door to a small room that became the ski patrol room. The ski patrol and first aid facilities were moved to the Wy'East Day Lodge after it was completed in 1981, and this room is now part of the Rachael Griffin Historic Exhibition Center.

Stone sign. 1937–1938. Basalt. Words carved in stone: "Mt. Hood Timberline Lodge erected 1936–1937 by Works Progress Administration in cooperation with Department of Agriculture Forest Service and Mt. Hood Development Association." Lower lobby entrance.

TEXTILES

Remaining original textiles include a few hand-woven samples and various appliquéd draperies that are kept in storage. In addition, several original hand-hooked rugs are displayed. Original textiles guide contemporary craftsmen as they re-create designs and select color schemes. The remaining original textiles are listed below.

APPLIQUÉD PATTERNS FOR DRAPERIES
Anemone. 1937–1938. Colored flowers, brown and green centers, and green leaves and stems on yellow background. Flower repeats five times. Panel is bordered in green. Two panels, each 62⅝ × 26½ inches. In storage.

Autumn Leaf. 1937–1938. Groups of three leaves—rust, green, and yellow—repeats four times on brown sailcloth. A pair of vertical green stripes runs down the sides of each panel. Two panels, each 74¹³⁄₁₆ × 30¾ inches. In storage.

Blue Gentian. 1937–1938. Blue and green flowers inside cream circles outlined in red on blue sailcloth background. Flower repeats six times. One panel, 61 × 45¼ inches. In storage.

Cat Tail. 1937–1938. Light green, brown, and khaki flower design in five repeats; with stripes top and bottom on green sailcloth background. Two panels. Dimensions of each panel: 72¹⁄₁₆ × 23⅝ inches. In storage.

Fish in River (also Fish and Wave, or Brook Trout). 1937–1938. Brown fish with yellow bellies and white eyes on rust background. Fish repeats five times. Three wavy yellow stripes of varying widths across bottom. Four panels, each 75⅝ × 30⅜ inches. In storage.

Indian Pipe Stem. 1937–1938. White, black, and light green flower pattern (three flower heads), repeats five times; stripes top and bottom on green sailcloth background. One panel, 74⅜ × 24¹³⁄₁₆ inches. In storage.

Phlox. 1937–1938. Five-pointed white flower with black center, repeats nine times on red sailcloth background. One panel, 75³⁄₁₆ × 40½ inches. In storage.

Shooting Star. 1937–1938. Double-headed pink flower with green leaves and stems on brown background. Flower repeats five times. 81½ × 52 inches. In storage.

Twin Flower. 1937–1938. White and red flower, repeats four times, on brown sailcloth background. One panel, 75⅝ × 31⅞ inches. In storage.

Zigzag. 1937–1938. Cream and black zigzag stripe across top and bottom of red sailcloth background. One panel, 77½ × 31⅞ inches. In storage.

HOOKED RUGS

Bricks. 1937–1938. Horizontal and vertical rectangle brick shapes form border of rug, made of blue and pink cotton plaids and prints. 33⅜ × 24³⁄₁₆6 inches. Brick design of this rug not found in patterns. Lower lobby or C. S. Price Wing.

Double "X". 1937–1938. Two Xs form pattern; made of light blue cotton. Background from cotton prints and plaids. 49⅝ × 24¹³⁄₁₆ inches. Similar rug design was used in the Bachelor Button guest room. Lower lobby or C. S. Price Wing.

Irregular stripes. 1937–1938. Shades of khaki in vertical pattern with several narrow horizontal stripes. Materials used are recycled uniforms and blankets. 65⅜ × 43¹¹⁄₁₆ inches. Pattern may have been used in Skyline room. Lower lobby or C. S. Price Wing.

Triangles (pyramid of six triangles). 1937–1938. Three sets of triangles combine to form pyramids or "mountains" at each end of the rug. Light and dark blue corduroy on a background of variegated khaki wool blanket and uniform material. 98⅜ × 63 inches. Repaired by CETA craftswomen in 1975–1977 using wool. Originally in Moon Over the Mountain guest room. Lower lobby or C. S. Price Wing.

Stairstep (two sizes). 1937–1938. Stairstep pattern in creamy white and light brown corduroy and black wool. 44½ × 32⅝ inches and 59¹⁄₁₆ × 35 inches. These rugs have probably been shortened and re-bound. Originally probably in the Zigzag guest rooms. Lower lobby or C. S. Price Wing.

Triangles (three in a row). 1937–1938. Mottled brown and khaki background in wool; two sets of three red triangles outlined in blue complete the pattern. 59¹⁄₁₆ × 18⅜ inches. Originally similar pattern was in Indian Pattern rooms. Lower lobby or C. S. Price Wing.

Wagon Wheel. 1937–1938. Red wagon wheel with blue center and outlined in blue. White cross behind wagon wheel extends to blue border. Background in khaki wool blanket material, all other colors in corduroy. 75⅝ × 55⅛ inches. Originally in Covered Wagon rooms. Rachael Griffin Historic Exhibition Center.

Wave. 1937–1938. Wave pattern in dark gray, cream, and dark blue corduroy on khaki background of dark khaki corduroy and light khaki recycled wool uniforms. 105 × 42½ inches. Repaired by CETA craftswomen in 1975–1977 using wool and other recycled materials. Originally probably in Fern, Fish, and Wave, or Fish in River, rooms. Lower lobby.

Zigzag (crossed elbow) and Mountain. 1937–1938. Diamond pattern in maroon corduroy on khaki background of

Wagon wheel hooked rug for the Covered Wagon guest rooms, 1937–1938. Corduroy and wool, 75⅝ × 55⅛ inches. Rachael Griffin Historic Exhibition Center.

recycled uniforms and blanket material. 69¾ × 42⅞ inches. Rug may have been cut. Restoration by CETA craftswomen 1975-1977 using cotton sweatshirts and wool pants. Similar pattern in Indian Pipe Stem and Anemone rooms; this rug may be a variation on that pattern. Lower lobby or C. S. Price Wing.

Zigzag outline by stripes. 1937–1938. Green stripes and lavender blue zigzag stripes in corduroy on a background or recycled khaki wool uniforms and blankets. 67½ × 44⅞ inches. Restoration by Florence Mackenzie, Timberline Restoration Project 1975–1976. Similar pattern used in several rooms, but color scheme is closest to Indian Woman and Dog. C. S. Price Wing.

WOVEN TEXTILES (MISCELLANEOUS)

Hand-woven samples. 1937–1938. Woven placemat in brown and white zigzag pattern, 17⅜ × 12⅜ inches; sample of a gold and tan pattern in wool and linen, 37¾ × 91¼ inches; a part-corduroy sample in brown, rust, lime, and green, 39¾ × 108⅝ inches; and a linen and wool sample in blue, mustard, and gold, 39 × 112⅝ inches, tagged with Margery Hoffman Smith's name. In storage.

Stairstep hooked rug, 1937–1938. Corduroy and wool, two sizes 44½ × 32⅝ inches and 59¹¹/₁₆ × 35 inches. Probably for Zigzag room. Lower lobby or C. S. Price Wing.

SELECTED BIBLIOGRAPHY

BOOKS, BOOKLETS, AND CATALOGS

Allen, Ginny, and Jody Klevit. 1999. *Oregon Painters: The First Hundred Years (1859–1959)*. Portland: Oregon Historical Society Press.

Arthur, Jean. 1998. *Timberline and a Century of Skiing on Mount Hood*. Whitefish, Montana: Whitefish Editions.

Barnes, Christine. 2002. *Great Lodges of the National Parks*. Bend, Oregon: W.W. West.

Berke, Arnold. 2002. *Mary Colter: Architect of the Southwest*. New York: Princeton Architectural Press.

Builders of Timberline Lodge. 1937. U.S. Works Progress Administration, Oregon Works Progress Administration. Portland, Oregon: Hallwyler Printing Company.

Camp Fire Girls and Boys. 1980. *Wo-He-Lo: The Camp Fire History*. Kansas City, Missouri: Camp Fire Girls and Boys.

Churchill, Clair Warner. 1936. *Mt. Hood Timberline Lodge: The Realization of a Community Vision Made Possible by the Works Progress Administration*. Portland, Oregon: Metropolitan Press.

Clark, Rosalind. 1983. *Oregon Style: Architecture from 1840 to the 1950s*. Portland, Oregon: Professional Book Center.

Color Schemes of the Bedrooms at Timberline Lodge. Circa 1937. U.S. Works Progress Administration, Oregon Works Progress Administration, Portland, Oregon.

Contreras, Belisario R. 1983. *Tradition and Innovation in New Deal Art*. Lewisburg, Pennsylvania: Bucknell University Press.

Creese, Walter L. 1985. *A Crowning of the American Landscape: Eight Great Spaces and Their Buildings*. Princeton, New Jersey: Princeton University Press.

Denning, Michael. 1997. *The Cultural Front: The Laboring of American Culture in the Twentieth Century*. London, England: Verso.

Dijkstra, Bram. 2003. *American Expressionism: Art and Social Change, 1920–1950*. New York: Harry N. Abrams.

Dodge, Nicholas A. 1975. *A Climbing Guide to Oregon*. Beaverton: Touchstone Press.

Falk, Peter Hastings, ed. 1985. *Who was Who in American Art*. Madison, Connecticut: Sound View Press.

Falk, Peter Hastings, ed. 1999. *Who was Who in American Art: 1564–1975, 400 Years of Art in America*. Madison, Connecticut: Sound View Press.

Fleischhauer, Carl, and Beverly W. Brannan, eds. 1988. *Documenting America: 1935–1943*. Berkeley: University of California Press.

French, Chauncey Del. 2004. *Waging War on the Home Front*. Corvallis: Oregon State University Press.

Gaze, Delia, ed. 1997. *Dictionary of Women Artists*. London, England: Fitzroy Dearborn Publishers.

Gilbert, Dorothy B., ed. 1947. *Who's Who in American Art*. New York: R. R. Bowker Company.

Gilbert, Dorothy B., ed. 1953. *Who's Who in American Art*. New York: R. R. Bowker Company.

Gilbert, Dorothy B., ed. 1966. *Who's Who in American Art*. New York: R. R. Bowker Company.

Gohs, Carl. Circa 1972. *Timberline: A Common Ground between Man and the Spirit of the Mountain*. Portland, Oregon: Metropolitan Printing.

Good, Albert H. 2003. *Patterns from the Golden Age of Rustic Design: Park and Recreation Structures from the 1930s*. Lanham, Maryland: Roberts Rinehart.

Grauer, Jack. 2004. *Mount Hood: A Complete History*, 3rd ed. Vancouver, Washington: Jack Grauer.

Griffin, Rachael, and Sarah Munro, eds. 1978. *Timberline Lodge*. Portland, Oregon: Friends of Timberline.

Harmon, Kitty, ed. 2001. *The Pacific Northwest Landscape: A Painted History*. Seattle, Washington: Sasquatch Books.

Harris, Jonathan. 1995. *Federal Art and National Culture: The Politics of Identity in New Deal America*. Cambridge, England: Cambridge University Press.

Hemingway, Andrew. 2002. *Artists on the Left: American Artists and the Communist Movement, 1926–1956*. New Haven, Connecticut: Yale University Press.

Henderson, George M. 2006. *Lonely on the Mountain: A Skier's Memoir*. Victoria, British Columbia: Trafford Publishing.

Hoefer, Jacqueline. 2003. *A More Abundant Life: New Deal Artists and Public Art in New Mexico*. Santa Fe, New Mexico: Sunstone Press.

Hull, Roger. 2005. *Charles E. Heaney: Memory, Imagination, and Place*. Salem, Oregon: Hallie Ford Museum and Willamette University Press.

Kaiser, Harvey H. 1997. *Landmarks in the Landscape: Historic Architecture in the National Parks of the West*. San Francisco, California: Chronicle Books.

Kennedy, David M. 1999. *Freedom from Fear: The American People in Depression and War, 1929–1945*. New York: Oxford University Press.

Kreisman, Lawrence, and Glenn Mason. 2007. *The Arts and Crafts Movement in the Pacific Northwest*. Portland: Timber Press.

Lee, Anthony W. 1999. *Painting on the Left: Diego Rivera, Radical Politics, and San Francisco's Public Murals*. Berkeley: University of California Press.

Lyford, Carrie A. 1940. *Quill and Beadwork of the Western Sioux*. Reprint. Boulder, Colorado: Johnson Books, 1979.

McArthur, Lewis A., and Lewis L. McArthur. 2003. *Oregon Geographic Names*, 7th ed. Portland: Oregon Historical Society Press.

McClelland, Gordon T. 1991. *George Post*. Beverly Hills, California: Hillcrest Press.

McDonald, William F. 1969. *Federal Relief Administration and the Arts: The Origins and Administrative History of the Arts Projects of the Works Progress Administration*. Columbus: Ohio State University Press.

McGlaugflin, Alice Coe. 1937. *Who's Who in American Art*, Vol. II. Washington, D.C.: American Federation of Arts.

McKinzie, Richard D. 1973. *The New Deal for Artists*. Princeton, New Jersey: Princeton University Press.

McNeil, Fred M. 1937. *Wy'East "THE Mountain": A Chronicle of Mount Hood Known to the Indians, who Worshipped it, as Wy'East; to the White Man, with Equal Eloquence, Simply as the Mountain*. Portland, Oregon: Metropolitan Press.

Melosh, Barbara. 1991. *Engendering Culture: Manhood and Womanhood in New Deal Public Art and Theater*. Washington, D.C.: Smithsonian Institution.

Morris, Richard B., ed. 1965. *Encyclopedia of American History*. New York: Harper & Row.

Niles, Philip. 2009. *Beauties of the City: A. E. Doyle Portland's Architect*. Corvallis: Oregon State University Press.

O'Connor, Francis V., ed. 1973. *Art for the Millions: Essays from the 1930s by Artists and Administrators of the WPA Federal Art Project*. Greenwich, Connecticut: New York Graphic Society.

Palmer, Joel, and John Palmer Spencer. 2000. *A Sight So Nobly Grand: Joel Palmer on Mount Hood in 1845*. Portland, Oregon: Oregon Historical Society Press.

Park, Marlene, and Gerald E. Markowitz. 1984. *Democratic Vistas: Post Offices and Public Art in the New Deal*. Philadelphia: Temple University Press.

Portland Art Museum. 1942. *C. S. Price: Retrospective Exhibition of Paintings 1920–1942*. Portland, Oregon: Portland Art Museum.

Portland Art Museum. 1951. *C. S. Price 1874–1950: A Memorial Exhibition*. Portland, Oregon: Portland Art Museum.

Robbins, William G. 1997. *Landscapes of Promise: The Oregon Story 1800–1940*. Seattle: University of Washington Press.

Runte, Alfred. 1991. *Public Lands, Public Heritage: The National Forest Idea*. Niwot, Colorado: Roberts Rinehart and the Buffalo Bill Historical Center.

Saab, A. Joan. 2004. *For the Millions: American Art and Culture Between the Wars*. Philadelphia: University of Pennsylvania Press.

Sargent, Shirley. 1982. *The Ahwahnee: Yosemite's Classic Hotel*. 2nd ed. Yosemite, California: Flying Spur Press.

Saydack, Roger. 1998. *C. S. Price: Landscape, Image, and Spirit*. Moraga, California: Hearst Gallery and St. Mary's College.

Sharylen, Maria. 1993. *Artists of the Pacific Northwest: A Biographical Dictionary*. Jefferson, North Carolina: McFarland & Company.

Sinclair, Donna, and Richard McClure. 2003. " 'No Goldbricking Here': Oral Histories of the CCC in the Columbia National Forest, 1933–1942." Portland, Oregon: Heritage Program Gifford Pinchot National Forest and History Department, Portland State University.

Steen, Harold K. 2004. *The U.S. Forest Service: A History* (Centennial edition). Seattle: Forest History Society and University of Washington Press.

Taylor, Nick. 2008. *American-Made: The Enduring Legacy of the WPA when FDR Put the Nation to Work*. New York: Bantam Books.

U.S. Works Progress Administration. 1942. *Furniture Designed and Executed for Timberline Lodge, Mt. Hood National Forest, under the Direction of Margery Hoffman Smith, Assistant State Director of the Federal Art Project in Oregon, and the General Supervision of Gladys M. Everett, State Director of the Division of Women's and Professional Projects*. 2 vols. Portland, Oregon: U.S. Works Progress Administration.

Wooley, Ivan M. 1959. *Off to Mt. Hood: An Auto Biography of the Old Road*. Portland: Oregon Historical Society Press.

Workers of the Writers' Program, Work Projects Administration in the State of Oregon. 1940. *Oregon: End of the Trail*. Portland, Oregon: Binfords & Mort.

Zaitlin, Joyce. 1989. *Gilbert Stanley Underwood: His Rustic, Art Deco, and Federal Architecture*. Malibu, California: Pangloss Press.

ARTICLES, REPORTS, AND UNPUBLISHED PAPERS

Allen, Cain. 2006. *The Lumber Strike Wanes*. Oregon History Project. Historical Records, Oregon Historical Society. www.ohs.org.

Ames, Muriel. 1967. "Timberline Treasures." *Oregonian, Northwest Magazine*. May 21.

Artists by Movement: Precisionism. http://www.Artcyclopedia.com/history/precisionism.html.

Balcomb, Mary N. 1980. "Paul Buckner: Sculptor." *American Artist* (June): 60–65, 102.

Barker, Neil. 2000. Portland's Works Progress Administration. *Oregon Historical Quarterly* (Winter) 101 (4): 414–41.

Bowen. Gwladys. 1938. "A Study in Harmony: That's Goal of Architecture and Fittings at Timberline." *Oregonian*. April 3.

Bowen, Gwladys. 1957. "Ex-Reed Ski Instructor Returns to Display Sports Wear Designs." *Oregonian*. November 13.

Bullock, Margaret. Circa 2000. *Back to Work: Oregon and the New Deal Art Projects*. Portland, Oregon: Portland Art Museum.

Cowbrough, Chris. 1978. "Colville's O. B. Turner: A 44-Year Labor of Love." *Farm Magazine* (December): 12.

Dawson, Oliver B. 1964? "The Old Blacksmiths." Unpublished manuscript. Division of Special Collections and University Archives, University of Oregon.

Dawson, Oliver B. 1975. The ironwork of Timberline. *Oregon Historical Quarterly* (September) 76 (3): 259–68.

Failing, Patricia. 1980. "Timberline Lodge: Showcase from the Depression." *Americana* (March/April) 8 (1): 32–38.

Flor, Frank. 1978. "Son Renews Father's Work." *Oregon Labor Press*. August 11.

Fortune. 1937. "Unemployed Arts . . . and how the government employs them . . . An Account of WPA's Four Arts Projects: their origins, their operation, their cast of 40,000, their audience of 70,000,000." (May): 159.

Frankland, James. 1937. *Report on Forest Service Activities in Connection with the Visit of the President's Party to Mt. Hood National Forest*. September 28. USDA, Zigzag Ranger District, Mt. Hood National Forest.

Fulton, Eleanor Ann. 1995. *Historic American Building Survey: Timberline Lodge*. HABS No. OR-161.

Gano, Ward W. The First Magic Mile Ski Lift. Undated, unpublished paper. Friends of Timberline Archive.

Gano, Ward W. 1983. Some Timberline Lodge Recollections. Unpublished paper. Friends of Timberline Archive. January 5.

Gano, Ward, and Robert Peirce. 1989. "Timberline Lodge—Mt. Hood, Oregon." *Classic Wood Structures*. American Society of Engineers. 75–81.

Goetze, Janet. 2005. "State's Consummate Woodcarver Dies at 89." *Oregonian*. November 19.

Gohs, Carl. 1969. "The House Which Artists Built." *Oregonian, Northwest Magazine*. January 5.

Goodrich, F. W. 1938. Federal Music Project Narrative Report for February 1938. RG 69, Oregon Administrative Records 651.311.

Greeley, W. B. 1927. "What Shall We Do with Our Mountains? How Completely Do We Want to Conquer our Western Wilderness?" *Sunset* (December): 14–15.

Griffith, Emerson J. Circa 1939. Timberline Lodge: An Experiment. Unpublished paper. Friends of Timberline Archive.

Heisler, Anne. 1981. Mt. Hood NF PIO, Greensheet, USDA—Forest Service, Region 6, No. 1822 (October 30): 2–3.

Horowitz, David A. 2004. "Martina Gangle Curl (1906–1994)." *People's Art and the Mothering of Humanity*. Oregon Cultural Heritage Commission.

"Howard Sewall: Oregon Artist." Undated paper. Friends of Timberline Archive.

Julius Meier (1874–1937). In *Oregon Biographies*. Oregon Historical Society. http://www.ohs.org/education/oregonhistory/Oregon-Biographies-Julius-Meier.cfm.

Kohnstamm, Richard L. 1986. "Notes from the Desk of RLK," in Patricia Failing, "The Challenge: One Man's Dream." *Timberline: A Love Story*, Judith Rose, ed. Portland, Oregon: Friends of Timberline and Graphic Arts Center Publishing Company.

Leeds, Valerie Ann. 2006. "Edmund Lewandowski's Mosaic Murals." *American Art Review* (April): 142–47.

Neuberger, Richard L. 1940. "Uncle Sam's Sun Valley: Region's Timberline Lodge is a hand-carved political storm center." *Coast* (January): 27–29.

Noles, B. J. 1976. *Oregonian*. October 20.

Oregonian. 1938. "Dig at Democrats, Lodge by Writer Brings Echoes." September 11.

Oregonian. 1956. "Second Snow Mishap at Mt. Hood Puts Stevenson Afoot in Storm." February 16.

Oregon Journal. 1981. "Arts Benefactor Margery H. Smith Dies." March 11.

Patterson, Rod. 1981. "Northwest Artisans to Furnish Day Lodge." *Oregonian*. September 17.

Patterson, Rod. 1981. "Supervisor Recalls Lodge's Furniture Built Without Plans." *Oregonian*. September 17.

"Report of Women's and 'White Collar' Projects Operating in State." 1936. Oregon Administrative Records (651.3), Records of the WPA (RG 69), National Archives at College Park, Maryland. December 12.

Richards, Leverett. 1955. "Timberline Lodge, Erected in Depression Period, Typifies Spirit of Oregonians." *Oregonian*. January 22–23.

Roosevelt, Franklin Delano. 1937. Dedication address at Timberline Lodge. September 28.

San Francisco News. 1938. "Oregon's Timberline Lodge is Tribute to Relief Labor." Oregon Administrative Records (651.109), Records of the WPA (RG 69), National Archives at College Park, Maryland. February 12.

Scott, Michael. 1979. "The Ski Lodge that the W.P.A. Built." *New York Times*. December 9.

Smith, J. Daniel. 1982. Architecture of the Northern Mountains and Forests: The Cascade Style. Friends of Timberline Archive. August.

Sports Illustrated. 1956. "Timberline: Triumph after Scandal." January 23.

Sports Illustrated. 1957. "Mt. Hood's Marchese." December 16.

Starr, Mary Elizabeth. 1941. The Textiles of Timberline Lodge. *Weaver* (April–May): 3–8.

Tucker, Kathy. 2002. "CCC Members Fight Fire in Willamette National Forest." Oregon History Project. Historical Records, Oregon Historical Society. www.ohs.org.

Tucker, Kathy. 2002. "Bonneville Dam Construction Workers Assembling Turbine." Oregon History Project. Historical Records, Oregon Historical Society. www.ohs.org.

Walton, Elisabeth. 1974. "Auto Accommodations." In *Space, Style and Structure: Building in Northwest America*, vol. 2. Ed. Thomas Vaughan and Virginia Guest Ferriday. Portland: Oregon Historical Society.

Waugh, Frank. 1920. Recreation Uses in the Mt. Hood Area: A Preliminary Report upon a Working Plan for the Accommodation of Recreation Uses in the Mt. Hood Area upon the Oregon National Forest. Unpublished paper.

Waugh, Frank. 1930. Public Values of the Mount Hood Area: Report of a special committee appointed by the Secretary of Agriculture to make a study of the features or qualities of major public importance of the Mount Hood area in the Mount Hood National Forest and the principles which should govern its management together with a summary of data compiled for the Mount Hood Committee by the United States Forest Service, North Pacific Region. Unpublished paper. June 9.

Wiener, Norman. 1989. The First Magic Mile Lift at Timberline Lodge. Unpublished paper.

Williamson, Francis E., Jr., Thomas Sherrard, and C. J. Buck. 1932. Forest Recreation Plan. U.S. Forest Service, Zigzag Ranger District. March 31.

Woolley, John, and Gerhard Peters. Franklin Roosevelt address at the dedication of Bonneville Dam, September 28, 1937, *The American Presidency Project* (online), Santa Barbara, California: University of California (hosted), Gerhard Peters (database). www.presidency.ucsb.edu/ws/index.php.

THESES

Cohen, Paul. 1985. *Timberline Lodge: Crisis and Contradiction*. BA thesis, Reed College.

Deering, Thomas P. Jr. 1986. *Mountain Architecture: An Alternative Design Proposal for the Wy'East Day Lodge, Mount Hood, Oregon*. Master of Architecture thesis, University of Washington.

Force, Rachel Gwen. 2004. *Blacksmith: The Significance and Preservation of O. B. Dawson's Ironwork for the WPA*. Master's thesis, University of Oregon.

Howe, Carolyn. 1980. *The Production of Culture on the Oregon Federal Arts Project of the Works Progress Administration*. Master's thesis, Portland State University.

Throop, Elizabeth Gail. 1979. *Utterly Visionary and Chimerical: A Federal Response to the Depression—An Examination of Civilian Conservation Corps Construction on National Forest System Lands in the Pacific Northwest*. Master's thesis, Portland State University.

Weir, Jean. 1977. *Timberline Lodge: A WPA Experiment in Architecture and Crafts*. 2 vols. PhD dissertation, University of Michigan.

Wickre, Karen. 1981. *An Informal History of Oregon's WPA Federal Theatre Project, 1936–1939*. Master's thesis, Portland State University.

Wood, Ann Claggett. 1996. *Mt. Hood's Timberline Lodge: An Introduction to its Architects and Architecture*. Master's thesis, Rice University.

INDEX